Lithuania in Crisis

NATIONALISM TO COMMUNISM,
1939-1940

INDIANA UNIVERSITY INTERNATIONAL STUDIES

Leonas Sabaliūnas

Lithuania in Crisis

NATIONALISM TO COMMUNISM,

1939 — 1940

INDIANA UNIVERSITY PRESS

BLOOMINGTON / LONDON

Published in Canada by Fitzhenry & Whiteside Limited, Don Mills, Ontario

Library of Congress catalog card number: 74-143247

ISBN: 0-253-33600-7

Manufactured in the United States of America

To the memory of J.N.-S.

CONTENTS

vii

PART THREE

The Economy: Problems and Tendencies

Contents

PART FOUR

German Seizure of Klaipéda: A Nation's Response

PART FIVE

Political Repercussions of the Outbreak of World War II

PART SIX

The Intervention of the Soviet Union

Contents

TABLES

FOREWORD

THE HISTORY OF ANY NATION IS INTERESTING, because history is about people; and people, in their infinite variety, are a source of never-ending interest. To read about a nation concerning which we know little, and to find it coming into clearer definition as we focus upon its particular problems and its special qualities, is a fascinating experience. To most persons in the Western world Lithuania presents the vaguest sort of image, and the literature upon it available in English, or in any language widely read in the West, is meager and all too often biased. Mr. Sabaliūnas deserves our thanks for presenting a scholarly, thorough, and absorbing study of one of the most fateful chapters in the life of the Lithuanian nation: the disappearance of its short-lived second period of national independence.

But the author has done more than this. He has given us an admirably documented case-study of an important historical phenomenon of the twentieth century: the breakdown of the liberal-democratic regimes created or reorganized in Eastern Europe after the First World War. Set up in an effervescence of Wilsonian liberalism, almost all of them collapsed under a combination of internal and external pressures. By 1938, before the Soviet engorgement had begun, only two of the East European states, Finland and Czechoslovakia, still retained the free and democratic institutions which all the belt of small states between the Arctic and the Aegean had enjoyed, on paper at least, a decade and a half earlier. It was not, then, well-functioning Western-style democracies that the Soviet Union absorbed in 1940 or dominated at the end of the Second World War. What happened in this region between the Paris peace settlement and Munich is a matter deserving much more thorough study than it has yet received.

Lithuania, as one of the first of these countries to abandon its liberal institutions, is of special interest. The lack of any real moral authority, as the voice of the people, on the part of the authoritarian regime that succeeded the democratic form became clear in 1939 and 1940. In Chapters X and XI Mr. Sabaliūnas portrays the internal disarray of Lithuania in its last two years of independence: a weakness that prevented a real national opinion from expressing itself when the supreme crisis came.

In the final analysis it probably would not have made any difference what kind of government Lithuania had in the contest between Germany and the Soviet Union: the little nation would have been subjugated in any case by the winner. It is the historic misfortune of the Estonians, the Latvians, the Lithuanians, and the Poles to lie on the military highroad between Germany and Russia; and whether it was the Teutonic Knights and the ambitious Hanseatic burghers in the thirteenth and fourteenth centuries or the Soviet politicians and military men in the twentieth century who took action, the interests of powerful neighbors have always overridden the rights and interests of the smaller peoples. The short-lived independence of the Baltic states in the twentieth century was made possible by the unusual fact that both Russia and Germany were losers in the First World War. As these two powers grew strong and a clash loomed between them, the chances that the small countries lying between them would be left alone vanished. Yet the loss of independence by the Baltic nations in 1940-1941 would have been more dignified and might have aroused deeper sympathy had these peoples been able to maintain, like Czechoslovakia, governments which could make a valid claim to representing their nations.

In his third chapter Mr. Sabaliūnas investigates the official
nationalism of Lithuania in the years of dictatorship, and the
reader finds himself listening to one more variation on a familiar
theme. The rejection of foreign ways and ideas, including liberalism; the contempt for inept parliamentary democracy as an
alien import; the emphasis on national will; the assertion that
the whole should have unlimited precedence over the individual
parts—all these traits reveal the same sort of "integral nationalism" that, in the case of larger nations, has received in recent
years such enlightening studies as those by William Buthman,
Michael Curtis, and Edward Tannenbaum for France and Fritz
Stern and George Mosse for Germany. The theory of the
"organic state," which Mr. Sabaliūnas analyzes in its Lithuanian
form, is familiar to us in the case of other countries from the
studies by Eugen Weber, Hans Rogger, Marvin Rintala, and
others. It is indeed true, as Mr. Sabaliūnas points out, that
"Lithuania was a piece of the Continent."

The principal part of our author's study, however, is not
concerned with the above-mentioned points. As the climax of
his narrative Mr. Sabaliūnas tells us in detail of the process by
which Lithuania was pushed into joining the Soviet Union.
From this exposition it is clear that the Lithuanians were not
permitted by their neighbor in the east to work out their problems in their own good time. The solution imposed on them was
the Soviet solution. We may assume that the decision made in
1940 was a permanent one, at least for the foreseeable future.
A quarter-century after the expulsion of the Nazis Lithuania is
firmly integrated into the Soviet system, and a generation has
grown up with constant instruction in Soviet values. To be sure,
Lithuania is still Lithuania. The traveler who visits the well-
kept-up baroque heart of Vilnius or delights in the clean modern-
ism of architecture and design that has made present-day Lithuania "the Scandinavia of the Soviet Union" will certainly not
think for a moment that he is in Russia. Yet whatever course the
Lithuanian spirit and Lithuanian culture steer, they will have to
remain within the warning buoys set up by Moscow.

Whether, in the long run, this fate is good or bad no one can say with certainty. One would be bold indeed to assert categorically that the narrow, arbitrary, bombastic regime in Lithuania in the 1930's was superior to the present Communist state, which, as elsewhere in the Soviet Union, has combined ruthless regimentation of thought and the methods of the police state with remarkable achievements in various aspects of life. It is conceivable that the Smetona regime might in time have permitted the development—or might have been pushed from below to yield to the development—of a more humane and free society than Lithuania had hitherto enjoyed, or enjoys at present. Chapters X, XI, XVI, and XVIII of the present study make it clear that such pressure from below existed, though it is equally clear that the Smetona government was able to resist the pressure until Soviet intervention weakened its position fatally. What possibilities for progressive change were latent in independent Lithuania must remain a matter for speculation. So must the question of whether a country as small and as poor in economic resources as Lithuania is a viable independent state in the twentieth century, quite aside from the problem of its military indefensibility against gigantic neighbors.

These remain theoretical questions. What does emerge from Mr. Sabaliūnas' study is the bleak fact that in the two decades from 1920 to 1940 the Lithuanians, like the East Europeans in general throughout their history, had little opportunity to shape their own destinies and institutions. Ambitious, short-sighted, intolerant and incompetent leaders at home or ruthless expansionists next door have usually decided the fates of these peoples. This chapter in the long story is not very cheerful reading; but it is very instructive.

Indiana University   CHARLES LEONARD LUNDIN

PREFACE

From 1795 to 1918 Lithuania was a part of Tsarist Russia. In 1918, at the conclusion of World War I, Lithuania, as well as Latvia and Estonia, was restored as an independent state. It remained independent for two decades, until the outbreak of World War II. In order to understand constitutional development in Lithuania during these interwar decades, one needs to be aware of the background conditions and trends in Eastern Europe generally. Lithuania became a parliamentary democracy in 1918 as did many states in that part of the continent. Unfortunately, its multi-party politics was conducted in an environment which lacked institutional stability yet which frequently demanded critical decision-making. In such an unfavorable climate, parliamentary government alienated a significant portion of the nation's population, which eventually discarded democracy itself. From 1927 to 1940 Lithuania had what some might call a temperate dictatorship, a form of authoritarianism that over the years acquired a Fascistic coloration. But authoritarianism may generate its own opposition, or so it was in Lithuania. Fragmented national parties, the arbiters of an earlier period, continued to exist and to oppose the authoritarian establishment. Reluctant to use excessive force, the government made no attempt to physically eliminate its opposition. Rather, it tried to render it impotent. However, government restraint was less in evidence when combating the Communist underground. Thus both the parliamentary and the authoritarian governments were burdened with the presence of political forces inimical to the basic organization of the state.

The proximity of Germany and Russia constantly affected Lithuania's system of government and her foreign policies, and threatened her very existence as an independent state. Toward the end of the interwar decades that threat became a reality to Lithuania. Collusion between Nazi Germany and Soviet Russia, inscribed in their treaties of August and September 1939, had cataclysmic consequences for many parts of Europe. For Lithuania, independence was first curtailed and then stifled altogether. In mid-1940 the Soviet Union annexed all three of the Baltic states, Latvia, Estonia, and Lithuania, and to this day they remain a part of Soviet Russia.

The pattern of political and economic development, the process of sovietization, the location, and perhaps even fate, make Lithuania a typical East European country. For example, the nature of the demands which the Russians presented to Lithuania in mid-1940 and to Czechoslovakia in mid-1968 were in many, though not all, respects identical: punishment of government officials objectionable to the Kremlin, formation of a government acceptable to Moscow, admission of Russian troops into the two states, and adoption of a mode of life similar to that in Russia. Yet there are aspects of Lithuania's experience which endow it with a significance that extends beyond her boundaries. For example, the study of the Lithuanian model is instructive in understanding authoritarianism as an instrument in the hands of those intent on a fundamental change of society. It augments the body of literature concerning systems of government which must deal with internal political movements bent on destroying the very systems within which they operate. It considers the uneasy position and limited effectiveness of moderate political parties under conditions favorable to extremist politics. The study also elucidates some of the problems of conducting societal relations in the presence of an intrusive Great Power diplomacy. Lastly, it deals with human behavior in crisis.

A study of Lithuania during the period 1939-1940 affords the opportunity to analyze a society which moves from initial domestic turmoil to later serious crisis. It is the purpose of this book to show the diverse problems facing Lithuania in terms of an analysis of crisis. Part I reviews Lithuanian domestic and foreign affairs in the interwar period. Parts II and III examine the politics and survey the social and economic conditions in the closing years of independent Lithuania. Parts IV, V, and VI consider three crisis situations: the loss of Klaipėda (Memel) to Germany in 1939, the impact of the outbreak of World War II, and the demise of Lithuanian independence in 1940.

Any success which this study might have owes much to those who gladly furnished access to basic Lithuanian materials. I am, therefore, pleased to acknowledge my indebtedness and my gratitude to them. I also wish to express my appreciation to those who otherwise aided me in the preparation of this work: Professors Alexander Dallin and Joseph A. Rothschild, my advisers at Columbia University, also Professor Alfred E. Senn, the late Consul General Jonas Budrys, Consul General Petras Daužvardis, Consul General Anicetas Simutis, Very Rev. Francis M. Juras, Juozas Audėnas, Alex J. Bachunas, Joseph J. Bachunas, Vincentas Liulevičius, Vincas Mašalaitis, Elizabeth Rubin, Kazys Škirpa, and Juratė Statkus-Rosales. I should also like to thank the Sisters of St. Casimir, Chicago, Illinois; the Sisters of Crucified Jesus, Brockton, Massachusetts; and the Marianapolis Preparatory School, Thompson, Connecticut. Special thanks are due to Professor Charles E. Helppie, of Eastern Michigan University, who read the manuscript and gave me the benefit of his competent judgments.

I am particularly appreciative of the generous support and advice which I received from Emilija and Vincas Rastenis.

The statements and interpretations in this study, unless indicated otherwise, are the sole responsibility of the author and thus do not necessarily reflect the views of any of the persons listed above. Any errors, of course, are the author's.

Ann Arbor, Michigan   Leonas Sabaliūnas
October, 1970

Lithuania in Crisis

NATIONALISM TO COMMUNISM, 1939-1940

PART ONE

Background: The Years
between the Wars

I

DOMESTIC AFFAIRS

CONSTITUTIONAL DEVELOPMENTS IN INDEPENDENT LITHUANIA are broadly divisible into three periods, the democratic, the authoritarian, and the period of partial retreat from authoritarianism. The democratic period lasted from the reestablishment of the Lithuanian state in 1918 to the end of 1926. The authoritarian period followed and continued from 1927 until the early part of 1939. The last period started in March 1939 and ended with the destruction of Lithuania's independence in June 1940. The socioeconomic setting in which these changes took place remained predominantly agricultural. Of the 3,080,100 people, a 1938-1939 total which includes the Klaipėda and Vilnius areas, 2,352,400 or 76.4 per cent depended on the land for their livelihood and 727,700 or 23.6 per cent lived in small towns.

The Democratic Period

THE TEMPER OF MIND in postwar Lithuania was one of radicalism,[1] and this radicalism of the democratic period was partly responsible for the onset of the second authoritarian period. Its probable sources were twofold: the proximity of revolutionary Russia and the psychology of an emergent Lithuania. For well over a century before World War I, Lithuania languished under the rule of Russian autocracy and the administration of Russian

3

bureaucracy. The common people, who were Lithuania's essence and the basis of her future national revival, had few rights and many obligations. The upper class was influenced by Polish culture, an influence whose origins date back to the time when Lithuania and Poland existed as a united state. The growing nationalistic intelligentsia viewed alien authority and the dearth of freedom as the two main causes of Lithuania's plight under the tsars. Thus, in the reconstruction efforts after 1918, Lithuanians relied upon their native strength while seeking additional freedom. The result was a glorification of the common people, and it produced sweeping reforms of a political, social, and economic nature intended to restructure Lithuanian society. Radical proclivities were especially strong among those leaders who had lived in Russia before they returned home to work for an independent Lithuania. Many of them were affected by Russia's revolutionary tradition and were prone to deal with problems in a radical way.

Postwar radicalism in economics occupied itself for the most part with land reform. Since about 76 per cent of Lithuania's population depended on agriculture for its livelihood, the distribution of land was a matter of primary concern. About 40 per cent of all arable land belonged to a relatively small number of landowners, who were generally of Polish orientation and who frowned on the idea of an independent Lithuania. Outmoded methods used before 1918, which made farming inefficient, called for change on economic grounds. Lastly, Lithuanians hoped that redistribution of land would help them halt the advance of Russian Communist forces, which in 1919 held a large part of Lithuanian territory. These considerations invited a radical solution of the land problem, and all political parties were committed to such a course. Reforms were set in operation soon after the establishment of Lithuania's independence. Land in excess of 80 hectares was expropriated, subject to compensation, and parceled out among small landholders and landless peasants. The character of the nation's rural society thus underwent a fundamental change.

Postwar radicalism in politics led to an extreme form of democracy. Like other states in Central and Eastern Europe, Lithuania embraced ascendant parliamentary democracy as its form of government. Its political spectrum consisted of three main forces which originated in pre-independent Lithuania, the Catholics, the Populists, and the Social Democrats.

The Catholic bloc comprised one of the main forces in postwar politics. It consisted of three political parties, the Christian Democratic Party, the Farmers' Union, and the Federation of Labor. At the core of the political structure was the Christian Democratic Party, which had assembled a considerable nationalist and Catholic following. The Party relied heavily on the Catholic clergy. Through them it succeeded in attracting a sizable number of women voters. It also found support among professional people. The Farmers' Union and the Federation of Labor were weaker partners in the bloc. The Federation of Labor had little support among urban workers, it showed more strength among rural laborers and small landholders.

Rather than as separate parties, these three groups should be regarded as different branches of one political movement whose unifying factor was the Catholic Church. The stratagem of breaking into three parties was largely intended to attract supporters from every sector of the nation's predominantly Catholic population. Catholic priests, most of whom were active in politics, impressed upon the faithful that it made no difference which group they supported at the polls, as long as they voted Catholic. In the Constituent Assembly elected in 1920 the Catholics had 59 deputies out of a total of 112.[2]

After the war Catholic leaders found themselves in a quandary. The radicalism of the democratic period made conservatism virtually synonymous with reaction and thus augured its defeat at the polls. Moreover, many Catholic politicians were relatively young men who had lived in Russia during the war and the revolution. The years they spent in that country left an imprint upon their attitudes and political behavior. These factors explain why Lithuania's political Catholicism soon after the war was

5

more progressive than it probably would have been under less disrupted conditions. However, of the three main political movements, the Catholic bloc was the least radical one.

The Populists formed the second main political force of the democratic period. They drew their strength largely from the rural population, especially from the small landholders, and attempted to represent their interests. In the elections of 1920 they won 29 of the 112 seats. The Populists were more radical than the Catholics but less radical than the Social Democrats. While their economic and social programs were not too different from those of the Catholics, basic ideological differences made cooperation difficult. The Populists expressed the sentiments of the liberal voters, especially those concerning relations between Church and State.

The Social Democratic Party was the most radical and least effective of the three main political movements. The Party's attitude was so strict that it frowned on any sort of cooperation with the Catholics. The Social Democrats relied primarily on the urban workers for political strength and elected fourteen members to the Constituent Assembly. Members of the Party were also active in local government, where they scored considerable gains.

For a number of years after the war the Catholics dominated Lithuanian politics. However, by 1926 their influence had begun to decline, and in the elections held in May of that year the Catholics lost their majority of seats in the Seimas (Diet). What caused this Catholic reversal? In 1925 a concordat had been concluded between Poland and the Vatican which, in effect, recognized Poland's interests as paramount in the unresolved conflict over Vilnius (Wilno or Vilna), a city and a territory held by Poland but claimed by both Poland and Lithuania. The ruling Christian Democrats' failure to parry this diplomatic setback, their introduction of a spoils system, the evidence of corruption in the government, and the sagging economy were largely responsible for the Catholic defeat at the polls. Control of the government then devolved upon the Populists and the Social Democrats, who formed a leftist coalition.

Lithuania acutely felt the insufficient development of her political culture. The postwar years of social and political flux soon alienated many of the country's conservatives and nationalists, who thought that factional strife exceeded permissible limits. Politics in Lithuania suffered from the prevailing tendency to view political issues from either an ideological or a religious point of view. Political parties were unduly concerned that their proposed solutions of concrete problems be fully consistent with their particular system of ideas. Such concern with ideology both delayed and depreciated compromise as an objective in politics. Further, the clergy were deeply involved in politics. The Social Democrats and the Populists treated Church officials, and the Church itself, as they did other political opponents, with little or no regard to the civilities conventionally shown to the ecclesiastical profession. Incessant and bitter party feuds made coalitions ephemeral.

Political conditions in Lithuania worsened when the Populists and the Social Democrats, who came to power in May 1926, began to implement their domestic programs. Measures which made the government distinctly unpopular in Catholic, nationalist, and military circles included the relaxation of restrictions on civil liberties, which resulted in an increase of Communist activities; the concessions which the coalition government had to make to the national minorities in order to win their support in the legislature; the removal from public service of a number of Catholic officials; the dismissal of some high officers from the army and plans to reduce the entire military establishment. In addition economic conditions failed to improve. Antanas Smetona, a prominent personality in the Lithuanian *risorgimento* and the republic's first President, recounted the threatening specter of the period as seen by the conservatives:

> The first interval . . . is the rule of all kinds of [political] parties, which proclaimed the widest possible freedom without discipline and harmony. By the end of 1926 that kind of freedom had brought our country to a point where the government was barely perceptible and where the promised freedom of each was preparing the bondage

7

of all Lithuania. Under such conditions, the state treasury was getting empty, there appeared swarms of unemployed, [and] the Seimas was about to appropriate millions of lits[3] for their aid. The interests of the farmers were forgotten, and dark mobs, led by Russianized chieftains, appeared in public . . . and insisted upon a Bolshevik government. Instead of jointly doing serious work, the Lithuanian parties in the Seimas wrangled constantly and allowed the national minorities to turn the helm of our state to and fro, as they saw fit. The entire country became uneasy; the Seimas and the government instituted by it became dejected, out of fear that it was giving in more and more to the unwholesome vagaries of impudent leaders. Men of obscurity threatened to deprive Lithuania's peaceful and industrious inhabitants of their property and to treat them as people were treated in Russia. Things got to a point where the police were no longer permitted to maintain order. Work was failing in the country, everything was becoming inert. Our covetous [Polish] neighbor was already quietly looking forward to the day when, after the disappearance of our government and the spread of disorder, not only the Vilnius territory but all of Lithuania as well, as a long coveted booty, would fall to its share.[4]

Change was on the way. As Smetona observed, "the general public was anxiously waiting for someone to deliver it from that danger. Divine providence has not forsaken it: with the dawn of December 17 Lithuania entered a new age."[5]

An Authoritarian Period

THE DAWN OF THE NEW AGE was the military coup d'état of December 17, 1926, through which a group of army officers wrested political power from the constitutional authorities. The coup ended the first or democratic stage in the development of Lithuania's political life and inaugurated the regime of Antanas Smetona.

Politically, President Smetona's Nationalist government was restrictive. It eventually outlawed all political parties but one—the Lithuanian Nationalist Union. This intermediary between President Smetona and the general public had emerged in 1924 as a party which relied on the well-to-do farm population and the intelligentsia. At that time, however, it was a relatively unimportant group; it was not the numerical superiority of its followers, but the boldness of its leaders that brought the Nationalist Union to power. Economically, the Nationalist government pursued a cautious and conservative course. Its direction of rural economy conformed to the interests of the relatively affluent part of agrarian society, such as the landowner of average or large holding. Culturally, the Nationalist leaders intended to capitalize on those elements in Lithuania's intellectual heritage which were distinctive in character. Smetona's authoritarianism was essentially an antidote to the earlier experiment with parliamentary democracy. The Nationalist regime persisted in its efforts to discredit that type of democracy and crystallize its own political principles. In the end, these principles acquired a certain psychological and political affinity with those of Fascism.

The creation on March 27, 1939, of a coalition cabinet of Nationalists, Catholics,[6] and Populists ushered in the third period in the politics of independent Lithuania. The formation of this government, known as the Černius government, forced the Nationalists to offer to the opposition concessions which tended to liberalize future political progress. Though of less consequence than the military revolt of 1926, the March realignment dealt a blow to Nationalist efforts to mold a monolithic society.

I I

FOREIGN AFFAIRS

POLITICAL DEVELOPMENTS AT HOME were always susceptible, and frequently ascribable, to the influence of events abroad. Thus it is necessary to preface the analysis of Lithuanian society with observations about international affairs. International relations in the Baltic area were molded by two elements, the main trends in the foreign policies of European powers, and the diplomatic environment distinctive of the area itself. In turn the setting of Baltic politics is more comprehensible if one distinguishes, in a general way, between the first half of the interwar period and the second. In the early years the leaders of many smaller nations were under the sway of Western ideas, institutions, and procedures. They were reluctant to adopt policies distasteful to London, Paris, or Geneva. Statesmen prepared their countries for what was viewed as a worthy membership in the League of Nations, whose establishment was the height of diplomatic idealism. Lastly, many were apprehensive about revolutionary Russia, not Germany. However, after only a few years, the era of hope began to fade. Attitudes and policies in many states underwent significant changes. The retreat from idealism produced a crisis of confidence in and a disillusionment with the West. In many countries the League of Nations was no longer considered the mainstay of their security. Finally, the fear of the Soviet Union receded somewhat and was replaced by growing concern with the recrudescence of Germany. In such a changing international context Lithuania pursued its domestic objectives and dealt with its problems.

In the years after the end of World War I the foreign policy of modern Lithuania sought the attainment of two main objectives, the maintenance of the country's independence and the acquisition of additional territories which the Lithuanians regarded as theirs. More specifically, the first objective was intended to dispel the prevalent opinion abroad that Lithuania was but an integral part of Russia and that their reunification was only a question of time. The first objective was to gain diplomatic recognition. With Lithuania's admission to the League of Nations in 1921 and its recognition by the Allied Powers in 1922 that objective was largely achieved. The second goal involved primarily Lithuania's efforts to gain possession of Klaipėda (Memel) and Vilnius (Vilna), an aim that presaged strained relations with Germany and Poland respectively.

Germany and Lithuania: Klaipėda Matter

INTERWAR RELATIONS between Lithuania and Germany chiefly concerned Klaipėda. German possession of Klaipėda and the neighboring areas dated back to the thirteenth century, when the Teutonic Knights commenced their campaign against Lithuania proper. The population consisted of Germans and Lithuanians, but it was difficult to ascertain their relative proportions. However, in the area as a whole the Lithuanians probably outnumbered the Germans, although Klaipėda itself was predominantly German.[1]

Areas coveted by the Lithuanians included the city of Klaipėda, the districts adjacent to it, and a part of East Prussia situated on the left bank of the Nemunas (Niemen). The Paris Peace Conference satisfied these claims only in part. The area that was finally detached from Germany, over German objections, and intended for Lithuania was a piece of land situated on the right bank of the Nemunas. It consisted of some 1,100 square miles and had a population of about 140,000. In diploma-

11

tic parlance this came to be known as the Klaipėda territory, and constituted the Klaipėda problem.

Contrary to the expectations of Lithuanians, the Klaipėda territory was not transferred to Lithuania immediately but, instead, was temporarily placed at the disposal of the Allied and Associated Powers. It was administered by a French High Commissioner in behalf of the Powers. The probable explanation of this action was the uncertainty about the future status of Lithuania in general. French and Polish diplomacy in particular was inimical to the interests of the Lithuanians.

The diplomatic tangle over Klaipėda made the Lithuanians pessimistic about the outcome of their endeavors. It was felt that the problem was nearing a solution; however, that solution was not expected to unite Klaipėda with Lithuania. The government at Kaunas (Kovno) became especially disturbed by the increasingly popular idea of making Klaipėda a free state. The Poles, and the French too, seemed to be inclined to support that idea rather than see Klaipėda attached to Lithuania. The Klaipėda Germans also favored such a solution. Some believed that conversion to a free state would facilitate eventual reunification with Germany. Others felt that independence would be advantageous economically. The Lithuanians concluded that they would not be able to effect the merger by peaceful means; hence they resorted to military action. Fighting commenced early in 1923, and Klaipėda soon became a part of Lithuania proper. The Powers sanctioned this fait accompli in 1924, when they concluded the Klaipėda Convention with Lithuania. The Convention recognized Lithuania's sovereignty over the territory and granted its residents local autonomy.

In 1928 Germany and Lithuania strengthened the existing territorial arrangements by signing a treaty designed to settle their border problems. However, the simmering discord between the German and Lithuanian residents in the Klaipėda territory did not subside. After the advent of National Socialism in Germany, conditions deteriorated markedly. Subsequent developments, namely, the retrocession of Klaipėda to the Reich on

12

March 22, 1939, must be considered in the light of Germany's resolve to extend its power in Europe. The seizure followed the annexation of Austria, the occupation of the Sudetenland, and the dismemberment of Czechoslovakia. Recovery of Klaipėda, confided the German Foreign Minister, was a "matter of honor."[2] What was a minor readjustment of frontiers to Berlin precipitated a major political crisis in Kaunas.

Poland and Lithuania: The Vilnius Issue

LITHUANIA'S RELATIONS with Poland were not completely neighborly. The main point of controversy was Vilnius. Vilnius was the capital of the Grand Duchy of Lithuania both before and after its union with Poland in 1569. Although its cultural environment was predominantly Polish and Jewish, Vilnius also became the mainspring of Lithuania's intellectual and political revival prior to 1918. Lithuanian nationalists viewed Vilnius as the center for a new and independent Lithuania. On the other hand, the unwillingness of many of the leading Poles to recognize the existence of an independent Lithuania was one explanation of the twenty-year crisis in Lithuanian-Polish relations. In general, the Poles hoped and worked for the restoration of the historical union between the two countries. The acquisition of Vilnius became the key to the fruition of their plans; for perhaps the Lithuanians, deprived of Vilnius, would succumb to the idea of union with Poland. Lithuania, however, was intent on being independent and determined to possess Vilnius.

Seizure of the city by the Poles on October 9, 1920 put a virtual end to all effective intercourse between the two countries for nearly two decades. Recovery of its historical capital became the primary concern of Lithuanian diplomacy. Lithuania's relations with neighboring states were often influenced, although not necessarily determined, by their attitude toward this objective.

Lithuanian efforts to regain the Vilnius territory were unsuccessful until the very end of the interwar decades. Initially, the League of Nations had attempted to resolve the dispute and

13

made several proposals to the parties concerned. Unfortunately, its intercession produced no mutually acceptable result. From 1922 on, the League seemed to be working only toward some kind of modus vivendi between the two sides; it refused to grapple with the controversy in a fundamental way[3]. Equally fruitless were Lithuanian efforts to find a solution by means of direct talks with the Poles. Neither side yielded. The Warsaw legislators made the Vilnius area an integral part of Poland, but the Nationalist party in Kaunas drafted a constitution which specified Vilnius as the state's capital.

Absorption in the recovery of Vilnius injected a measure of rigidity into the foreign policies charted by the Kaunas government. Lithuania viewed Poland as an implacable enemy and held Warsaw responsible for the "permanent danger of international banditry." Such a posture of enmity distinguished Lithuania's diplomacy throughout a good part of the interwar years. Parenthetically, antagonism between Kaunas and Warsaw was not unwelcome to either Germany or the Soviet Union. Moscow's diplomatic support of Lithuania may have helped the latter to assume and persist in such an attitude of hostility. For when Soviet support failed to meet Lithuanian expectations, as was the case at the time of the Polish ultimatum to Lithuania in 1938, Lithuania softened its opposition to Poland.

Hostility between Lithuania and Poland generated frequent border disputes. In March of 1938 a Polish soldier was shot to death on Lithuanian territory, which brought the two countries to the brink of war. The incident culminated in a Polish ultimatum to Lithuania, demanding the establishment of diplomatic relations. On March 19 the Kaunas government submitted to diplomatic pressure and accepted Poland's terms. This averted an armed conflict, but the unfriendly attitude toward the Poles remained.

Despite the unfriendly popular sentiment, official relations between Kaunas and Warsaw improved considerably after the ultimatum. It seemed as though the forced establishment of diplomatic ties created that necessary basis without which no meaningful change in policy was possible. In the closing months of 1938 the two governments initiated talks intended to clear the way for the restoration of normal relations between their countries.

What accounted for these moves? Dissatisfaction with the support the Lithuanians received from Moscow during their diplomatic confrontation with Poland appears to have been one reason for the change. The character of European diplomacy in the 1930's offers another possible explanation. Renewed emphasis on national interest and power undermined the faith that the Lithuanian government had once put in the League of Nations and collective security as peace-keeping means. The readjustment in Kaunas, which was made possible by the establishment of diplomatic relations with Warsaw, reflected this disillusionment, as well as the growing concern about Lithuania's security. Limited rapprochement with Poland did not signify any fundamental shift in Lithuania's foreign policy. As further discussion will indicate, its course was one of neutrality. However, the improvement in relations with Poland meant that Lithuania was determined to enhance its security by mitigating one of the main sources of unrest in the Baltic area.

The Russians and Lithuania

AFTER WORLD WAR I, the establishment of normal ties between Lithuania and the Soviet Union (embodied in numerous treaties of a political, economic, and legal nature), and frequent references by both sides to their amicable relations, indicate that, on the whole, both the Russians and the Lithuanians were content to coexist in peace for two decades. Neither the small-scale revolutionary activities of the Lithuanian Communists nor the habitual exclamations of the Communist International were allowed to interfere with relations between the two states. The legal basis of these relations between Lithuania and the Soviet Union was the Treaty of Peace concluded on July 12, 1920. The political and psychological basis, however, lay in their mutual animosity toward Poland.

The years of generally adequate, and at times close, relations with the Russians are divisible into three periods. For a number of years after 1920 relations with Russia were dormant. Western sentiment at the time frowned on any kind of close association with Communist Russia. Lithuanian diplomats were often seen in the Western capitals but not in Moscow. Further, there was at first a deep mistrust of Soviet motives among many Lithuanian leaders. Many doubted whether anything could be gained through agreements with the Russians. They felt that when it became opportune for the Russians to promote their revolutionary goals, Moscow would disregard any previous commitments contrary to those goals. Lastly, the Lithuanians showed no inclination toward an active Russian policy because, they felt, the Kremlin authorities were unwilling to implement certain provisions in the Treaty of Peace. Relations between the two countries thus were good but not close.

The treaty of nonaggression concluded on September 28, 1926, brought the period of comparative inaction to an end. Under its terms, Lithuania and the Soviet Union agreed to conduct their mutual relations on the basis of the Peace Treaty signed in 1920. They pledged to respect each other's sovereignty and territorial integrity. Further, the two governments promised to abstain from acts of aggression against each other and to refuse all support to any third parties committing an act of aggression against one of the signatories. Each promised to dissociate itself from any economic or political coalition prejudicial to the interests of the other. Finally, the signatories consented to settle all potential disputes not settled by diplomatic means by creating an ad hoc Conciliation Commission, to be governed by a separate agreement.[4]

In seeking an agreement with Moscow, Lithuania wanted mainly to break the grip of Polish pressure. In a separate note appended to the treaty, the Soviet government recognized the Lithuanian claim to the Vilnius territory and thus strengthened Lithuania's diplomatic position. The Soviet Union, for its part, was attempting to break out of a diplomatic isolation. Its treaty

16

with Lithuania (together with similar agreements which the Soviet Union had already made with Afghanistan, Germany, and Turkey) contributed to the gradual disintegration of the cordon sanitaire against Russia. The Kremlin leaders were also seeking to prevent the growth of Polish influence in the Baltic area. They were apprehensive about the possible creation of a single bloc of nations, under Poland's leadership, along Russia's western frontiers and they feared an understanding, however unlikely, between Poland and Lithuania. Conclusion of a treaty with Lithuania was thought to be one way of hampering such unpleasant possibilities.

The treaty of nonaggression started a period in which Lithuania and the Soviet Union forged what some have termed a "special relationship." Partial congruence between the foreign policies of the two states in the Baltic area antedated the treaty of 1926. However, that correspondence was made more significant and precise by the treaty.

The third period in Lithuanian-Soviet relations must be viewed against a different background, that of the emergence of National Socialist Germany and the threat to Russian security that the Kremlin leaders saw in this development. Moscow was becoming increasingly concerned lest a German conquest of the Baltic states be the first step in that country's assault upon the Soviet Union. Its attitude toward the Baltic states began to change. After 1934 Lithuania cooperated closely with Latvia and Estonia. The third period in Lithuanian-Soviet relations is therefore discussed in the context of Lithuania's cooperation with those two states.

Estonia, Latvia, and Lithuania

THE FOREIGN POLICIES OF LITHUANIA and those of Latvia and Estonia showed considerable divergence in the first decade of the interwar period and an increasing amount of similarity in the second. It is convenient to review these changing interests by looking into two projects of Baltic unity which inspired a good

17

deal of diplomatic activity after the end of the war. It was thought that one way in which the old idea of Baltic solidarity might be brought closer to reality would be formation of a close tie among Lithuania, Latvia, and Estonia. This potential alliance was referred to as the smaller Baltic union. Another goal was the creation of a larger bloc that would include Finland, the Baltic states, and Poland. Warsaw was particularly eager to have such a combination. Poland hoped that the bloc, under its leadership, would coordinate the foreign policies of the member states. This project came to be known as the greater Baltic union. Lithuania, in effect, favored the first possibility and opposed the second. The Kaunas government declared that Lithuania stood ready to participate in any kind of union provided that such a union was based on independence and equality of its member states. It insisted, however, that Poland aimed at hegemony in the area, a design that precluded Lithuania's entrance into the proposed union.

The smaller Baltic union was developed in the 1930's; but the greater Baltic union failed to materialize for several reasons. At a time when confidence in the League of Nations was still prevalent, many attached dubious importance to regional understandings. Also, divergent interests of the different states made any attempt at coordination a difficult task. Latvia and Estonia, for example, favored such a union and supported Poland in her efforts to form it. Fear of Bolshevism was greater in those two states than in Lithuania because of the geographic proximity of the Soviet Union. Finland, on the other hand, preferred to remain neutral and declined to take part in the proposed union. Finally, Lithuania's opposition to Poland prompted the former to establish closer ties with the Soviet Union, which in turn regarded any coalition under Poland's leadership as detrimental to its security.

In the 1930's the interests of Lithuania, Latvia, and Estonia acquired greater consonance than in the preceding period. Their foreign policies aimed at cooperation among themselves and neutrality with respect to others. The conclusion of the German-

Polish nonaggression declaration in January of 1934 and the failure of the powers to come to an agreement on a scheme of collective security in Eastern Europe gave the Baltic governments the needed impetus finally to arrive at some closer and more explicit communion among themselves than had previously existed. On September 12, 1934, they signed the Treaty of Good Understanding and Cooperation and thereby framed what came to be known as the Baltic Entente. The three governments agreed to confer periodically on all questions concerning their foreign relations. They further agreed to help one another politically and diplomatically and to coordinate their diplomatic and consular activities. Lastly, the treaty envisaged peaceful settlement of all potential disputes among them.[5] Pursuant to the understanding, a number of Foreign Ministers' conferences were convened between 1934 and 1940 to discuss foreign policy matters which were of common concern. Formation of the Baltic Entente showed that the three republics were alert to dangers posed by the emergent Germany and were determined to safeguard their independent existence by as close an intra-Baltic cooperation as appeared to be possible.

A National Dilemma

THE MOUNTING ANTAGONISM in the ideological camps of the European powers confronted the Baltic states with two vital policy options. Association with either Germany or the Soviet Union was one alternative; a policy of neutrality was the other. The Baltic states chose to be neutral. Early in November 1938, representatives of the three governments met at Tallinn to draft neutrality laws. All three finally adopted such laws in late 1938 and early 1939. They imposed restrictions on the entrance and sojourn in the Baltic republics of warships, armed merchant vessels, and military aircraft of warring countries. In addition, the laws set forth other precautionary measures aimed at minimizing the danger of provocations.[6]

Lithuania's Foreign Minister referred the neutrality bill to an extraordinary session of the Seimas in Kaunas on January 10, 1939. His speech before the legislature revealed the rationale which prompted the Baltic states to imitate a Scandinavian practice dating back to the years before the outbreak of World War I. The Foreign Minister reasoned that such an explanation of the rights and obligations of a neutral power had helped the Scandinavian states to stay neutral in World War I. He added that Lithuania's statement of its rights and obligations was a proper and helpful step in attempting to steer that country clear of any potential conflicts among other powers. The Foreign Minister further intimated that the authors of the bill intended to dispel any possible doubts the neighboring governments might have about the course the Lithuanian government chose to follow. Lithuania was determined to prevent the commission of any acts which would tend to irritate or to affront the neighboring powers.[7] Neutrality thus remained the policy to which the Baltic states were firmly committed until the last days of their independent existence.

The ultimate destruction of the Baltic states resulted from German and Soviet policies. With the rise of Nazism, the Kremlin expected the Baltic countries to be friendly with the Soviet Union, and with it alone. On the one hand the numerous official pronouncements of the Soviet leaders registered their satisfaction with existing Soviet-Baltic relations, yet on the other hand commentators, military personnel, party members, and government officials in the Kremlin voiced mounting apprehensions that Germany might transform the three states into involuntary accomplices in an anti-Soviet crusade. Until the Czechoslovakian crisis, Moscow's recurrent demands for exclusive friendship were not explicitly formulated. However, in the early part of 1939 the Soviet attitude became crystallized. The formerly vague claims became a specific Soviet demand for veto powers on Baltic foreign policies. The Baltic states refused to comply.

After the fruitless negotiations between the Soviet Union and the Western powers during the summer of 1939, Germany and the Soviet Union signed the Pact of Nonaggression on August 23 (and a secret supplementary protocol on September 28). Among other things, the Baltic states were consigned to the Soviet field of action. Thereupon Moscow forced on them the so-called treaties of mutual assistance, stationing in their territories a limited number of Russian troops. The Soviet action restricted substantially the independence of the three republics.

Control of the Baltic area without its actual annexation did not satisfy the Soviet government. The Kremlin leaders were apparently determined to seek security through territorial expansion. After Germany's assault upon western Europe, the Russians moved into the Baltic. They occupied the three countries in June 1940, and later incorporated them into the USSR. The destruction of the Baltic states had been accomplished.

PART TWO

The Polity: The Nationalists and Their Opponents

THE TENETS OF MODERN

LITHUANIAN NATIONALISM

DEMOCRACY IN POSTWAR EUROPE was generally a brief experiment. In the majority of European nations it eventually succumbed to the forces of authoritarianism. In spite of differences, the various authoritarian movements on the Right exhibited many elements in common. Central in importance was their all-encompassing nationalism.

The advent of authoritarianism in Lithuania occurred on December 17, 1926. Why this particular corner of the world was not made safe for democracy is not the primary concern of this book. We are discussing here the consequences of this failure, namely modern nationalism in Lithuania from 1927 to 1940. In this essay modern nationalism includes the doctrinal concepts of the members of the Lithuanian Nationalist Union, formed in 1924, and of other individuals who contributed to the main body of Nationalist principles. Similarly, the term Nationalists refers mainly, but not solely, to members of the ruling Lithuanian Nationalist Union; it also includes other individuals who were generally sympathetic to the existing form of government.

Honoring President Antanas Smetona, the principal Nationalist journal surprised no one when in 1939 it openly conceded that "it is no secret that since 1927 Lithuania has been led not by some group of persons, not by some institution, but by one man."[1] Because this veteran personality had succeeded in presiding over the nation's destiny both during its moments of

25

grandeur, as in 1918, and in its days of despondency, as in 1940, the study of the Nationalist movement must first of all be a study of the political thought of its President. Other men made weighty contributions to Nationalist theory and practice, but in the final analysis Smetona alone was responsible for both.

National Unity and National Uniqueness

THE FIRST FACTOR which defined Smetona's political endeavors was his idea of national unity. This was the criterion by which he judged the quality of his country's civil life.[2] With uncommon consistency, his last major address in 1940 presaged national unity as the basis for postwar reconstruction, just as in 1907 he had thought it necessary to publish a new periodical expressly for that purpose.[3] In the intervening decades the means had changed, but the predilection for unity had not. Year in, year out, the apostle of unity and his disciples had lectured their fellow countrymen on every conceivable occasion that all individual views must be subservient to the demands of national unity. A truly indivisible nation was to be forged by uniting the people in a common cause, and a Nationalist administration was to be the instrument of national unity.[4] In order to keep the contrast alive between the liberal democracy before 1926 and the new regime, the Nationalists vigorously and persistently countered all the basic tenets of the old system.

The unity which the Nationalists had volunteered to bring about was teleological; its grand design was the realization of national potentialities. A descendant of the formative decades of preindependent Lithuania,[5] nationalist ideology, as it evolved before World War II, was implanted in a categorical affirmation of faith in the nation's future. "Ever more successfully and joyfully we shall create the Great Lithuania," exulted a Nationalist author. "Now comes the time of the concentration of Lithuanian national energies, of the consolidation of will, and, finally, of the true flowering of the ways of creation."[6] The Nationalists' quest for Lithuanian ways of life underscores their conviction that

26

their predecessors had imitated the Western model; hence, they began with an adroit denunciation of everything which seemed alien to the Lithuanian soul. "Pacifist wild talk," "sickly cosmopolitan ideas," "noxious gases and intoxicants," "foreign winds" and "foreign gods," "ideological scholasticism," "intellectual superstition" were some of the colorful gibes the Nationalists used in their scornful campaign against liberal democracy. Smetona once said that Lithuania had been "insulted" by liberalism and that there would be no return to it.[7] The nation had to discover not only its own form of government but also its own way of life. In doing so, the Nationalists particularly treasured qualities innate in the land and the people which distinguished one nation from another.[8] However, the Nationalist writers failed to identify any of these qualities. Instead, they merely placed emphasis on the need for individuality and hoped that ultimately, "in the process of our nation's life and work," this would produce a national culture which would make the country "an inimitable phenomenon of the universe," which would "justify" the nation's existence.[9]

The reasons for such concentration of attention on purely Lithuanian traits are traceable in part to the nineteenth century, to the disillusionment with the West in general, and to parliamentary democracy in particular. "In the speeches of the 'great' Western statesmen we once looked for lofty ideas and a true concern with the needs of mankind," confided a disaffected Nationalist. "Now we merely skim through those speeches. Now we are almost sure that we will find there either the official and insincere statements about the 'great principles' which no one believes any more and which are never put into effect, or demagoguery, or a formal justification of some evil, or, finally, the betrayal of impotence."[10]

National consciousness originates unawares, imperceptibly. To impart meaning and direction to it is the work of the educators, the intelligentsia.[11] By sketching and elucidating new vistas for future years, Antanas Smetona substantiated his own belief that "a nation without consciousness is no nation, and

27

that a nation without leaders is no nation: both are necessary."[12] He was resolved to give his nation both purpose and leadership.

Providing the people with leadership turned out to be a less exacting undertaking than drafting a national ideology. The Nationalists were reluctant to define the essential qualities of their concepts and were puzzled about just where this cultural autarchy would lead. The new man, no longer simply a citizen but a national figure, was above all interested in action, in striving for the ultimate. One proposition proved to be incontrovertible: the new ideology must grow out of the native soil. As Smetona vividly put it, "the Italians have their marble, the Germans their iron, and we have our clay, wood, and stone."[13] Such was the inception of the national movement which, in the words of a young proponent, proceeded "to foster national consciousness, to promote solidarity [and] the sense of destined togetherness, and to [cherish] love of one's land, one's traditions, work, duty, and the irresistible struggle for . . . a better future."[14]

To create such a nation meant to enhance cultural, not political, energies, for only cultural production attests to the fullest expression of the national spirit. Modern Lithuania, unlike historical Lithuania, was determined not to overlook the importance of national culture as the base upon which the state was founded.[15] The new leaders turned their backs on the medieval grand dukes, whose resourceful statecraft in the fourteenth and fifteenth centuries had neglected the development of a national culture.

In theory, modern nationalism was attended with deference to humanism. With the excesses of 1917 over and forgotten and the cataclysm of 1940-1945 still in the future, the Nationalists cherished the humanist tradition and hoped to become worthy successors of the gens humanissima. Confident that the welfare of one nation is a contribution to the welfare of the entire family of nations, Jonas Aleksa recorded the moral fervor of nationalism when he exclaimed, "we shall finally declare war on animosity, malice, envy, obsolescence, indecency, and infamy."[16]

28

There is reason to assume that Lithuanian politics was modified to a considerable extent by fidelity to ethical norms.[17]

The repudiation of parliamentary democracy was not confined to the disavowal of a form of government; it meant parting with a way of life. The Nationalists were not content merely to establish a new government but aspired to bring about a thorough change in the very structure of society as well. In theory the Nationalist transformation promised to be all-encompassing. "The nation-state is essentially a totalitarian state," asserted Antanas Maceina. "The totality in a nation-state is nothing but the permeation of public life with national elements."[18] In one of his addresses, President Smetona commented on the totality of aspirations and obligations:

> Not *pars* but *tota*, not some part of the nation but its totality shines in the hope of our free country. Not the needs of any one social class but the welfare of all . . . must be the nation's concern The government's orientation, which we say is national, prepares ways for itself from one end of our land to the other, not only in breadth but also in depth. . . . Through various public cultural institutions, through educational, agricultural, credit, industrial, and trade organizations, through the nationally conscious organizations [the government] . . . deliberately aspires, as if by means of some girders, to associate with the public at large. In this manner it reaches for and comes to the nation's solid base with all its characteristic features. . . . Led by its government in such a manner, so educated and roused, the public becomes organized. In other words, it becomes conscious of itself, an orderly nation, knowing what it is and what it wants.[19]

Stout words echoed throughout the land, striking a totalitarian note which was not lost upon the army, the schools, the economy, and the arts. "The army command is now concerned not only with the education the soldiers get but even more so with their indoctrination";[20] the purpose of education is to foment a national society, or "total pedagogics in a young nation-state, seeking a monolithic national body and a collective soul";[21] "a nation-state, as a matter of course, presupposes a national

29

orientation in art."[22] Nationalist ambitions appeared to be without limit.

The Assertion of Authority

HAVING DISCARDED THE LIBERAL FAITH, Lithuania, like other states in eastern Europe, sought a new framework to act within. According to Smetona, there were three possible options: Communism, Fascism, and authoritarianism. He selected the last for his country. Authoritarianism was defined as a form of government in which all institutions were constituted and operated in conformity with the predominance and responsibility of one person's will, and which excluded all legal means to oppose the will of the leader.[23] Authoritarianism was essentially a means to an end for the Nationalists. The realization of a conscious transformation of society which the Nationalists hoped to achieve was inconceivable without a monopoly of power. And when the President said "unity without discipline is impossible,"[24] he merely bowed to the demands of the logic of power. Despite the emphasis on education and indoctrination, which was abundantly supplied by the Nationalist ideologue, authoritarian power was the beloved instrument of the President.

Smetona distinguished between Fascism and authoritarianism. The affinity between the two was readily perceptible, but the differences were not. On several occasions President Smetona had echoed Benito Mussolini's advice that Fascism was not for export. Having branded his country's adoption of parliamentary democracy as an unfortunate import of foreign ways, the President was astute enough not to appear to be doing the same thing with Italian Fascism. "The Fascist state," he reasoned, "is a nation's form, and the nation itself—its content."[25] National content is a living phenomenon, creating at all times new forms of self-realization—both in the life of an individual and of a nation.[26] And because the experiences of one nation are unlike those of another, the cultural synthesis would retain national individuality. Lithuania would not embrace Fascism in its

30

entirety, but it would be affected by Fascist experience.[27] The Nationalist establishment did not develop into a Fascist state, but the doctrines which the Nationalists espoused were based on Fascist thought.

The Nationalists, with some support from Catholic intellectuals,[28] had persistently assailed the liberal democrats for having failed to offset ample individual rights with commensurate obligations. The new government would restore the proper balance by inducing all citizens to esteem tradition, discipline, authority. In habitual exhortations to old and young, to soldiers and farmers, by written and spoken word, the Nationalist President was indefatigable in his efforts to enhance order and discipline by continual references to a citizen's absolute obedience to his leaders:

> Today the leadership principle is everywhere being considered as the basic law in life. . . . Line up . . . toward the top, toward authority, toward the leader! Only this will make united action and united work possible. . . . Having devoted themselves to government authority, [the Nationalists] must not surrender to any outside influence. Should something be not clear to you, wait for explanations from above. . . . Trust only those who stand at the helm of the state. . . . Be calm and patient! In case of need, your thoughtful government officials will explain to you and will warn you how and what to guard against, how and what to defend. Obey them and do as you will be told.[29]

Another qualitative change wrought by the Nationalist regime was its emphasis on action. According to the Nationalists, their liberal predecessors talked much and acted little. Now it would be different. Antanas Smetona insisted that members of a Fascist society must always be on the move, for Fascism was an organization of work. Lithuania had to hasten onward because dangers surrounded her; she was constrained to race against time, he urged. At the end of the war most people had hoped that the soldier would be able to put away his sword and go back to his plowshare. But, continued the President, this had not happened. On the contrary, continental powers again were at odds with one another. Their armies and even their entire populations were being mobilized for an eventual challenge of power. The implications were clear. Nations would have to be drilled like armies, and discipline and harmony would have to displace freedom and dissent. There was no time to waste on parliamentary chatter, when there was serious work to be done quickly, in accordance with the dictates of the leadership principle.[30] Frequent allusions to the ominous foreign threat surrounded Nationalist reforms with a barrack-like atmosphere and a sense of urgency. Most of these dangers were real, the Nationalists had no need to invent them.

The ardent Nationalists, both party members and their intellectual coadjutors, were in accord on one far-reaching purpose, namely, to activate the Lithuanian character and to bring about a "psychological coup."[31] Stasys Šalkauskis analyzed this object of the Nationalist program: "The Lithuanian is not a voluntaristic but a contemplative type, with a noticeable inclination to an eastern quietism. He is patient, persevering, rather passive, and often even sluggish. He is a subtle observer of the world and people, in harmony with nature's rhythm, and peacefully disposed in his relations with others. . . . The Lithuanian is not inclined to tackle his future problems actively and resolutely, . . ."[32] Other writers, too, had studied and deplored the Lithuanian's "passive character," which was said to have been responsible for his disinclination to resist energetically the misfortunes that often were his lot.[33] The new man would have to be a Westerner, an activist, and the Nationalists would see to it that he became one.

The Organic State

NATIONALIST CONSTRUCTION is attainable only in an organized society. Smetona believed that the pluralist Lithuanian society must be converted into a monolithic community. Certain implications then followed with bitter logic. Fascism did not answer the demands of individual freedom, but only of individual interests. Instead of formal rights, the "organic" state provided for individual needs and security.[34] The nation was not a loose mass of people but an "organic" whole. Only such a nation could convey a true impression of its will. The tabulation of votes, a typically democratic contrivance, was a mechanical and therefore imperfect representation of the nation's will. Afflicted with internal contradictions, liberal institutions must surrender to the authority of a Leader who alone could achieve domestic harmony, for only one person's will could bring about ultimate unity. The balanced individual, one whose rights did not exceed his obligations, became the mainstay of society.[35]

Members of the "organized society" were not to compete among themselves; rather, they were to labor in harmony for the greater good of the entire nation. Work for mutual existence was to supplant the struggle for individual survival. Relations between capital and labor became an object of government attention. There were to be no strikes or lockouts to advance the conflicting interests of labor and management. A common standard of justice was to be applied.

Life in the new society would be organized through unified financial, economic, and cultural associations. And the association of associations would be the compact nation itself.[36] The role of the individual in such a well-ordered society was traced by a Nationalist editor, who advised that "the nation can be structured in such a way that the performance of any state service would constitute an active participation in the nation's common destiny. By an appropriate system of organizations every citizen can be made a part of such a trend in which he would feel himself a significant particle of order. . . . We conceive a nation so organized as integrated on a professional and functional basis into the political, economic, and cultural work of the state."[37] The Leader would exert discipline and harmony would spread through this organized whole of individual activities: "In all areas of culture, doing any kind of work, one must be guided by these principles. That is how the schools must operate, every institution, every organization or association, the press, the written and spoken word. A work of such proportions is conceivable [only] in consolidated organizations. This must be plainly visible in agriculture, industry, trade, and various other branches of private economy. Such today is the general direction everywhere. . . . Leadership is everywhere. . . ."[38] In an "organic" society the execution of work is the domain of manifest will and is reserved for appointed individual leaders. The thinking, on the other hand, is the province of a select collective. Antanas Smetona, who had participated in both, suggested the following division of labor: "Where in any work will manifests itself, an appointed individual leads; and where anything is being considered, selected men think. Consequently, leadership must everywhere be individual, from top to bottom, [and] in conformity with a selected collective. Only in this manner can a nation be spirited, enduring, progressive, vigorous, and, finally, united."[39]

The constitution of 1938 was the epitome of Nationalist theories. A punctilious embodiment of Smetona's political philosophy, this basic law conferred on the Seimas and the State Council only advisory and deliberative functions; invested the President with practically unlimited powers; and established ministries to direct public affairs in conformity with the Leader's will. Faithful to the intrinsic nature of authoritarianism, the Nationalist document left no legal means to countervail the Presidential will with any other.

The Lithuanian Nationalist Union

THE PRINCIPAL INTERMEDIARY between the Nationalist government and the general public was the Lithuanian Nationalist Union. Unlike political parties in the democratic countries, the Union as such was not expected to formulate its platform and campaign for political power. With an approximate membership of 13,000 men and women,[40] its task was to popularize the ideas of its leader. Discipline, the President was prone to remind, must originate with him, then pass through his administration into the Nationalist Union, from which it would devolve upon the

34

man in the street.[41] In order to carry out its responsibilities, the party had to be in close communion with the government and other Nationalist organizations, and had to have an intimate knowledge of a multitude of public activities. Party functionaries were often spurred by the President to set about their mission by exhibiting efficiency in the management of their particular affairs and by propagating in word and deed the Nationalist doctrines.

However, there were some Union members who believed that their duties were weightier than those of an agent; that, in fact, they were the decision makers. The Leader of the nation thereupon corrected them: the party merely influences the government, it does not direct it.[42] However, in the actual course of politics this concept of the division of labor was not as perfect as the President had suggested.

Educational Policies and Youth

AN OBJECT OF SPECIAL NATIONALIST CONSIDERATION was the country's youth. The two pillars upon which the education of a third of a million[43] students had rested were religious and national traditions. President Smetona dictated that religion was to be the rule, and its absence the exception. Ancient Lithuania, he pointed out, was religious and tolerated all faiths; and such it had remained until the present day. Having said that much, he then made it clear that education was to have a national orientation too.[44]

In their delineation of educational policies, the Nationalists were disinclined to tolerate in classrooms any universalist tendencies. They insisted that teachers impress upon boys and girls that national mindedness was the crucial pivot of culture.[45] By 1939 the country's leading pedagogical journal inferred that the "dry and abstract values" which had formed the basis of instruction in earlier years now had given way to the "intimate, living, and Lithuanian reality," and that this change attested to the triumph of the idea of national unity.[46] The school was regarded as a nucleus of nationalist society and as a model authoritarian republic, where students were to be the citizen-followers while the teachers were worthy leaders who directed them toward the ideals of truth, welfare, and beauty.[47]

The Union of Young Lithuania, a Nationalist offshoot for youths over eighteen, supplemented the regime's efforts to indoctrinate the country's younger generation with chauvinism. Devoid of originality, it echoed the Leader's ideas and blindly vowed its complete loyalty to him. The organization called on its 40,000 members to absorb the meaning of national liberty and always to be prepared to give their all to defend it. Youths were also admonished not to stain their honor as Lithuanians by such practices as marriage with foreigners.[48] Of all its programmatic statements, the group was most explicit about the leadership cult. Its chief officer, Alfonsas Kaulėnas, summarized the stringent posture: "The Union of Young Lithuania operates on an authoritarian basis. It knows only one leader—the Union Chief, the Nation's Leader, Antanas Smetona. Consequently, all that fails to originate with his thought and the general direction he has decreed is alien and unacceptable to the Union of Young Lithuania. Young Lithuania steadfastly believes that the nation can be united only when . . . the will of one leader prevails."[49] In their unconditional surrender to supreme authority, the *jaunalietuviai* (Young Lithuanians) were drilled to obey orders even if they failed to grasp what they were all about. "Surely," they would remark laconically, "one cannot always waste time on explanations, when one must act and act fast."[50]

Seven other Nationalist youth corporations were also voicing their ultrapatriotic sentiments and authoritarian faith in schools of higher education. In unison with the Young Lithuanians, they deified the splendor of their country's past, rated national traditions highly, and solemnly promised never to forfeit the nation's freedom: "Sooner will iron turn into wax and rock into water than will we desist from our purpose."[51] In the eleventh hour of Lithuania's independence the loyalty of most of the younger

36

generation continued to be militantly devoted both to its Leader and to its country.

Successes of the Nationalists

EVALUATION OF THE NATIONALISTS' SUCCESSES and failures is hampered by the difficulty of ascertaining and measuring the degree and depth of patriotism and nationalism. The regime was obsessively concerned with both. In political theory authoritarianism had made far-reaching inroads and appeared triumphant. Unquestionably it had legions of devotees among those who explicitly espoused it (as was the case with the Nationalists) and among some Catholics; but it also attracted a throng of fellow travelers who simply shunned democracy. If the Nationalists failed to convert to the new faith as many citizens as they had hoped to, they had nonetheless succeeded in neutralizing diverse strata of society who were formerly their opponents.

The most significant gain the Nationalists made in their deprecation of parliamentary democracy was the measure of theoretical support that their modern nationalist creed gained from Catholics. The establishment of cordial relations between the two groups focused first on educational policies, which were based on peaceful coexistence between religious and national traditions. "Religion and nationality," propounded a Catholic philosopher, "are the two basic elements in man's life which impart meaning to this life and make it precious."[52] The passage could have been attributed to President Smetona himself. Equally reinforcing was the confluence of Catholic and Nationalist ideas on the "organic" structure of society. Another philosopher, the highly regarded Stasys Šalkauskis, explicated the position which some Catholics assumed: "As a matter of principle the Catholic world view is prone to defend the organic and hierarchic organization of society and . . . to consider best that form of government which brings the monarchic, aristocratic, and democratic elements into a most perfect union."[53] And when a Catholic politician openly embraced "authoritarian democracy"

37

as the most suitable form of government for Lithuania under the circumstances,[54] the Nationalists rightly supposed that their leadership principle enjoyed a measure of Catholic support.[55] For such agreeable assistance the Nationalists replied in kind: they paid salaries to Catholic clergy and appropriated generous sums to Catholic schools, seminaries, monasteries, and churches.

Nationalist Failures

DESPITE THE SUCCESSES of the Smetona regime, by the eve of World War II the Nationalists had become bogged down. The Nationalist campaign was not confined to any one segment of society; consequently, its effects were equally diverse. The Nationalist theoretical challenge had been total, but when united action was called for, the public answered with apathy. Universal public indifference and deep political discord on the eve of the Soviet assault suggest the chasm that severed Nationalist theories from the pulse of everyday life. Both popular disengagement and national disunity are amply documented. "Colorless," "passive," "stagnant," "baconized"[56]—these were some of the disparaging terms hurled by intellectuals, especially leftists, at Lithuania's youth and the general public.[57] Stasys Šalkauskis reflected Catholic ambivalence when he flouted the Nationalists by declaring "our passivity, inclination toward servility, a horizon closed to wider interests, a predilection for cunningness, and that monstrous envy which cannot tolerate the emergence of true personalities have now again found for themselves a most favorable ground."[58] The stifling atmosphere was particularly distasteful to the country's leftist intellectuals, the domestic outcasts who wanted none of the Nationalist doctrines. They lived with the hope that the future would eventually bring a new birth of freedom, when they would speak a language the coming generations would be able to understand, a language not unlike the thunder of a cannon.[59] They did not have to wait much longer.

National unity, the raison d'être of the Nationalist movement, was seen as fantasy rather than as reality. From a seemingly inexhaustible diversity of adjectives, "great," "true," "real," "iron," "constructive," used to depict unity, none characterized it more fully than "elusive." The Catholic and Populist press on one side and the Nationalist media on the other battled ceaselessly. A Nationalist spokesman conceded that the regime in general and the leadership principle in particular remained alien to a great many people, and that the government was in retreat.[60]

What were some of the causes which accounted for Nationalist failures? Two major developments may be cited: a dilution of the dynamic revolutionary nature of the movement and a reluctance to use force against the opposition. Conservative in social and economic policies, the President failed to satisfy his younger followers who had hoped for a more vigorous and more militant administration than the senior party members were willing to institute.[61]

The President's disinclination to resort to arbitrary and excessive compulsion to impose his will caused a gap between the logic of totalitarianism and the compromising nature of politics. There appears to be some truth in the allegations by a number of dejected younger Nationalists that President Smetona was content to broach his political philosophy in general terms, while allowing a good deal of freedom, too much for the taste of most party members, to those who interpreted it and put it to use.[62]. This is not to imply that Lithuania's was a liberal regime. The common recourse to police measures, the protracted ban on all opposition parties, the broad powers bestowed on district executives, and the existence of forced labor camps, all negate such a conclusion. Those repressive acts actually employed by the government were sufficiently severe to generate widespread discontent, but they were inadequate to give effect to the essential conditions implicit in Nationalist political theory. This ambiguity suggests that President Smetona might have been content with a less dictatorial form of government than had in fact evolved. Occasional testimony by former members of both the government and the opposition also indicates that the destruction of liberal democracy was not intended to be permanent.[63] Perhaps there was some thought of a presidential democracy, that is, a form of democratic government under which the chief executive is not responsible to the legislature. Had this been in vogue on the continent, it might have reconciled the President's beliefs with the means he was willing to apply to realize them. But President Smetona was primarily an exponent of national unity, not of democracy. To gain the first, he forsook the second.

THE CENTERS OF OPPOSITION

The Catholics

THE MOST EXTENSIVE OPPOSITION to the Nationalist regime emanated from Catholic quarters. However, the dissolution of the Christian Democratic Party and the abrogation of its right to take part in the country's political life restricted the Catholics from acting as a cohesive political group.[1] There continued to exist until the very end of independence a nucleus of Catholic leaders, both senior clergymen and their younger secular collaborators, whose general position was thought to be representative of the Catholic bloc. In 1939 1940 the Catholics resembled a pressure group contending for special interests more than a regular political party. Nevertheless, Catholic influence in political, economic, and cultural areas could not be doubted.

To say that Catholics were in opposition to the Nationalists is not a full appraisal of the Catholic position. However, it is more difficult to tell what they were endeavoring to do, than it is to understand what they were fighting against. A Nationalist writer had good reason to assert that "so far ... the young Christian Democrats lack an intelligible political ideology. It is not clear whether they tend toward an authoritarian or a democratic regime."[2] Some of them were publicly committed to an "organic" and hierarchic composition of society; others preferred a simple authoritarianism. Some, like Professor Šalkauskis,

41

would have preferred the superimposition of the hierarchical Catholic hegemony upon the organic state the Nationalists were constructing.[3] Others denounced the one-party regime and sided with individuals and institutions battling for political rights.[4] And still others hoped for an administration in which the best men of all convictions would work together.[5] However, the emergent Catholic consensus, overshadowing the profound but less immediate differences concerning the nation's future political organization, pleaded for more representative government and the restoration of civil rights. In one editorial after another the Catholic press vigorously assailed the Nationalists' pretensions of serving as sole intermediaries between the government and the people; they condemned their exorbitant claims as unconstitutional, absolutely groundless, and abnormal. In sum, politics under dictatorial conditions made the Catholics ambivalent; they both supported and opposed the Nationalists. In theory, a segment of the Catholic elite placed a good deal of emphasis on various strands of authoritarianism, thereby reinforcing many of the Nationalist ideas. But in practice, this affinity with the Nationalists did not prevent many other Catholics from advocating more permissive government and from seeking political influence, goals which made them the rivals of the Nationalists.

In addition to the influence which the Catholics acquired through their extensive press, they drew considerable strength from the varied social and cultural activities which they carried on among old and young. Their campaign among workers was highly successful. The Union of Christian Workers, a professional association with 52 chapters throughout the land, emulated the Communists in striving to attract the loyalty of the workers. It supported labor's economic demands, provided for numerous recreational opportunities, organized courses on home economics, and formed separate sections to meet the needs of young workers.[6] In some instances its accomplishments were so marked that the workers themselves would rid their meetings of Communist speakers.[7]

Associations formed for the purpose of teaching students and children to serve God and country were organized as affiliates of Catholic groups for adults. Meetings, Communion services, Christmas parties, and a variety of devout exercises were arranged. Fragmentary statistics and a possible overlap in membership render it impracticable to suggest an accurate picture of Catholic numerical strength. However, a survey of the Lithuanian press furnishes adequate grounds for the following estimates of membership in some of the major Catholic organizations:[8]

Organization	*Estimated Membership*
Catholic students "Ateitis"	6,000
Catholic children "Angelaičiai"	55,000
Union of Christian Workers	10,000
Union of Catholic Women's Organizations	112,000
Catholic rural youth "Pavasaris" (men's division)	40,000

The Populists

ALTHOUGH ITS FULL POTENTIAL cannot be estimated with complete accuracy, a second source of resistance to the Nationalist supremacy was the veteran Lithuanian Peasant-Populist Union, commonly referred to as the Populists. A democratic party in pre-Nationalist years, the Populists tallied approximately one-fourth of the total vote. In 1939-1940 they persistently criticized the Smetona dictatorship for the suppression of individual rights, favored radical agrarian reforms,[9] tended to support a planned economy, and deplored public indifference to the affairs of state. Not unlike the Catholics, the Populists worked out their attitudes at private meetings in Kaunas, which were frequented by such esteemed party figures as the former Prime Minister Mykolas Sleževičius and the onetime President Kazys Grinius.

Even before the formation of the Černius administration on March 27, 1939, the two principal sources of opposition to the government had agreed to coordinate their anti-Nationalist campaign. The initial stage of the joint operation, which in late 1938 and early 1939 brought about an abortive anti-Nationalist manifesto in Klaipėda, goes back to the top level Catholic and

Populist conversations initiated in the spring of 1938. Frequent consultations between the two parties were prompted by their resolve to impress upon the citizens their belief that the Nationalist government had neither popular confidence nor popular mandate to administer the country. Joint action necessitated a joint declaration of principles. This, however, was no easy accomplishment as the allies, despite their animosity toward the Nationalists, were themselves far apart ideologically. They often clashed over questions such as Church and State prerogatives.[10] The compromise which was finally achieved owed much to the growing influence in Catholic quarters of younger secular leaders. Essentially, the common platform published late in 1938 was a demand for the restoration of democratic government. However, it envisaged a restriction on the activities of splinter parties and expected the future President and the ministers to sever their party affiliations upon assumption of office.[11]

The ensuing association of the Catholics and the Populists with the political following of the dictatorial ex-Premier Augustinas Voldemaras[12] made the return to democracy a somewhat attenuated objective. The triple alliance, ratified by opposition centers in Kaunas, set up a new political front calling for a form of government based on national unity and discipline,[13] an appeal totally devoid of originality. The nature of its political propositions, its modus operandi, and such incidentals as the Fascist salute it had adopted cast a shadow of doubt on the group's democratic authenticity.

The Nationalist regime quickly suspended the journal published in Klaipėda by the opposition triple alliance. The new political front itself discontinued its operations when it threw its support behind the Patriotic Front that gained momentary popularity in the wake of German occupation of Klaipėda.[14] Yet the existence of a united Catholic and Populist opposition was evidenced by the parallel editorial opinions of their dailies in the capital.

The Social Democrats

IT IS NOT SURPRISING that the most pertinaciously democratic political movement was also the most shattered one. The Lithuanian Social Democratic Party, a third core of opposition which earlier claimed a considerable labor following and a membership of 3,000, for years was not conceded the privilege of publishing even a single newspaper. Only in 1939 did it secure authorization to "toy" with a modest monthly.[15] Sensitive to the Catholic-Populist opposition's dubious adherence to democratic principles, the Social Democrats remained aloof from the Catholic-Populist axis, choosing instead the desolate and ineffective path of unaffiliated opposition.

The Army

HABITUALLY CONTRAVENING President Smetona's advice to display a nonpartisan interest in politics broadly defined, the Lithuanian army frequently intervened in the course of domestic events in a manner unintended by the chief executive. Because of these extracurricular activities, the military profession is briefly considered here as a political factor. The precarious privilege of intervening in interparty quarrels seems to have been reserved for the army's upper echelons. The ordinary soldier was instructed by his superiors to keep aloof from any active participation in party politics either on the side of the Nationalists or of the opposition.[16] Instead, he was offered a required three-stage civics course, intended to familiarize him with the soldierly virtues, the military and political history of his country, and the nation's aspirations. Additional lectures on Lithuania's geography, economy, political institutions, and underlying policies were foreseen for the future.[17] Military journals published for the army's rank and file normally abstained from party politics, too.

In 1926 army officers had brought Smetona to power. However, by 1939, especially under the leadership of Stasys Raštikis, they could not be, and were not, relied upon to back the President unequivocally. It is difficult to ascertain the political views of the officers. It is sufficient to point out that the majority of the senior officers favored conservative policies and usually stood by the chief executive. On the other hand, the dynamic personality of Professor Voldemaras continued to attract admirers among the younger officers who were displeased with Smetona's moderate course.[18] Besides determining the enemies abroad, the military could be counted on to do some plotting against their adversaries at home. The expensive military establishment, which annually absorbed more than a quarter of the total government revenue, had grown into an imposing force rivaled only by the political dexterity of the President.

THE COMMUNIST UNDERGROUND

LITHUANIA'S SUCCESS in gaining and reinforcing its independence from Russia after the end of World War I condemned the Communists to twenty years of underground existence. Incessant hostility between nationalists[1] and Communists issued from divergent ideological commitments. The nationalists wanted Lithuania to be an independent state; the Communists subordinated national aspirations to the demands of the class struggle and expected Lithuania to become part of Soviet Russia.[2] The congruity of political program and action between the Russian and the Lithuanian Communists during the interwar decades made the Communist Party of Lithuania, in the eyes of the nationalists, a medium of a foreign power. Thus, the Communist alternative concerned Lithuania's very existence. The stakes were high, and at the time compromise seemed to be impossible. The nature of domestic politics did not fundamentally affect the hostile attitude which the two parties assumed toward each other.

Communist Strategy and Tactics

EARLY COMMUNIST PLANS for Lithuania depended largely on events and policies in Russia. In 1920, the victory of a Communist revolution in the West still appeared to be possible. The outcome of the Polish-Russian war, then in progress, was one

47

determinant of such a possibility. In the summer of 1920 it
seemed that Russia would win that war, and the Communists
were jubilant. Many in Moscow hoped that Russia's successes
at the front would induce the proletariat in other countries to
take up arms for the Communist cause.

The inroads of the Red Army animated the Lithuanian Communists, too. A Provisional Revolutionary Government was
established on Lithuanian territory which was retaken by the
Russians from the Poles. The Lithuanian Communist leaders
considered the time opportune for an uprising against the government in Kaunas. They made the necessary preparations and
sent instructions to local Communist organizations, telling them
to be ready for action. The purpose of these activities was the
establishment of a Soviet government in Lithuania.[3] However,
Communist plans aborted because the progress of the Red
Army proved to be ephemeral. Russian reverses in the war with
Poland destined the victory of the Communist revolution in the
West to an indefinite delay. The delay, in the case of Lithuania,
lasted two decades. Adverse circumstances prevented the Russian army from absorbing Lithuania in 1920, but a propitious
turn in events enabled it to accomplish that purpose in 1940.
In the interim, Communists in Lithuania made every effort to
survive as a cohesive group.

The strategy of the Communist Party of Lithuania for the
years following the Polish-Russian war was worked out at a
congress held in 1921 in Königsberg. Its immediate task was to
approach the masses, radiating influence throughout the lower
segments of Lithuanian society. Specifically, the Communist
plans called for an alliance of two groups, the urban and rural
workers and a portion of the farming population, the small
landholders. The Communists hoped that in their struggle
against the government the farmers with medium sized holdings
would adopt a neutral, if not a favorable attitude. These decisions and expectations were inspired by Lenin's writings, by
the experiences of the Bolsheviks in Russia, and by the resolutions of the Comintern's third congress.[4] In subsequent attempts

48

to implement these plans, the Communists put forth economic demands beneficial to labor and the small farmers. Their covert participation in government elections, labor union activities, and the cooperative movement was intended to win for them as broad a range of influence as possible.

The next congress of the Communist Party of Lithuania convened in 1924. Meeting in Moscow, the delegates reviewed the record of the preceding three years and appeared rather pleased with it. Two accomplishments were considered noteworthy, the increase in ideological and organizational strength and the additional popular support for the Party.[5] The congress made no changes in strategy. It simply told the Party organizations to make use of the public's dissatisfaction with government policies by supplying the people with political meaning and direction. The congress did, however, alter some of the tactical means. For example, the attempt to appeal directly to the rank and file members of other socialist parties, a device known as the united front from below, replaced earlier attempts at joint action through agreement with the leaders of those parties, known as the united front from above.[6] Refusal by the leaders of other socialist parties to collaborate with the Communists in the past made such a change necessary.

The military coup in late 1926, which brought the Nationalists to power, augured a precarious future for the Communist Party. The Communists themselves referred to the next four or five years as a time of crisis.[7] Changes in Lithuania's domestic politics prompted the Communist leaders to call another conference, which was held in Moscow in 1927. Empowered to act as a congress, it entered into a critical examination of past operations and enunciated the general direction which the Party was to adhere to in the years of Nationalist supremacy. The next comparable congress was convened only in 1941. The decisions made in Moscow[8] spurned the use of any sporadic conspiracies against the Kaunas authorities. Instead, they asserted that the Lithuanian regime could be overthrown only by a well-planned mass uprising of workers and peasants led by the Communist Party. The

49

peasants in question were primarily the hired agricultural labor-ers,[9] but small landholders and even farmers with medium sized holdings were not excluded. In fact, the conference decided to intensify the Party's efforts to win the support of the farmers of medium sized holdings. The delegates reaffirmed the need to link the struggle for the economic progress of workers and peas-ants with that for their political goals. They also agreed that those committed to such a struggle should not be led to rely upon outside help; rather, they should be educated to have faith in their own energies. Lastly, the conference decided to set up a number of illegal organizations for work in Lithuania, but it added that legal means of action must not be overlooked either.

The Communist Party had survived the crisis produced by the Nationalist takeover. This hopeful conclusion issued from a conference of Party leaders held in 1933. However, the delegates were not at all satisfied with the Party's over-all achievements. They conceded that their failure to attract a sizeable following was of major significance. The conference felt that the causes of this failure were an improper application of the united front tactics in some cases and their utter disregard in others. More-over, the conference noted that in fighting for the cause of labor the Party had not always put forth demands which the workers cared most about, but had instead accentuated requests alien to their immediate needs. Many local Communists were irritated by the priorities given to the interests of international Commu-nism and of the USSR over local requirements. Their earlier grumble that "Moscow issues the directives and we fools carry them out" was corroborated by a defector who, in 1939, had testified that to Communists in Lithuania the orders from abroad not infrequently seemed altogether senseless, because they failed to meet the needs of labor. For instance, strikers who sometimes did not even know what they were striking for were induced to demand that England pull its troops out of China, that Italy cease fighting Ethiopia, and that the German government release Ernst Thälmann, demands which were all fairly remote.[10]

The conference impressed on the delegates the need to correct these operational errors. Specifically, it ruled against further attemps at concerted action through agreement with the leaders of the Social Democratic Party, whom it upbraided for alleged collaboration with the government. Instead, it urged its followers to go directly to that party's rank-and-file members. In conclusion, the conference again reminded the workers not to expect outside help but to rely on their own strength and to be prepared to give their lives for the sake of the revolutionary cause. The delegates hailed the future day when the Communist Party would lead an insurrection against the regime and inaugurate a Soviet government in Lithuania.[11]

The threat to Russian security that the Kremlin leaders saw in the emergence of National Socialist Germany was probably the main reason for important tactical changes effected throughout the world Communist movement in 1935. The seventh congress of the Communist International spurred its member parties to propose to the Social Democrats, Populists, and other parties the formation of a broad anti-Fascist alliance commonly known as the popular front.[12] The attempt to form such a coalition in Lithuania came in July 1935, when the Communist Party decided to approach the leaders of the Social Democrats, the Populists, and the Socialist Zionists, but it also persisted in its campaign to undermine the strength of the rival parties by a direct appeal to their rank-and-file members and supporters. The Communists were instructed not to insist on a dominant position in any coalition that might be created, but instead to work on equal terms with the others.[13] Communist efforts to put together an anti-Fascist coalition produced virtually no result. The failure to frame such a coalition indicates that despite the expedients employed, the Communist Party found few if any partners willing to engage with it in any kind of concerted action.

Organization and Members

COMMUNIST ACTIVITIES in Lithuania flowed principally through three channels: the Communist Party of Lithuania (Comintern

Section), Lithuania's Communist League of Youth, and the Lithuanian Red Aid. The main, although not the most popular, vehicle was the Party.

As early as April 1918, agents from Moscow appeared in Vilnius and began to build a Communist organization in Lithuania. Soon they founded the Communist Party of Lithuania and Byelorussia, a hybrid symptomatic of the early Bolshevik intention to merge Lithuania and Byelorussia into one Soviet republic.[14] However, Lithuania's success in preserving its independence made that type of organization unsuitable. In 1920 the two were divorced, and Lithuania acquired its own organization, the Communist Party of Lithuania.

One determinant and indicator of any group's potential is membership. However, the discussion of the Communist Party's numerical strength encounters two problems. One is determining the actual number of members; the other is determining their effectiveness. Evidence suggests that a number of the Party's local and intermediate organizations were so shattered and inert as to deprive their membership lists of much of their meaning. Their poverty of accomplishment was due to numerous and diverse causes: an actual membership short of the purported one, desertion from the Party, inactivity of the primary organizations, broken communications between the regional centers and their primary organizations, and a disorganized state of regional leadership.[15]

The attempt to determine the precise membership in the Communist Party faces difficulties. Factors responsible for the lack of certainty include the following: a dearth of reliable information, discrepancies in available data, failure to distinguish between members living in detention under the State Security Department and those still enjoying their freedom, and failure to distinguish between members residing in Lithuania and abroad. Recognizing such limitations, Table 1 presents estimates of Party membership.

The period when Lithuania struggled to maintain and reinforce its independence from Russia inflicted severe losses on

52

the Communist Party. Many of its primary organizations were smashed, while those that remained lost contact with one another. Some Communists lost their lives fighting the nationalists, others were arrested and detained in custody, while still others were forced to flee the country.[16] Thus, Table 1 indicates that the Party survived this period with an approximate membership of 863 in 1920.

Russian gains in the war with Poland in the summer of 1920 heightened Communist activities in Lithuania. Membership in the Party rose to about 1,300. However, the increase in numerical strength was a momentary one, and membership soon began to fall. In 1922 it stood at only 211. A government decision to intensify its repressive measures against the Communist Party was one cause of this marked decline, while the repercussions of the Polish-Russian war were another. The expectation of a quick and easy victory in mid-1920 prompted a number of people to join the Party. When the victory failed to materialize, many of the less determined members became disillusioned and left the Party—or were expelled.[17] These adverse developments, in turn, gave rise to further problems: violations of Party discipline, failure to attend meetings, and the inclination to discontinue work among the citizens at large in favor of work within the Party.[18] Lastly, the collapsed condition to which the organization was reduced generated discord among the leaders of the Party.

Later, however, persistent efforts enabled the Communists to rebuild their organization and find new supporters. In the months before the Nationalist seizure of power late in 1926, the Party was believed to have a membership of more than 500. But the dawn of the Nationalist period dealt another blow to the Communist Party. Its illegal publications were a registry of failures. They show that Party committees in the city and region of Kaunas, both in an area of preponderant activities, were "dead organs." They further disclose that "the primary organizations were not doing anything," and that there were practically no such organizations in places of work. In general, the Communists

53

TABLE 1

MEMBERSHIP IN THE COMMUNIST PARTY

Year	Number of members
1918	800
1919	n.a.*
1920	863
1921	1,300
1922	211
1923	298
1924	800
1925	n.a.
1926	507
1927	254
1928	n.a.
1929	750
1930	650
1931	n.a.
1932	500
1933	750
1934	1,100
1935	1,850
1936	1,942
1937	1,499
1938	n.a.
1939	n.a.
1940 (before the occupation)	1,500

* Not available.

Note on Sources: The table is based on the following Communist sources: B. Sudavičius, *LKP kova už darbininkų klasės vienybę (1934-1937 metai)* (The Struggle of the CPL for the Unity of the Working Class, 1934-1937; Vilnius: Valstybinė politinės ir mokslinės literatūros leidykla, 1961), p. 29; A. Gaigalaitė and others (eds.), *Lietuvos TSR istorija* (History of the Lithuanian SSR; Vilnius: Mintis, 1965), III, 165 and 283; E. Šopa, "Buržuazinės diktatūros nuvertimas ir Lietuvos įstojimas į Tarybų Sąjungą" (The Overthrow of the Bourgeois Dictatorship and Lithuania's Entrance into the Soviet Union), *Lietuvos TSR istorijos bruožai* (Aspects of the History of the Lithuanian SSR), ed. J[uozas] Jurginis (Kaunas: Šviesa, 1965), p. 71; S. Atamukas, *LKP kova prieš fašizmą, už tarybų valdžią Lietuvoje 1935-1940 metais* (The Struggle of the CPL against Fascism, for the Soviet Government in Lithuania, 1935-1940; Vilnius: Valstybinė politinės ir mokslinės literatūros leidykla, 1958), pp. 48, 50, 56, and 63; A. Beržinskaitė, *LKP veikla auklėjant Lietuvos darbo žmones proletarinio internacionalizmo dvasia, 1927-1940* (The Activities of the CPL in Educating the Working People of Lithuania in the Spirit of a Proletarian Internationalism, 1927-1940; Vilnius: Valstybinė politinės ir mokslinės literatūros leidykla, 1962), p. 8; S. Lopajevas, *Lietuvos komunistų partijos idėjinis ir organizacinis stiprėjimas, 1919-1924* (The Increase in Ideological and Organizational Strength of the Communist Party of Lithuania, 1919-1924; Vilnius: Valstybinė politinės ir mokslinės literatūros leidykla, 1964), pp. 46, 81, 97, and 100; *Partijos darbas* (Party Work), no. 8 (August 1932), p. 97; Institute of Party History, "Lietuvos komunistų partijos istorijos apybraiža" (A Sketch were more or less isolated from the public.[19] Precise figures on membership for the years immediately following the Nationalist victory are not available. However, there is reason to think that the Party was decimated. In mid-1932, a time when the crisis was considered to be over, the membership was still below 500.

Membership in the middle of the 1930's was on the rise. The increase was partly due to the relaxation of the rules for admission of new members effected in 1935. Sectarianism, which had characterized the Party in previous years, was discarded in favor of a more inclusive organization. Loyalty, agreement with Party decisions, and willingness to work toward the establishment of the dictatorship of the proletariat were henceforth to be sufficient qualifications for membership.

From 1937 to the Soviet occupation of Lithuania in mid-1940, the Party managed to keep its membership at about 1,500,[20] despite purges and police repressions. Table 2 shows that on the eve of Russian annexation, many Communists were relatively new members who had joined the Party during the preceding three and a half years. This would tend to corroborate the conclusion reached by the State Security Department that the Party not only had succeeded in finding new support to take the places of comrades isolated by the police, but also had continued to increase its total membership.

Lack of reliable information precludes an inquiry into the Party's social composition before 1940. However, Communist sources reveal that seven months after the Soviet occupation, 65.8 per cent of Party members were white collar workers. They further indicate that in February 1941, only 13.5 per cent of members were industrial workers.[21] Communist influence was

---

of the History of the Communist Party of Lithuania), *Komunistas* (The Communist), no. 11 (November 1967), p. 107.

The estimate for 1927 is based on recent Communist disclosures that "about 50 per cent" of the total party membership had been arrested by the Nationalists soon after their seizure of power late in 1926. See A. Marcelis, "Dėl padėties Lietuvos Komunistų partijoje po fašistinio perversmo" (On the State of the Communist Party of Lithuania After the Fascist Coup), *Komunistas* (The Communist), no. 8 (August, 1966), p. 68. The estimate for 1930 is based on an article placing the total membership between 600 and 700. See *Balsas* (Voice), July 25, 1930, p. 586.

TABLE 2

MEMBERSHIP IN THE COMMUNIST PARTY AS OF JANUARY 1, 1941
(according to length of service)

Period of Initiation	Number of Members	Percentage of Total Membership
Before 1921	28	1.1
1921-1925	44	1.8
1926-1930	283	11.4
1931-1936	729	29.1
1937-1939	557	22.2
1940: Before the occupation	190	7.6
1940: During the occupation	673	26.8
Total	2,504	100.0

Note on Sources: The table has been derived from a report which Party Secretary Antanas Sniečkus gave in 1941. See A. Butkutė-Ramelienė, *Lietuvos komunistų partijos kova už tarybų valdžios įtvirtinimą respublikoje 1940-1941 m.* (The Struggle of the Communist Party of Lithuania for the Consolidation of Soviet Power in the Republic, 1940-1941; Vilnius: Valstybinė politinės ir mokslinės literatūros leidykla, 1958), p. 167.

The table apparently includes a number of Communists who were living abroad before the occupation but returned to Lithuania after the occupation.

generally stronger in small industrial and commercial firms which had succeeded in evading government controls in independent Lithuania and which had oppressed their employees by substandard conditions of work. In such places the workers were alienated and disgruntled, tending to pay more attention to what the Communists had to say.[22]

The primary organizations, known as cells, were the base of the Party pyramid. According to the rules, they were not to have more than seven members. However, some primary organizations failed to abide by these rules and had a much larger membership.[23] Between the primary and the national organizations were the regional formations, of which there were fourteen in 1936.[24] This structure lasted until the reforms of 1938, when it was decided to abolish the regional organizations. The reforms were intended to synchronize the Party apparatus with the units of administration into which Lithuania was divided.[25]

The chief instruments of Communist operations were strikes, demonstrations, and clandestine publications. As a case in point, during 1935 the Communist underground activities inside Lithuania included: publication of nine issues of *Tiesa* (Truth), an organ of the Party's Central Committee with a circulation of 2,000; seven issues of *Kareivių Tiesa* (Soldiers' Truth), the Central Committee's organ for soldiers, circulation 2,000; eleven issues of *Darbininkų ir Valstiečių Jaunimas* (The Youth of Workers and Peasants), an organ of Lithuania's Communist League of Youth, circulation 1,000; and between thirty-six and forty-nine proclamations. Moreover, the Communists were responsible for approximately thirty-five strikes in which 5,400 workers took part.[26] Communist political slogans generally decried the persecution of "revolutionaries," demanded the release of political prisoners, called for additional rights for workers and peasants, resisted any improvement in Lithuanian-Polish relations, and pursued a pro-Soviet course.

Subsidiary Organizations

MEMBERS OF LITHUANIA'S COMMUNIST LEAGUE OF YOUTH (Komsomol) did not fare as well as their senior comrades. Diligence by the security organs, interfactional quarrels among the members themselves, and the sectarian nature of the organization made the Komsomol a failing body as late as 1936. The young Communists distributed revolutionary leaflets, hoisted red flags, and spent much time with individual employees in small shops, but the results were meager. They failed to establish contacts with larger groups of young workers in the factories; moreover, it appears that they themselves were not at all enthusiastic about political education.[27] After the seventh congress of the Communist International, the Komsomol altered both the nature of its activities and its organizational structure with a view to making itself more attractive to younger citizens. For the most part, the innovations corresponded to the changes effected by the parent Party.[28] This readjustment enabled the youth group to double its small membership, which by mid-1940 reached approximately 1,000. This total may include a number of Komsomols

57

who were also members of the Party, since in earlier years all Party members under 21 (or 23 according to some sources) were at the same time members of the Komsomol.[29]

The Lithuanian Red Aid (MOPR)[30] was by far the most popular pro-Communist organization in the country. After the reforms initiated throughout the Communist movement in 1935, membership in MOPR increased from 145 in 1931 to 1,250 in 1936, and to approximately 6,000 in 1940.[31] The Red Aid included a sizable leftist but not strictly Communist following. Moreover, it had a host of regular contributors whose numbers are impossible to identify. A number of businessmen and leftist intellectuals, especially after the establishment of Soviet military bases in Lithuania late in 1939, made regular payments to it in order to be on the safe side. A functionary of the Communist Party is reported to have said in 1940 that "we had always been able to keep a large and active group of sympathizers around us all through the illegal days."[32]

The main purpose of the Red Aid was to raise funds for the assistance of revolutionaries who were suffering arrest, imprisonment, and exile. Inasmuch as figures for the last years of the interwar decades are unobtainable, it is necessary to revert to earlier data for some estimates of the extent of its transactions. Table 3 lists the organization's finances for the second half of 1935. Some 60 per cent of the total contributions raised in Lithuania came from Kaunas.[33] Furthermore, it appears that foreign aid was negligible and that the bulk of finances was raised at home.[34] In the closing years of the decade, the contributions probably increased, reaching a monthly average of 6,000 lits.[35]

The months before Lithuania's absorption by the Soviet Union saw an increase in Communist activities. Two main developments animated the Communist underground. One development was the deteriorating social and economic conditions that beset the Lithuanians after the loss of Klaipėda, the affliction of European war, and the acquisition of the heterogeneous Vilnius population; and the other was the encampment in

58

TABLE 3

SEMIANNUAL FINANCIAL STATEMENT OF THE LITHUANIAN RED AID
JULY—DECEMBER, 1935
(*in lits*)

Receipts		*Expenditures*	
Balance from the first half of 1935	957.15	Grants to political prisoners	11,794.85
Contributions in Lithuania	19,680.90	Grants to prisoners' families	3,500.10
From MOPR in Moscow	3,600.00	To deportees and freed prisoners	1,500.00
From abroad	126.30	Medical aid to freed prisoners	2,000.00
		Legal aid	328.00
		Press	561.00
		Travel	1,140.40
		Miscellaneous	2,246.20
Total	24,364.35	Total	23,070.55

Source : *Raudonoji Pagalba* (The Red Aid), No. 16 (April, 1936) quoted in Juozas Daulius [Stasys Yla], *Komunizmas Lietuvoje* (Communism in Lithuania; Kaunas : Šviesa, 1937), pp. 110-111.

Lithuanian territory of the Red Army late in 1939.[36] Unlike the ordinary Russian soldiers, the political commissars failed to comply with their treaty obligations not to meddle in Lithuanian affairs. Under orders to assist local Communist activities, they attended Party meetings and tried to establish contacts with workers in Vilnius. Furthermore, for purposes of military construction they employed Lithuanians of Russian descent, who were presumed to be susceptible to revolutionary propaganda.[37]

The program of the Communist Party contained both its habitual slogans and some new allegations. It continued to insist on political rights for the workers, freedom for political prisoners, and legalization of the Party. It also included the following specific demands of a political and economic nature: mobilization of all forces against the Nationalist government, work for the unemployed, higher wages, and improvement of peasant conditions. Lastly, in addition to all of these objectives, the Communists accused the Lithuanian government of bad faith in executing the terms of the October 1939 treaty with the USSR.[38]

In December 1939, the Party modified its tactics once more. Again it placed emphasis on the divisive approach, directing its attention to the average followers of non-Communist parties but refusing to have anything to do with the rival leaders, especially the Catholics and the Populists, who had aided the Nationalists by entering the coalition government in March.[39] The Communist attitude toward the Social Democratic leadership was an exception. Unlike the Catholics and the Populists, the Social Democrats were on exceedingly bad terms with the Kaunas authorities, so much so that their participation in any coalition government was out of the question. One may conjecture that the absence of any collaboration between the Marxists and the Nationalists was a factor which accounts for Communist overtures in January 1940, to the Social Democratic leadership to cooperate against the government. Communist disinclination to have any dealings with the leaders of the other political parties was fully reciprocated. For no matter how persistent their proffers of joint action in the past, no matter what name they went under, the response to them, first by the Social Democrats and later by the other groups, was always the same—negative.

Summary

THIS SUMMARY OF THE COMMUNIST MOVEMENT in Lithuania requires several additional observations. The Communist underground had brought forth a number of professional revolutionaries who were committed to radical reforms of a social, economic, and political nature. More significantly, they were committed to such strong and close association with a foreign power that the very idea of an independent Lithuania was anathema. Ample evidence attests to the Lithuanian Communist Party's affiliation with the Soviet Union, including the choice of Moscow as the place of some of the most important Party conferences and congresses, the occasional selection of prominent Russians to serve on the decision-making organs of the Lithuanian Party, the approval of Lithuanian-initiated actions by the organs of the Communist International or those of the Communist Party of the Soviet Union, and the vision of Lithuania as a future member of the Soviet Union. However, the government succeeded in keeping Communism a marginal force in Lithuania. The conclusion emerges that from the beginning of the interwar period to its end the Communist Party was perennially on the verge of a crisis.[40] Standing alone, the local Communists did not constitute any appreciable threat to a people with as highly developed a sense of national consciousness as the Lithuanians.

PART THREE

The Economy: Problems and Tendencies

PROBLEMS ON THE LAND

Economic and social problems paralleled the political difficulties which gripped Lithuania in 1939-1940. The fact that a great many citizens became distinctly unhappy and felt that something had gone awry in their country was a phenomenon overlooked by none. Since during this period Lithuania was an agrarian country, it was the agricultural sector of the nation's economy which held the key to Lithuania's economic problems.

Farm Productivity and Surplus Population

At the end of the interwar decades some 77 per cent of the country's population depended on agriculture for its livelihood. This fact is attributable to a number of circumstances. Heavy industry, which had made some progress in Lithuania before 1918, was crippled by the forfeiture of Russian markets in consequence of the establishment of an independent Lithuanian state. The large investment in local industry of foreign capital,[1] interested primarily in the supply of cheap agricultural raw materials and in a market for its output, was not conducive to industrial growth. The agrarian majority tended to conserve rural supremacy,[2] and the government was disinclined to borrow abroad at high interest rates.[3] The state of the economy was precarious because of the high percentage of the population engaged in agriculture, because of a scarcity of available land,

and because of a low rate of productivity. This confluence of adverse circumstances generated an unfortunate situation, commonly referred to as agricultural overpopulation which occurred throughout most of Eastern Europe. Table 4, which shows the indexes of agricultural production for Lithuania and the neighboring states, does not reflect real income, but it does include an approximate representation of that income. An estimate of Lithuanian surplus agricultural population is presented in Table 5. Without exploring the causes responsible for modern Lithuania's cumbrous inheritance, these realities of rural life made apportionment of land and farm policies questions of paramount concern to the entire population.

Agrarian Reforms

THE ORGANIZATION OF LITHUANIA'S RURAL ECONOMY was established by governmental land reforms after World War I. The agrarian reform was viewed as a means of adjusting the excessive demand for land to its limited supply. It was accomplished at the expense of the large estates and was not solely an economic enterprise. The reform was motivated by three underlying considerations. Economically, the bankruptcy of the large estates and the obsolete communal farming techniques which derived from tsarist Russia impelled the legislators to adopt a radical program for change. Socially, the fact that a small number of proprietors owned vast areas of land was viewed by the new leaders as an intolerable inequity. And, politically, the national government could not overlook the incompatibility between the Lithuanian commoners, who fought for the new republic and who were promised land as a reward, and the Polonized landed aristocracy, who frowned on the idea of an independent state.[4] The reconstruction, which lasted throughout the interwar years, ended in 1939. The results of this agrarian reform appear in Table 6. The redistribution of land weakened the position of the Polonized landowning element in Lithuania, created 38,747 new farm settlements, and provided 26,367 small landholders with additional lots. In view of future

66

TABLE 4

INDEXES OF AGRICULTURAL PRODUCTION PER PERSON DEPENDENT ON
AGRICULTURE, PER MALE ENGAGED, AND PER HECTARE OF AGRICULTURAL
LAND, BY COUNTRIES, 1931-1935 AVERAGE
(Europe — 100)

	Per Person Dependent on Agriculture	Per Male Engaged in Agriculture	Per Hectare of Agricultural Land
Estonia	99	103	69
Latvia	111	103	80
Lithuania	73	74	69
Poland	49	56	75
USSR	39	41	—
Germany	195	191	181

Source: Adapted from League of Nations, Economic, Financial and Transit Department, *Economic Demography of Eastern And Southern Europe*, by Wilbert E. Moore (Geneva, 1945), p. 35.

difficulties that beset agriculture, it is important to realize that by favoring the new settler and the small landholder, the government brought into being a large number of small individual farmsteads, ranging in size from 8 to 12 hectares.[5] Allotments of such size were considered both necessary and sufficient to provide the farmer's family with means of subsistence and to utilize the family labor potential.

TABLE 5

« STANDARD » AND « SURPLUS » AGRICULTURAL POPULATIONS, AROUND 1930,
ASSUMING EXISTING PRODUCTION AND EUROPEAN
AVERAGE PER CAPITA LEVEL
(in thousands)

	Population Dependent on Agriculture	"Standard" Population Assuming European Per Capita Level	"Surplus" Population Number	Per Cent
Lithuania	1,657	1,205	452	27.3
Latvia	1,036	1,149	− 113	− 10.9
Estonia	626	624	2	.4
Poland	19,347	9,425	9,922	51.3

Source: Adapted from League of Nations, Economic, Financial and Transit Department, *Economic Demography of Eastern And Southern Europe*, by Wilbert E. Moore (Geneva, 1945), pp. 63-64.

TABLE 6

REDISTRIBUTION OF LAND

1919–1939

	Hectares	Per Cent of Total
I. Land distributed for permanent ownership		
1. To schools, organizations, asylums, etc.	927.0	0.1
2. To parish churches	1,616.3	0.3
3. For cemeteries	410.5	*
4. To employees and laborers for homes	3,287.5	0.4
5. To new settlers	362,117.1	50.0
6. To small landholders	90,628.9	13.0
Total	458.987.3	63.8
II. Land distributed for temporary use		
1. To state institutions	34,931.1	4.8
2. To institutions of local government	2,598.6	0.4
3. To private persons and organizations	10,742.9	1.5
4. For community pastures	29,214.2	4.0
Total	77,486.8	10.7
III. For miscellaneous uses	183,808.0	25.5
Grand total of land affected by reform	**720,282.1**	**100.0**

Source: Adapted from Lithuanie, Centralinis statistikos biuras, *Annuaire statistique de la Lithuanie: 1939*, XII, 108–110; Anicetas Simutis, *The Economic Reconstruction of Lithuania after 1918* (New York: Columbia University Press, 1942), p. 28.
* Less than one-tenth of one per cent.

Studies of the consequences of agrarian reforms are fragmentary. However, there is some information pertaining to the distribution of farms according to size. Table 7, based on an agricultural census of 1930, was compiled in independent Lithuania; Table 8 was displayed by the Communists subsequent to their seizure of power. These two tables, in addition to incidental observations on the trend in agriculture, permit several tentative conclusions concerning the outcome of the land reform. They also reveal unintended developments which, at the end of the second interwar decade, became acute problems.

The statistics for 1930 indicate that the mainstay of the Lithuanian economy consisted of small individual holdings,

TABLE 7

DISTRIBUTION OF FARMS ACCORDING TO SIZE,
1930

Farm Size (hectares)	Number of Farms	Per Cent of Total Farms	Cumulative Per Cent of Farms	Area (hectares)	Per Cent of Total Area	Cumulative Per Cent of Land
1—2	13,797	4.80	4.80	18,862	0.44	0.44
2—5	39,666	13.80	18.60	135,214	3.13	3.57
5—8	45,882	15.96	34.56	295,307	8.64	10.41
8—10	32,355	11.26	45.82	287,590	6.66	17.07
10—12	28,060	9.76	55.58	304,612	7.05	24.12
12—15	31,512	10.97	66.55	419,123	9.71	33.83
15—20	33,236	11.57	78.12	569,921	13.20	47.03
20—30	34,197	11.90	90.02	826,593	19.14	66.17
30—50	20,597	7.17	97.19	762,894	17.66	83.83
50—100	6,476	2.25	99.44	425,025	9.84	93.67
100 and over	1,602	0.56	100.00	273,373	6.33	100.00
Total	287,380	100.00		4,318,514	100.00	

Source: Lithuania, Central Bureau of Statistics, *Recensement agricole en Lithuanie* (Kaunas, n.d.), I, 22.

TABLE 8

DISTRIBUTION OF FARMS ACCORDING TO SIZE,
1940

Farm Size (hectares)	Number of Farms	Per Cent of Total Farms	Cumulative Per Cent of Farms	Area (hectares)	Per Cent of Total Area	Cumulative Per Cent of Land
Up to 2	41,240	11.62	11.62	38,930	0.86	0.86
2—5	56,070	15.80	27.42	198,590	4.41	5.27
5—20	196,180	55.29	82.71	2,188,980	48.57	53.84
20—30	38,630	10.89	93.60	938,470	20.82	74.66
30—50	15,950	4.50	98.10	614,500	13.63	88.29
50 and over	6,724	1.90	100.00	527,487	11.71	100.00
Total	354,794	100.00		4,506,957	100.00	

Source: Butkutė-Ramelienė, p. 117. According to other sources, the number of farms in the 5 to 20 hectares category was 190,890. See Cimbolenka, ed., p. 57; Truska, p. 118.

ranging from 5 to 100 hectares. They accounted for over 90 per cent of the land in use for agriculture. However, contrary to the intentions of postwar land reformers, the estates had not disappeared. While the number of new settlers and small landholders in the indigent category of 1 to 5 hectares was sizable, approximately 18 per cent of the total number of farmers, the share of land which they possessed amounted to approximately 4 per cent.

The statistics in Table 8 for 1940 must be viewed with the following qualifications. The large increase of farms below 2 hectares is partly due to the omission from Table 7 of all holdings below one hectare. Mainly subsidiary sources of livelihood, the number of such holdings in 1940 was 22,200.[6] In 1930, they amounted to 21,290 or 0.2 per cent of the total agricultural area.[7] Some discrepancies between the two tables are attributable to territorial changes effected in 1939. Although it is difficult to verify the above data in their entirety, the literature in 1939-1940 which strongly criticized the progressive parcellation of farmland[8] offers additional support to the implications derived from the tables.

The statistics published by the Communists attest to the growth in the intervening years of a rural population which could barely subsist on its small land allotments. By patronizing the relatively affluent rural society, the owners of average and large holdings, Nationalist legislators were largely responsible for the widespread destitution of agriculture. The impoverishment of village commoners was evidenced by public sales of property, by the reduction in size of their plots, and especially by the fact that at least 22 per cent of the recipients of land were eventually compelled to relinquish their holdings.[9] By reason of government laxity in taking legal action to force the payment of debts, the real value of agricultural sales by auction cannot be determined with certainty. The total arrears, in redemption dues and other indebtedness, which the revenue officials were instructed to collect from the new settlers amounted to 35,406,282 lits by 1938. The following statistics relate to the

71

possessions of small farmers and denote total indebtedness and the number of public sales in the course of the critical years:[10]

Year	Number of Public Sales in Agriculture	Indebtedness in Lits
1936	1,560	5,386,802
1937	1,653	9,732,665
1938	1,036	6,232,031
1939	746	3,400,000
1940 (Jan.-May)	351	1,385,597

The condition of the weaker farmers amounted to a qualitative modification of postwar reforms, the repercussions of which bred social, economic, and political discontent among the prostrate peasants. What were some of the causes of this state of affairs?

The postwar land reform laws had substantially altered the nature of farming. Principally, the communal organization of agriculture was replaced by individual farming. The breadth of this rural transformation is illustrated by the fact that the amount of land converted into individual settlements approximated one-third of the state territory. While beneficial to the national economy as a whole, the reorganization of the provincial way of life had some disadvantages. The abolition of certain customary rights, such as access to pastures, formerly held in common with the entire village population, was detrimental to the interests of the small landholders and the landless peasants.[11]

Contrary to the intentions of agrarian reformers, the large estates were not eliminated from the national economy. In 1929 the Nationalist authorities departed from postwar legislation by raising the expropriation-free maximum from 80 to 150 hectares. The consequences of this conservative counterreform are illustrated in Table 9, which shows the number of estates and the land they controlled.

There were other factors that afforded advantages to the large landholders. The experimental farm was one of them. Leased by the Ministry of Agriculture to the original landowner with a view to cultivating choice livestock and grain, the experimental

72

TABLE 9

UNEXPROPRIATED ESTATES,
JANUARY 1, 1940

Size in Hectares	Number of Owners	Arable Land and Forests in Hectares
Up to 80	649	51,792.5803
80—90	57	4,989.0966
90—100	75	7,187.8812
100—110	89	9,461.2981
110—120	57	6,606.6835
120—130	53	6,629.3890
130—140	37	4,978.8712
140—150	580	88,426.5304
Total	**1,597**	**180,072.3303**

Source: Elsbergas, p. 197.

farm proved to be an "escape clause" utilized by the estate owner to exceed the 150 hectare ceiling in order to preserve his holdings. For many years this expedient deprived the reform officials of power to distribute sizable areas of land to new settlers and small landholders. However, the management of such farms came under mounting criticism from various quarters.[12] The last years of the interwar decades afforded evidence of growing government pressure on the trustees of public land to live up to the terms of the contract with the Ministry of Agriculture or face the loss of privileges. Nevertheless, some 43 large experimental farms outlasted the regime which invented them.

Among other privileges conferred upon the landed aristocracy were the right to retain fertile soils, the possibility of keeping estates intact de facto by means of fictitious apportionment among relatives, the high indemnification for expropriated areas, and the low rents paid for experimental farms.[13]

Finally, the government failed to strengthen the effect of the redistribution of land by regular and adequate aid to the beneficiaries of the reforms. Unlike numerous other developments under examination, the want of such support does not suffer from insufficient documentation.[14] Postwar reform laws did not limit the right to obtain land by either the ability or indeed the intention to work it. In the early period of independence, all those who volunteered to fight for Lithuania's independence, were rewarded with land. However, the need to appease the small landholders and the new settlers by extensive measures of support diminished. The economic laws of natural selection, abetted by Nationalist agrarian policies, either eliminated the unstable element from this sector of the national economy or left it on the brink of poverty.

The Price Scissors in Agriculture

THE OUTBREAK of war in September 1939 aggravated the farm situation. Initially, the farmers were not at all disturbed by the European crisis. Bacon could be as good as gold provided the government preserved a lucrative neutrality. However, the farmers quickly changed their minds. The single benefit the war brought about, namely, facility in selling farm produce, was more than offset by the reappearance in all its severity of that age-old anomaly, the "price scissors." There arose a divergence in prices between manufactured and agricultural goods which worked to the disadvantage of the farmer. The prewar year most adverse to the farmer had been 1935. Subsequently, the terms of trade between manufactured and agricultural products improved, and in 1938-1939 farm purchasing power became stabilized. Table 10 attests both to the relative price stability before the outbreak of hostilities and to the sharp rise that attended it. According to the Central Bureau of Statistics, during the first nine months of war the general price index moved upward some 46.6 per cent. But of particular harm to the rural economy was the unequal rate of increase in commodity prices between manufactured goods, which went up as much as 55 per cent, and farm prices, which increased only 43 per cent. Scarcity of such essential farm supplies as nails, hobnails, yarn, soap, glass, iron, and wire raised their prices astronomically. Moreover, hoarding minimized the supply of some important articles,

74

TABLE 10

PRICE INDEXES, 1938 = 100

	1939									1940				
	IV	V	VI	VII	VIII	IX	X	XI	XII	I	II	III	IV	V
General	100.3	100.4	99.9	99.9	98.4	99.9	106.8	115.3	123.4	128.4	134.7	141.9	142.5	144.3
Food and agricultural produce	100.6	100.9	98.9	98.7	95.1	97.8	104.5	109.0	115.9	121.8	129.0	139.6	139.7	140.3
Raw materials and semifinished goods	101.2	101.0	101.4	101.7	101.9	101.5	110 3	120.6	129.1	133.3	138.5	140.4	140.7	143.5
Manufactures	97.3	97.6	98.4	98.6	98.7	100.4	105.1	119.3	129.1	134.9	139.8	147.5	149.4	152.1

Source: *Statistikos Biuletenis*, nos. 5-6 (May-June 1940), p. 52.

credit purchases dwindled, and service costs soared. Because of the Price Administrator's inability to enforce government regulations on price ceilings, remote rural areas suffered from especially unfavorable terms of trade with the towns. This plight prompted a migration of many countrymen into the towns.

Shortage of Farm Labor

A PHENOMENON which in 1939-1940 discomfited not only agriculture but the entire economy was the serious shortage of farm labor. In the nineteenth century, when the Lithuanian birth rate was high and labor mobility virtually nonexistent, there was no shortage of labor. Subsequent migrations to Russia and to America, which in pre-World-War-I years attracted some 20,000 Lithuanians annually, diminished the supply of labor, but the situation was far from alarming. However, just before the end of the interwar decades urban unemployment emerged simultaneously with a rural labor shortage. This baffling situation provoked incessant public debates directed at finding some feasible solution.

In 1930 hired farm employment comprised 153,764 men and women, constituting 15.5 per cent of the total labor force permanently engaged in agriculture. That number included a small amount of child labor utilized for minor services.[15] The somewhat liberal Communist estimates for 1939-1940 placed the total at about 200,000 workers.[16] As attested to by government statistics reproduced in Table 11, at the start of 1940 agriculture was still in need of some 35,000 laborers. The high rate of urban unemployment was in startling conflict with the registration of some 22,000 people who were able but not willing to work the land, and with the fact that Lithuania was supplying labor to neighboring countries. The shortage of agricultural workers brings into relief the abnormal state of the economy.[17]

Postwar agrarian reforms had enlarged the amount of land under cultivation and had also intensified farming, which, in turn, increased the demand for rural labor.[18] But the supply of

TABLE 11
SHORTAGE OF FARM LABOR
1940

Adult male laborers	11,735
Female laborers	14,250
Junior male laborers	4,008
Shepherds	4,100
Others	1,196

Total 35,289

Source: *Lietuvos Ūkininkas* (The Lithuanian Farmer), December 21, 1939, p. 2. The estimate fails to include the Vilnius territory acquired in 1939.

laborers who were inclined to work the land was insufficient. Opportunities for employment in industry, trade, transport, construction, and drainage projects occasioned an exodus from the rural districts.[19] Lastly, in addition to the positive attractions of the cities there existed a negative complex of rural social and economic conditions which contributed to the exodus. The deteriorating terms of trade resulting from the war made the farmworker's life extremely difficult. This prompted him to do nothing rather than go back to the landowner. Late in 1939 a provincial newspaper had written:

... a large portion of [rural] workers usually have no permanent employment. In the summer they work the fields for the larger farmers and in the fall they return to their tattered, and often rented, sheds, and roam about wondering what to do next. Before them—a long and rainy fall, and then the cold. And that spring. ... Ah, how far the spring, when the farmer will be in need of his hands. One has to tighten his belt and stare with an envious glance at a public official, wearing marketed clothes, or at a satiated farmer. Anxiety mingles with anger that with his healthy and strong hands he cannot even earn a living. Many thoughts of all sorts, among which almost always is the thought that not all citizens are equal, enter his mind. Is it possible that some worker might be wrong in thinking so? Is it possible that he had not read the laws and the constitution? But supposing he had, is it not all the same? Truly no one cares about him, no one enters him in the files of the unemployed, no one offers him any assistance, no one supplies him with a job. Nowhere is he insured against unemployment, accident, and hunger.[20]

77

This passage portrays the unfortunate seasonal farm worker. Other laborers who resided near the surviving estates and who worked them on a permanent basis vied in misery with the roving seasonal employees. Enjoying a measure of employment security, these "true serfs of our age, [these] most unfortunate people," differed from the serfs of tsarist years only in that the landlord could no longer offer them for sale or exchange them for a dog.[21] They lived their lives without hope of a better day, as revealed in another vignette from the lives of the village proletariat:

There is a large estate here—with more than 300 hectares—called Doviatova. From times past people have many unpleasant memories about it. But of greater importance [than their recollections] is that which now clearly catches one's eye. The estate is up to its ears in debt ... The poor landowner himself lives in poverty and so do his laborers. Ragged, weary, some fifteen families subsist here in their rotting, dilapidated huts. .... So many families and there is no well. Water has to be carried from the neighbors, from afar. The cottages are located more than half a kilometer away from the estate. There are no stables near the cottages. With pails in their hands, [the peasants] walk to the estate to look after their cattle. And this goes on and on.[22]

It was from such circumstances that the farm laborer tried to escape. And as he did, the entire economy became more disarrayed. Unlike the demand, the supply of labor was diminishing. Workers requested high wages, and the farmers, because of the unfavorable terms of trade, could not afford to pay them. Without benefit of sickness and old-age insurance, bonuses for children or premiums for length of service; with no minimum wage law, no organized labor movement to protect his interests, and no one to be concerned about his food, clothing or state of health, the rural worker found himself at the mercy of the farmer who hired him.

In view of the variable state of the national economy, it is difficult to determine the real income of various occupations. But a rough representation is attainable, as indicated in Table 12.

It reveals an unequal distribution of wealth which reserved the lowest place on the socio-economic scale for the rural worker. Their invidious lot is adequately documented, and the documentation appends a humble chapter to Lithuanian history.

Social Stigma of Rural Labor

IN ADDITION to economic hardships, social inequality appears to have been a subsidiary cause of the migration of agricultural workers to the towns. The laborer complained that the employer did not eat at the same table with his help, that he often indiscriminately blamed servants for minor infractions, that he was inconsiderate of the needs of his workers, that he scoffed at an employee who chanced to have a newspaper by labeling him a "professor," and that his daughter did not dance with a hireling. In short, he made life on the farm miserable indeed.[23] In some cases female domestic help, because of urban unemployment, would be prevailed upon to labor in the country. But, they often kept their place of employment secret, for fear that relatives would frown upon an occupation which was viewed as socially inferior to work in town.[24]

According to one commentator, Lithuania was developing an upper class. This process was somewhat artificial. It did not necessarily reflect differences in income, but was rather a result of the intention on the part of the intelligentsia or the civil servants to be an upper class.[25] It is not at all clear what direction future developments might have taken had Soviet occupation been averted. Evidence indicates a process of social stratification; yet it caused mounting apprehension among influential individuals and political organizations who apparently desired to bring it to a halt.

Conflicting Calls for Action

THE COMPLICATIONS of the rural economy generated much talk and little action. Government determination to do something to

79

TABLE 12

MONTHLY WAGES IN LITS FOR SELECTED OCCUPATIONS,
1939-1940

Occupations   *Wages*
(in Lits)

GOVERNMENT

Member of State Council	2,000
Chairman of the *Seimas*	2,500
Assistant to the Chairman of the *Seimas*	1,800
Secretary of the *Seimas*	1,500
Seimas representative	900

MILITARY

Highest officer, highest category	2,900
Intermediate officer, intermediate category	1,075
Lowest officer, lowest category	425

CIVIL SERVICE

First (lowest) category	180
Sixth category	288
Twelfth category	648
Eighteenth (highest) category	1,200

INDUSTRY

Skilled labor (Kaunas average)	247
Skilled labor (Lithuanian average)	222
Unskilled labor (Kaunas average)	149
Unskilled labor (Lithuanian average)	123
General Lithuanian female average	96

AGRICULTURAL LABOR

All-year male laborer	35
All-year female laborer	27
All-year junior male laborer	22
All-year junior female laborer	18
Shepherd	12
Seasonal male laborer (spring term)	78
Seasonal female laborer (spring term)	57

MISCELLANEOUS

Public works employee	117
Lumberer	163
Postmaster	214
Grade school teacher	173
Saleswoman in a grocery store	140
Rural cooperative employee	135

Note on Sources: The table has been derived from fragmentary materials published in Lithuanian periodicals. See *Annuaire statistique...*, XII, 140-141 and 188-189; *Talka* (Collective Action), April 15, 1939, p. 153; ibid., June 1, alleviate the diminishing supply of farm labor was elicited by intense public concern. In a plethora of resolutions and articles citizens registered their opinions about the labor problem. They urged the administration to find means to mechanize agriculture[26] and by so doing to decrease the demand for labor, to provide farm employees with adequate housing, to shorten their working hours, to arrange for recreational facilities in the country, and to adopt a system of labor incentives.

On the other hand, the agrarian interests called for the application of stern measures against migratory labor. They were annoyed at the government practice of paying unemployment compensation to urban newcomers who had refused to work on the land. Reproachfully the landowners reminded the Kaunas authorities that in the previous 12 years agriculture had received only 15.6 million lits in government subsidies, amounting to 1.3 million a year, while in 1939 alone the urban unemployed received a total of 6 million lits.[27] When they offered jobs to these unemployed, the landholders were often told that it was better to starve to death than go back to the farm.[28] Consequently, representatives of the landowners believed that drastic action was necessary against laborers who declined to return to the village, especially against "idlers" who instigated "serious workers" not to work for less than 1,000 lits a year.[29]

1939, p. 224; *XX Amžius,* December 21, 1939, p. 7; *Lietuvos Aidas,* April 1, 1940, p. 7; Žiugžda, IV, 637; *Lietuvos Žinios,* July 5, 1940, p. 6; ibid., July 30, 1940, p. 10; *Tautos Ūkis,* April 20, 1940, p. 290; ibid., May 25, 1940, p. 410; *Vyriausybės Žinios,* July 11, 1924, p. 2; ibid., August 29, 1936, p. 2; ibid., January 28, 1937, pp. 5-6.

With the exception of figures for military, civil service, and government officials, who were paid strictly specified salaries, most estimates were computed on a 26-day basis. The totals in government and military categories do not include housing and representation allowances, extra payment for conferences, and other subsidiary sources of income.

Monthly averages for rural workers, with the exception of seasonal employees, include a small payment in kind. On the other hand, they do not include dwelling quarters, meals, and sometimes even clothing provided by the employer. The figures do not reflect the income of married couples, who received less in cash and more in kind than the single laborers. Finally, the quoted averages suffer somewhat from the inclusion of the low-paying Vilnius districts.

In the miscellaneous group the lumberer's average takes in the 30 per cent bonus paid by the local government, but other figures exclude the indeterminate allowances for dwelling quarters and heating.

Government Remedies

GOVERNMENTAL REMEDIAL ACTION proved to be a concession to landed interests. Any intentions some might have had to mitigate rural distress by substantive reforms were discarded. Instead the government resolved to unravel a major social and economic tangle by resorting to superficial means. In December 1939, the Council of Agriculture, the top advisory agency to the Ministry of Agriculture, which the government had created earlier in the year, recommended better protection of state frontiers so that laborers could not enter foreign territory to find more profitable employment.[30] In April of the next year, in an overt blow at migratory labor, the Ministry of the Interior urged government agencies to refuse work on public projects to all urban applicants who failed to meet a three year residence requirement. This action prompted a leading journal of economics to suggest other ways of dealing with the problem, such as raising the rural standard of living.[31]

Anxious to eliminate all intermediaries who supplied labor to needy farmers at a profit, the Ministry of Agriculture chose to intervene in hiring practices. It instructed the landholders who were short of help to register with offices of local government and to select their own representative, or to accept a government appointee, who would travel wherever labor could be found and do the hiring for the entire neighborhood.[32]

The final step in government efforts to ameliorate the vexatious problem was the labor legislation of May 6, 1940,[33] which envisaged the establishment within the Ministry of the Interior of an Office of Labor Administration. Like previous enactments, the new law had little to offer the worker. The sponsors of the bill had hoped to ensure a purposeful utilization of the nation's labor potential, to direct workers to positions regardless of personal choice, to train young men and women for various vocations, and to organize public works in order to absorb the urban unemployed. However, the legislators' primary concerns were to arrest the movement into towns, to prevail on urban newcomers to return to their rural communities, to curb the hiring for domestic help in towns of persons living in the country, and to introduce a system of compulsory labor.[34] It is difficult to know whether these measures would have sufficed to assuage this particular labor problem. However, judging from the cursory manner in which so intricate a matter was handled, there was no ground for optimism.

VII

URBAN CONDITIONS

AT THE END of two decades of independent existence, nearly a quarter of the Lithuanian population lived in expanding urban communities. In 1939-1940, despite noticeable unemployment, housing shortages, and other hardships attendant upon rapid development, the cities continued to attract sizable numbers of new residents. Their annual rate of population increase amounted to 3 per cent, with internal migration responsible for 2 per cent.

The absence of comprehensive family living studies[1] makes impossible any precise analysis of the conditions of life. However, the growth of a middle class in the towns was attended by a parallel augmentation of low-income groups, industrial laborers, craftsmen, petty white collar workers, the unemployed and the underemployed. Low wages, partly revealed by Table 12, and the distressingly high cost of living guaranteed a bleak future for these urban residents. The bulk of their precarious means of existence consisted of earnings by the head of the household; income from subsidiary employment came to an insignificant amount.

Increased Cost of Living

IN THE YEARS before World War II the real standard of living had been undermined by the progressive disparity between labor income and the cost of living. The war months, as shown by

84

TABLE 13

INDEX NUMBERS OF COST OF LIVING
1929 = 100

	1939		
		X	55.1
		XI	57.6
I	52.4	XII	60.6
II	52.8		
III	52.5		*1940*
IV	52.6	I	62.6
V	52.7	II	65.3
VI	52.4	III	69.0
VII	52.4	IV	69.2
VIII	51.8	V	70.3
IX	52.8	VI	70.9

Source: League of Nations, Economic Intelligence Service, *Statistical Year-Book of the League of Nations*, 1939/1940 (Geneva, 1940), p. 210.

index numbers reflected in Table 13, only accelerated this trend. In order to offset the marked rise in the cost of living, early in 1940 the government decided to raise workers' salaries by 5 to 15 per cent and to award a single winter bonus.[2] However, this additional income did not materially affect the 34 per cent increase in the cost of living which had occurred since the outbreak of hostilities in September 1939.

The state of the national economy weighed heavily upon the common wage earners. This is well illustrated by Table 14, which lists the monthly minimum cost of living for single adults and for families of two and five. Particularly pertinent to the living conditions of urban labor are the considerably higher averages reproduced in Table 15. The two tables, along with the available income figures, indicate the difficult circumstances of the ordinary worker. Some employees, especially the skilled ones, earned a tolerable living. But others were reduced to poverty as their real incomes did not keep pace with the rapid rise in the cost of living. This statistical profile is substantiated by contemporary accounts. In the winter of 1939 the Catholic *XX Amžius* (Twentieth Century) had reported on the living conditions of a typical family of five. The head of the household was a public works employee paid 6 lits a day, a wage above the

TABLE 14

THE MONTHLY MINIMUM COST OF LIVING IN LITHUANIA
(*In Lits*)

FOR A SINGLE ADULT

	Food	Clothing	Living Quarters	Heating & Light	Misc.	TOTAL	For a Family of Two	For a Family of Five
MONTHLY AVERAGE FOR 1939	25.57	7.15	13.35	13.99	3.18	63.24	103.3	153.6
June, 1939	24.89	6.95	13.20	13.03	3.06	61.13	100.53	149.44
December, 1939	27.90	8.62	14.10	17.00	4.25	71.87	115.74	172.70
March, 1940	33.14	9.51	14.00	19.68	4.18	80.51	130.64	196.69
May, 1940	33.37	10.30	14.10	19.25	4.13	81.15	132.75	200.26

Source: *Statistikos Biuletenis*, nos. 5-6 (May-June 1940), p. 53.

TABLE 15

THE MONTHLY MINIMUM COST OF LIVING FOR A SINGLE ADULT
IN SELECTED CITIES AND THE URBAN AVERAGE
(In Lits)

	1939		1940					
	VI	XII	I	II	III	IV	V	VI
Kaunas	92.4	101.7	104.4	120.2	118.5	117.7	119.2	115.3
Šiauliai	73.9	88.5	86.6	88.6	93.4	92.1	92.9	93.2
Vilnius	—	—	93.1	97.9	99.7	99.0	97.2	98.7
URBAN AVERAGE	67.7	78.9	82.1	85.4	89.3	90.3	91.6	90.6

Source: *Statistikos Biuletenis*, No. 7 (July 1940), p. 82.

average 4.50 lits in this category. The national minimum cost of living for a family of five amounted to 173 lits monthly. The monthly salary of this worker was 156 lits, which approximated the Kaunas wages for unskilled labor, 149 lits. Even with slightly better-than-average earnings, his income fell considerably short of the requirements for meeting the minimum urban cost of living, especially since the urban minimum for a family of five was higher than the national estimate. To make both ends meet, the laborer was constrained to work hard and to restrict the purchase of food as much as possible.[3]

Besides the soaring cost of living, the war caused other discomforts for the average wage earner. Shortages of raw materials impelled a number of firms to cut down production and to reduce employee working hours. It is, however, next to impossible to evaluate these over-all losses.[4]

Housing Shortages

AN UNUSUALLY SEVERE URBAN PROBLEM was the shortage of housing, especially in Kaunas. Rents in that city, sometimes 100 or 120 lits a month for a single room, were thought by some to have been among the highest in the world. Not infrequently soaring rents absorbed as much as 50 per cent of workers' earnings.[5]

Like many other sectors of the national economy, home construction was in the domain of free enterprise, unregulated by governmental control. Twenty years of progress in urban construction was climaxed in 1938-1939 by record investment totals, as shown in Table 16. Ultimately, however, such construction only

TABLE 16

INVESTMENT IN URBAN CONSTRUCTION
(In Thousands of Lits)

	1938	1939
Total for general construction	53,000	66,000
Total for residential construction	34,000	45,000
Kaunas total for general construction	22,000	33,000
Kaunas total for residential construction	12,000	25,000

Source: *Economic and General Bulletin*, no. 1 (January 1940), p. 11.

benefited the prosperous urbanites, since it proved to be beyond the reach of the many impecunious citizens who wished to settle in towns. Thus, urban construction failed to meet the demands generated by internal migration, and the poor were forced to seek shelter in substandard quarters on the outskirts of urban communities.

In 1939 the Kaunas municipal authorities resolved to grapple with the housing problem. The Mayor summoned the City Council to a session and demanded action. In a grotesquely inadequate proposal which would have been funny had it not been tragic, the Mayor petitioned the councilmen to alleviate the housing shortage by appropriating funds for the construction of four small houses, to be rented to the impoverished laborers. One member took the floor to confess that so ineffectual a resolution was hypocrisy. He was apprehensive lest the proposed measures, evidence of "remorse of conscience" and nothing more, embarrass the Council before the public. However, the unperturbed majority of municipal leaders voted in favor of the Mayor's "relief" program.[6]

In accordance with a cabinet instruction of May 30, 1939, the Committee of Construction opened an investigation into the

housing situation. It set up a special commission whose procras-
tinations caused it to outlive the last two governments of independent Lithuania. The commission reached the decision that the
solution to the problem needed more studying, more planning,
more preparation. In addition to these findings, the investigators
recommended the following extraordinary measures to expedite
"social construction": construction of living quarters for workers,
craftsmen, and petty white collar employees, adoption of incen-
tive credit policies, relief from real estate taxes, and a program
of mass construction of inexpensive workers' colonies.[7] If not too
little, these suggestions were surely too late. When the Russians
descended on their Baltic neighbors in 1940, they found a swarm
of workers' families subsisting in far-off huts, barracks, and
basements and a score of other people studying their travail.

The laborers, like the small landholders and the new settlers
who profited from postwar land reforms, remained unprotected
against the powerful competitors for credit. As in agriculture,
there was genuine public concern, but the administration neglected to act vigorously. Failure to solve the housing problem was
one of the more conspicuous gaps in the record of the Lithuanian
regime.

Unemployment, Public Works, and Relief

UNEMPLOYMENT was yet another major difficulty. Because of
seasonal work, temporary part-time occupations, restrictions on
the registration of the unemployed, and a wide divergence in
the unemployment figures quoted in nationalist and Communist
sources, any attempt to ascertain the jobless total accurately is
hazardous. It is only necessary to point out that estimates for
June 1, 1940, range from 22,657 cited by nationalist sources to
76,452 in Communist sources.[8] The figures seem to have excluded the Vilnius area, which Lithuania regained in 1939. According
to its Mayor, Vilnius had some 15,000 jobless workers in the
first part of 1940.[9] Keeping in mind the exclusion from the files
of registered unemployed of all newcomers who had lately left

89

the provinces and all urban residents who had not lived in the cities for three consecutive years, nationalist estimates tend to be markedly conservative[10]; the Communist ones, though somewhat inflated, are probably closer to the facts.

Another indication of the worsening trend in the labor situation is the information concerning public works. During the first six months of 1940, between 6,000 and 9,000 laborers were supplied jobs at various public works projects,[11] and it was hoped that eventually as many as 11,000 unemployed could be aided in this manner.[12] Moreover, government sources estimated in March that expenditures on public works in 1940 would amount to 8,269,640 lits, an increase of 57 per cent over 1939. The acquisition of eastern Vilnius districts and the rise in unemployment as a result of the wartime slump in production were believed to have been responsible for so noticeable an expansion of emergency measures. Expenditures could have increased further, for it was not at all unusual for the legislators to use their original appropriations for unforeseen needs at a later date. Just such an increment for public works in 1939 made up 33 per cent of the original allowance. The money would have financed year-long projects envisaged for every district, with the Vilnius area alone using up 3,757,500 lits.[13] Another means of relief, providing work for some 25,000 people, was lumbering. However, the bulk of those who benefited from lumbering were small landholders, and it is not at all clear how many of them were urban laborers.[14]

Besides creating jobs for the idle workmen, public authorities were constantly searching for other solutions, short of radical reforms, to alleviate the sufferings of the society's unfortunates. Sporadic measures such as the preliminary sketch of a social assistance act, the sale of fuel at lower prices, and the possibility of allocating city jobs to those who needed them were intended to ameliorate the worker's lot.

Along with relief programs administered by the government, several civic groups volunteered their services in assisting destitute nationals. Cumulative data concerning such civic measures are not available; however, national news reports give reason for presuming that they were extensive and substantial. Local Catholic and citizens' organizations were active in succoring workers with large families, providing the poverty-stricken with free medical care, clothing, and housing, helping those parents who needed such aid to educate their children, and assisting the elderly and the beggars. These social organizations tried, as best they could, to lift the poor out of their squalor. But their means fell short of the need, and the over-all tangible effects proved to be negligible. The conventional relief approach initiated by the government did not have any noticeable effect on the condition of labor. Discontent mounted. "With a heavy heart I must confess that I had hoped to see better living conditions in my native state," lamented a laborer who in 1918 volunteered to fight for his country. "We, workers, are not looked upon as human beings. It is impossible for us to read newspapers, to find out what is really going on. Everybody is making fools of us. Some life we have!"[15] Gradually the depressed life of the worker alienated him from the sense of community. It was feared that in the absence of forceful measures to improve his lot, "love of one's country," pride in its "glorious past," and other civic virtues would be undermined. The four political parties responded to these economic and social grievances in different ways. The Nationalists were dilatory, the Catholics and the Populists occasionally exposed bad conditions, but only the Communists for their own reasons viewed them in all their seriousness.

VIII

THE COOPERATIVE MOVEMENT

WHEN LITHUANIANS spoke of the public interest or of its primacy over the private interest, they usually alluded to the state or to institutions controlled by the state. Popular consensus endowed the state with the all but exclusive right to declare what constituted the national interest. However, a significant minority, members of the cooperative movement, believed that their private interest coincided with the public good, and they worked tirelessly to convince others of this.

The Cooperative Way

COOPERATION, extolled by its proponents as a condition indispensable to the progress of the Lithuanian peasantry, answered a dual purpose. Primarily, it sought to improve the material welfare of the economically vulnerable peasant masses. But over and above their economic concerns, the cooperative societies served a variety of social and civic functions. "Our cooperative organizations, like no one else, are dedicated to the service of the popular masses, their social well-being, and the speediest possible development of their moral and material potentialities, as the most reliable fortifier of our nation's independence and growth,"[1] asserted Petras Šalčius, Lithuania's ranking exponent of cooperatives, before conferees from the three Baltic republics. The cooperative movement undertook the education of its members in the elementary attributes appropriate to good citizens:

> A nation and its economy are not merely a sum of economic goods and the amount of business done, but millions of live and conscious human beings who must know not only how to produce economic goods each by himself but how . . . to take the field—in an orderly and joint manner—as one man, and how, in time of need, even to die for the nation's welfare and its future. Only that nation will succeed in accomplishing this which even in time of peace knows how and is able to discuss and to do things together. . . . This training can be supplied only by cooperation, which even in time of peace accustoms people to the idea that many things can be accomplished only by a concurrent effort, which teaches men to act jointly, choosing as a base of this action not the interest and well-being of some one individual but the welfare of all. This is as much as to say that cooperation must . . . be a school of joint action . . . where each [individual] becomes inured to adjust his interest to the interests of others, to compel the submission of his will, his vagaries or caprices to the general will of the majority.[2]

Indeed, the devoted protagonists of the cooperative movement asserted that it "seeks the welfare of the whole [by] engaging wide popular masses in creative work, based on economic reality, and [by] proclaiming the multiple solidarity of all societies and all nations, mutual respect of interests, fraternal cooperation, and universal peace."[3]

Membership in Cooperatives

THE BEGINNINGS of Lithuanian cooperation can be traced to the last quarter of the nineteenth century. However, not until the reestablishment of the country's independence in 1918 did the movement acquire significant proportions. In the interwar decades the idea of cooperative effort had attracted numerous supporters from among the nation's intelligentsia, farmers, and laborers. They founded hundreds of credit, insurance, consumers', and producers' cooperative societies, to further the economic well-being of small and medium-sized farm groups who, as a result of post-war land reforms, were the mainstay of Lithuanian agriculture. The types of cooperative and the number of registered cooperative societies are listed in Table 17. Membership in the cooperative movement is shown in Table 18. With assets estimated at more than 200 million lits,[4] the 1,332 registered societies (not including establishments in the Vilnius area) were consolidated into six cooperative unions. Spurred by

TABLE 17

COOPERATIVE SOCIETIES
1938-1939

Type of Cooperative	Number of Societies	
	1938	1939
Credit	398	401
Stores and consumers'	251	275
Manufacturing	228	224
Insurance	2	2
Miscellaneous	409	430
Total	**1,288**	**1,332**

Source: Simutis, p. 35.

TABLE 18

MEMBERSHIP IN THE COOPERATIVES
1938-1939

Type of Cooperative	Number of Members	
	1938	1939
Credit	134,087	137,163
Trade	23,480	29,284
Dairy	18,688	22,019
Miscellaneous	11,886	11,886
Total	**188,141**	**200,352**

Source: Petras Šalčius, "Lietuvos kooperacijos judėjimas 1938-1939 metais" (The Lithuanian Cooperative Movement in 1938-1939), *Talka* (Collective Action), June 15, 1940, pp. 322-326.

government assistance, the collective operations became so extensive that by 1939, according to one economist, there was not a single country household which did not deal with the cooperatives in one way or another.[5] In a declaration which he read to the *Seimas* on April 5, Prime Minister Jonas Černius acknowledged the weighty contribution which the farm cooperatives had made in fostering the economic and cultural progress of the nation's peasantry, and he further pledged to continue the government's support of their activities in the future. On the whole, cooperation fared well in 1939. Although the Central Union of Dairy Cooperative Societies had a more profitable year in 1938 than in 1939, the total sales of all cooperative societies surpassed those of the previous year by 13 per cent.[6]

The cooperationists had problems, too. It was a matter of common knowledge that genuine popular interest in cooperative labor, so extensive in postwar years, was waning. A dispirited follower had to concede that with the exception of a few members, most had only a vague idea of what cooperation really was, although the cooperatives, with a membership of 200,000, were the largest formal organization in the nation.[7]

Beggarly Means

SOME COOPERATIONISTS conceded the truth of the allegation by economic commentators that collective action was a "beggarly means," resorted to by less developed nations not by preference but by the necessity of accelerating economic growth. An increasing number of able, educated, and ambitious individuals deserted the cooperatives to take up business independently. According to their disapproving former associates, they were "selfish" people, usually store managers and lesser attendants, who wanted to get rich quickly. They could be found in almost every town. On the other hand, there were common grievances expressed by disillusioned cooperationists. They pointed to restrictions of freedom to realize individual ideas and to maximize individual potentialities which were attendant upon collective action.

95

"Many heads but little sense, much talk but little work," asserted those who, in the eyes of cooperative devotees, wished to live off the labor of others.[8]

Government, the Camel in the Tent

GOVERNMENT OPENHANDEDNESS toward cooperative enterprises, evidenced by preferential legislation and financial aid totalling some 60,000,000 lits,[9] encumbered the beneficiaries with a measure of interference in their internal affairs. Some cooperative workers felt that government meddling went too far and were distinctly annoyed by it. The Central Union of Dairy Cooperative Societies concluded that government decision makers were apt to pay no heed to the opinions of cooperatives, especially rural cooperatives. Governmental policies were frequently at odds with the attitudes of members of provincial cooperatives. An editorial in a cooperative newspaper regretted that:

> ... principles of the authoritarian form of government and of the planned economy find an ever wider application ... in the administration of various sectors of our country's life. It seems that in a sense such tendencies exert influence upon the life of our cooperative organizations, too .... More and more the cooperatives sense the "protection" of certain agencies, and they can no longer solve independently many problems—not only the more important ones but trifling too—but must act according to instructions. Plans for the distribution of profit, estimates of expenditures and receipts are being meticulously amended and changed by certain commissions.[10]

The journal continued by pointing out that such circumspect guidance from above hampered the activities of cooperatives by choking their creative initiative and dispiriting them in general. It counselled the administration to curb its interference in the affairs of cooperatives, lest nothing remain cooperative about their efforts but the name plate on the door.[11]

Internal Failures of Cooperatives

COOPERATIVES ALSO SUFFERED from a number of technical and operational imperfections. All things considered, employment in cooperative societies had very little to offer. Monthly salaries of 120 to 150 lits for salesmen, clerks, and bookkeepers were tolerable. But over-all working conditions, long hours, and uncertainties about health insurance and old-age pensions prompted employees to seek jobs elsewhere, drained away members, and discouraged new applicants.[12]

As attested to by members and customers, the inadequate services of many cooperative stores were a source of considerable dissatisfaction.[13] Campaigning for better service, the cooperative weekly frequently reproved its model salesman, a good-natured but somewhat remiss country lad, for dripping kerosene into a herring keg, for negligence in fulfilling promises made to customers, for reading novels while on duty, for failing to get up in the mornings to open the store on time, and for other similar lapses. The cooperative storekeepers were always apprehensive lest displeased buyers frequent private retailers instead. Toward the end of 1939 the Council of Agriculture was considering the adoption of a plan to allay these fears by markedly increasing the number of cooperative stores in provincial towns.[14]

Cooperative Propaganda

ONE CANNOT SAY that backers of cooperation were inactive in the face of these reverses. Quite the contrary, their efforts at checking the setbacks lacked neither energy nor ingenuity. In fact, it would be difficult to find a group which could have outdone the cooperative functionaries in the techniques of propaganda. "The sixth congress of cooperatives must turn into a huge ... manifestation that cooperation in our country is alive, creative, determined to surmount all obstacles and to go into ever new fields of activity in the future."[15] Soviet seizure prevented the convention from meeting. However, the campaign for popular support

97

left listeners with the impression that "poverty cannot be con-
quered without cooperation because there are too many individual exploiters, and we will not have enough time to satiate them
all."[16] By means of an individual approach, public lectures,
parades, and town festivals, which attracted tens of thousands
of spectators and participants, the sedulous leaders carried their
message directly to the masses. The cooperative organ *Talka*
(Collective Action) addressed its readers in simple, comprehensible stories, cartoons, and poetry intended to demonstrate the
superiority of cooperation. Its series of moralizing pictorial
sketches showed how children could form cooperatives; how
amply the cooperative rewarded a conscientious manager who
withstood the devil's temptations to squander public funds and
to cheat customers at the scales; how a salesman persuaded a
panicky lady not to hoard salt but, instead, to buy only one
pound; how that same salesman made a donation to the army in
the hope that the soldiers, upon return, would join the coopera-
ative; and how a customer advised the storekeeper to clean up
the place and to display merchandise in the show window,
instead of just staring through it. *Talka* and the men and women
of the cooperatives made every effort to impart substance to their
slogan that cooperatives were the nation's economic and spiritual
strongholds.

THE GREAT DEBATE

WHEN ONE WRITER PORTRAYED the Lithuanian state as a banker, an industrialist, a merchant, a navigator, and a hotelkeeper,[1] he called attention to a notable feature of the country's life, namely, the government participation in management and production, regulatory measures, and substantial investments of capital in major industries. Notwithstanding such widespread involvement, the Nationalist regime eschewed a planned economy. Instead, it stimulated private initiative to expand manufacturing and trade. Indeed, many observers characterized the government's economic philosophy as intrinsically liberal.

Problems with Classical Economic Liberalism

IN NO SECTOR of the nation's economy was governmental interference shunned more than in industry and trade, especially the latter. "Trade," complained a reformer, "will probably be the only branch of the economy which manages its affairs according to obsolete liberal principles, conforming neither to the spirit of the times nor to the over-all needs of the national economy."[2] The critic had not intended to convey the impression that the government was indifferent to industrial growth, for such was not the case. He did find fault, however, with the allegedly excessive freedoms of the businessman who could commence almost any transactions he pleased, choose for his firm any site he preferred, and get along without any requirements of professional competence. Such benevolent disengagement on the part of the Kaunas authorities resulted in industrial deficiencies which in 1939-1940 were subjected to mounting criticism by some of the nation's economists.[3]

The developments with which the economic specialists were concerned included the sluggish rate of industrialization and some ills accompanying production. Aside from lack of experience and administrative imperfections at the cabinet level, the nation's economists blamed the government for its failure to rationalize the progress of industrial growth. In this sense government noninterference in industry was in line with its lackadaisical housing and agricultural policies.

The chief method the government adopted to bolster industrial expansion was a policy of protectionism. Secured from foreign competitors by high tariffs, infant firms rapidly increased in number. With outworn machinery purchased abroad and a readily available labor force at home, manufacturers supplied consumers with high-cost, low-quality goods, accumulating handsome returns for themselves. Instead of showing improvement, the situation deteriorated. The public continued to overpay, the lucrative firms continued to multiply, and industry began to suffer from overinvestment and overproduction. A number of these ill-managed, uneconomical concerns operated below their capacity, not infrequently as few as three or four days a week. The proliferation of these infant firms did not result in the desired rate of economic growth.

Movement Toward a Planned Economy

BY AND LARGE, the Nationalists did not question the primacy of free enterprise. They reserved for possible government intervention only those projects in the national economy which were beyond the resources of private investors. By 1939-1940 the relationship between the government and the economy had been subjected to severe criticism from many influential quarters.

Large segments of the population were alienated from the government by the convergence of deep-seated difficulties, such as the failures of land reform, the problems concerning urban and rural labor, the inequality of wages and its social and political consequences, the slow pace of economic growth, and lastly the start of World War II and the subsequent disorganization of foreign trade. As problems spread, the number of acceptable policy alternatives dwindled, until gradually both the politicians and the economists began to concentrate their attention upon economic rationalization as the only solution. A decade earlier, liberal politics had been discredited; now the liberal economy was threatened. Indeed, the very term became all but synonymous with obsolescence. More acceptable terms such as "rational," "guided," or "planned" economy gained in currency.

The Catholics, the Populists, and a group of economists affiliated with the journal *Tautos Ūkis* (National Economy) surged into the forefront of those advocating far-reaching governmental intervention in the economy. But the Nationalists were reluctant to make bold innovations. The attitude of the cooperative workers appears to have been equivocal. To the extent that rationalization meant the imposition of restrictions on private enterprise, the cooperationists were all for it. On the other hand, the cooperative press refrained from taking a side in the debate concerning the need for governmental intervention in the economy. The extent of rationalization, both in the torrent of recommendations adopted or considered and in the administration's policies, remains subject to dispute; yet the trend toward the regulatory state was unmistakable. Most of the leading parties and pressure groups leaned in the direction of a planned economy. Only some older Nationalists were less inclined to go along with this particular cause.

Influencing this trend in Lithuania were the examples provided by neighboring Germany and the Soviet Union. Notwithstanding their dissimilar forms of government, both produced the impression that, unlike the liberal democracies, which valued individual interests, they stressed the welfare of the whole.[4]

101

In contrast with liberal beliefs, social and political theorists argued for a new relationship between the individual and the state. They insisted that the modern state had the duty and obligation to protect the welfare of the individual and to guarantee every national at least a minimal means of subsistence.[5] Just how the state could best respond to this dictate was but a tactical point. What mattered was the principle of intercession on the part of the state for the individual's material welfare. The backers of the regulatory state now emphasized comprehensive planning with a view to the public good. The likelihood that the "invisible hand" of the classical economists would not actually harmonize individual self-interest with the general well-being was becoming increasingly obvious to the reformers. One adherent to these new theories in individual and state relations interpreted the essential character of a regulated economy as follows:

> The ideas of "guided economy" are vigorously assailing all positions, and it is now possible to assert positively that a planned economy is neither a bluff nor an episodic phenomenon derived from the economic crisis [of 1929-1933] but a fact of economic policy of epochal significance. . . . Mindful of vital national interests and prone to afford all its citizens the most comfortable means of living and promoting cultural growth, the state cannot be impeded by the interests of a privileged individual. . . . With a view to the common good it dictates concrete objectives to the national economy and adopts appropriate economic policies in order to accomplish these objectives. [The state assumes such prerogatives] because it is responsible for the nation's welfare, for the nation's history. It sees to it that all have work and bread, that all are able to take part in the nation's cultural activities, that all are able to provide their children with a decent education, that medical care be accessible to all, and so on. And this criterion is the only just criterion to determine the fairness of any law.[6]

While the course toward rationalization was plain, the claim that the existing structure of the economy already embodied its essential characteristics, that planned economy was a "fact," must be dismissed as premature.

The Flax Debate

THE 1939-1940 DISPUTES concerning government intervention in the economy were not confined to specialists and civil servants. On the contrary, they attracted the attention of all citizens interested in the nation's economy. Many felt the need of government intervention for the benefit of all, but few polemicists knew either what constituted the general welfare or how much government action would be necessary and sufficient to attain it. The organization of the flax industry illustrates this point. For most purposes, the flax industry can be viewed as a microcosm of the entire economy, and its specific problems and solutions exemplify the general conditions.

In 1939, because of inadequacies in organizing the production and marketing of a valuable export crop, flax, that industry became a candidate for exhaustive reforms. Three groups proposed changes: the Jewish dealers, who had been in the trade for many years; the Lithuanian middlemen, who had only recently shown interest in the industry; and the cooperationists, who persisted in their efforts to drive private merchants out of business and to consolidate all transactions in their own hands. Past efforts by the cooperatives had repeatedly failed to encompass the whole of the flax trade because of vigorous opposition from private business interests. Their renewed campaign to secure monopolistic rights in marketing and export again threatened private businessmen with loss of income. Having advised the Jewish merchants to invest their capital elsewhere, and seeing no pressing need for Lithuanian capital, the representatives of the powerful Central Union of Agricultural Cooperative Societies resolved on May 26, 1939, to disregard "the calculations of some businessmen." Instead, they proposed to solve the flax difficulty in a way most advantageous to the producers themselves.[7] Convinced that private firms accumulated profits for a "handful of

103

millionaires" at the expense of "masses of poverty-stricken people," they concurred in reiterating the widely accepted view that the public interest would be served best if individual initiative were circumscribed.[8]

In December 1939 the collective interests scored initial gains when the Council of Ministers, under the influence of Catholics and Populists, decided to reserve the entire flax trade for a cooperative concern especially established for that purpose. However, adjusting the radical cabinet action to a course more in keeping with the Nationalist regime's view of the organization of economy, the influential Finance Minister Ernestas Galvanauskas subsequently authorized a private firm to buy flax. On April 30, 1940, he publicly explained why he had done so, arguing that the exclusive privileges requested by the cooperative societies were advantageous to the national economy in some ways but detrimental in others. Accordingly, he crystallized the problem by reserving the export of flax to a cooperative firm operating under government supervision, and by authorizing both the cooperatives and private businessmen to purchase flax from the producers. In this manner, the Minister believed, competition in domestic trade would be preserved.[9] However, the Finance Minister's qualification of the earlier cabinet ruling caused the cooperationists to protest bitterly. They denounced the solution as an inadmissible subordination of the general welfare to individual pursuits. On May 4 the convention of the Chamber of Agriculture, an institution with cooperative preferences, blamed the Ministry of Finance for "sacrificing the interests of all farmers to a small group of persons" and unanimously appealed to the government to eliminate all private firms from the flax trade.[10]

Increasing Emphasis on Cooperative Action

THE CONTROVERSY and resolution of the problems in the flax industry were typical of cooperationist thinking and action. The agrarian interests, especially through the Populist press and, to a lesser extent, through the Catholic media, promoted their cause against the private sector. Ultimately, the government would have to step in as a conciliator. More often than not the cooperative side would acquire greater gains than its private rivals, but they were usually not as extensive as it expected. The cooperative expansionists maintained that they did not intend to put an end to individual initiative. They merely refused "to feed the private interest" any longer.[11] In short, they advocated a secondary role in the nation's economy for the individual businessman.

Cooperative aspirations were profusely supported by the Populists, whose *Lietuvos Žinios* (News of Lithuania) fully supported the cooperative planners for displaying a willingness to commence a new venture.[12] Of all the major political parties and pressure groups, the Populists, together with the economists and commentators affiliated with them, were most identified with the cooperatives' objectives. The Catholics did not fall far behind the Populists. However, Catholic writers were more moderate than the Populists; they emphasized not so much the diminution of private enterprise as its conformity with national objectives.

Support for private businessmen issued from two sources. These were the Nationalists in general[13] who were disinclined to deviate appreciably from their conservative course, and the Ministry of Finance in particular. Ernestas Galvanauskas, who consented to head that Ministry in November 1939, asked for and received discretionary powers in shaping the nation's fiscal, industrial, and trade policies. For years an influential figure in economic and political quarters, his views and the measures he initiated were partly responsible for balancing public and private concerns.

Minister Galvanauskas is believed to have favored a guided economy, including the government's obligation to outline national goals and its right to oversee the implementation of these goals. He spurned the extreme possibilities of either a liberal economy or an economy completely managed by the government. For the purpose of having profitable commercial intercourse with such powerful neighbors as Germany and the

Soviet Union, the Minister of Finance stressed the need for several centralized firms with exclusive rights to trade in certain specified areas. Yet he also stated positively that at home competition would not be denied.[14]

The agrarian interests in general and the cooperative lobby in particular expressed their views with self-righteous oversimplification. Their argument that total harmony existed between rural cooperative interests and the general well-being was untenable. Spokesmen for collective action insisted that all they cared about was the good of the country while private businessmen looked only to profits.

Another position they advanced was that rural cooperative aims coincided with purely Lithuanian interests. This proved to be a well-timed and well-directed argument. The displacement of Jewish middlemen by Lithuanians was a prospect entertained by both cooperative workers and private businessmen. The cooperationists gave prominence to their own Lithuanian character, and they scored so high in popular esteem that on one occasion Finance Minister Galvanauskas thought it advisable to caution them against transforming cooperation into something beyond the reach of critical examination.[15]

Stronger Government Sanctions

THE PROCESS of rationalization and direction-from-above embraced ever wider areas of national life. Nationalist Lithuania had for so long undervalued individual rights and emphasized obligations that it did not hesitate to invade and to suspend individual freedoms for the sake of "a weighty social obligation"[16] to rid the country of social and economic ills. The way was now clear to increasing interference in the citizens' everyday affairs. As problems multiplied, so did the scope of public encroachment on the private domain. Many believed that only the community made it possible for an individual to exist, therefore every member owed a debt to society. As if in repayment of a loan, the individual was put under obligation to live a life beneficial to the

106

entire community. If he proved to be indifferent to the duties of a citizen, it was incumbent upon the state to take corrective action. Hence the state needed greater powers.[17] The particular kinds of sanction thought proper for the government to exercise included its right to introduce *compulsory* insurance in agriculture, to *proscribe* the parcellation of farms, to *remove* owners who had mismanaged their farms, to *eliminate* private businessmen from certain occupations, to *compel* idlers to work, to *prohibit* the export of labor, to adopt *drastic measures* to stop labor migration into towns, and to aid women by *imposing punishment* upon drunkard husbands. Government actions of this nature received much attention. They had the consent of the majority of those actively engaged in determining social and economic policies. However, there was less interest in defining the proper limits of public authority.

Council of National Economy

A MOVE in the direction of planning took place on April 17, 1939. The government announced the creation of the Council of National Economy, an advisory body on all social and economic matters, consisting of representatives from business, government, and academic institutions. This prestigious body was instructed to draft a comprehensive plan designed to step up the rate of economic growth.[18]

For a group meant to assume the dominant role in planning the nation's economy, the Council proved to be a noteworthy failure. Reportedly, it had envisaged an increase in its membership and the formation of a number of commissions to investigate specific problems. But before it produced a plan of any kind, the Council went into summer recess and did not reconvene until half a year later.[19]

An Economic General Staff

THOUGH THE COUNCIL underwent a gradual eclipse, the realization that a higher rate of growth could be brought about only

107

by means of vigorous and coherent direction from above survived, and was embodied in a law enacted on May 11, 1940. Designed both to expedite economic development and to parry any disruptions the war might bring, the new legislation incorporated the Finance Minister's thinking and invested him with extraordinary powers. In effect, Ernestas Galvanauskas was made the head of the nation's economic apparatus. To quote Prime Minister Antanas Merkys, the action made the Ministry of Finance like "an economic general staff."[20] The Finance Minister was authorized to establish export and import firms and to exercise supervision over foreign trade in general; to intervene decisively in industry and trade by prescribing the volume of production, by ordering plants to procure the necessary raw materials and means of production, by distributing labor, by instructing industrial firms to share available commodities, raw materials, and fuel, and by determining prices, wages, and the terms of sales and purchases; and he was further authorized to take any other measures necessary to increase the nation's productive capacity.[21]

Before the bill became law it underwent critical examination in the Seimas. It was also discussed at the dairy industry convention in April 1940 and at the conventions of the Chamber of Agriculture and the Chamber of Commerce, Industry and the Crafts in May 1940. Major opposition to it arose from agrarian interests, which were apprehensive lest the proposed enactment confer upon the Minister of Finance far-reaching powers, set too low a value upon agriculture and unduly stimulate finance, industry, and trade.[22] This fear, which was not totally unjustified, exposed to view the rivalry between the rural cooperative interests and their political representatives, such as the Ministry of Agriculture, and the urban financial, industrial, and commercial establishments, with the Ministry of Finance as their spokesman. A definitive victory for either side would have had a critical effect on the future structure of the economy, and both groups were fully aware of the consequences. In general, the cooperationists and their supporters detected a trend inimical to their pursuits, and they were thoroughly annoyed by their inability to supplant private businessmen.[23]

The elevation of the Ministry of Finance into a central authority with appropriate executive powers was an example of the kind of emergency measure which the lawmakers were prepared to endorse while still shunning more radical solutions, such as an economy planned and administered by the government. The last important piece of legislation in independent Lithuania maintained restricted economic pluralism within the fabric of a guided economy. Whether or not these reforms would have been adequate to correct accumulated difficulties must remain conjectural. The Soviet annexation of Lithuania intervened to cut short her independent experiments.

PART FOUR

German Seizure of Klaipėda:
A Nation's Response

X

AUTHORITARIANISM IN RETREAT

THE RISE OF NAZI GERMANY was cause for concern to many European nations. The particular source of Lithuanian uncasiness was Germany's desire to recover Klaipėda (Memel). The Klaipėda problem made the Lithuanian authorities rather pessimistic about future relations with Germany. They believed that the problem could not be resolved without far-reaching concessions to the Germans which the Lithuanians felt they could not make. From 1935 on, government officials in Kaunas regarded Germany as a peril to Lithuania.[1] Military and political leaders frequently alluded to the dangers which surrounded Lithuania and led the people to believe that the nation's liberty would be defended against any attempt to violate it. Thus, the popular reaction to the loss of Klaipėda was highly emotional.

Resolution to Resist

RETURNING HOME from Switzerland, Lithuanian Foreign Minister Juozas Urbšys stopped in Berlin to pay a call on German Foreign Minister Joachim von Ribbentrop. In the name of the Führer, Ribbentrop presented Urbšys with a demand for the return of Klaipėda, a "burning matter" to Germany.[2] On March 22, 1939, Lithuania yielded.

The surrender of Klaipėda to Germany struck Lithuania with unprecedented effect. Never in its brief political renaissance,

113

whether in the time of the early wars for independence or in the later months of decline, had a blow by an enemy caused the Lithuanian people to demand with such resolute unanimity the realization of national unity and the defense of the nation's liberty. None called for war against the western power, but the general consensus was never to retreat again. Yet at no previous time was the nation's will to defend itself so divorced from its potentiality to do so as at that moment. Consequently, as in past and future exigencies, popular sentiment, which was prepared for the worst, had to submit to official prudence, which could only hope for the best.

In anticipation of a spontaneous eruption of nationwide indignation, the Council of Ministers hastened late on March 22, 1939, to declare a state of emergency in all of the country's districts, with the exception of those adjacent to Germany.[3] This precautionary move placed additional powers to cope with potential unrest in the hands of security organs.

In the forefront of the universal uproar, the Christian Democrats and the Populists, the principal parties of Lithuania's loyal opposition, proceeded to channel the mounting discontent in two directions. They urged the citizens to retain their confidence in the nation's future, and they advocated the institution of a more representative government than the one which had presided over the country's destiny for over a decade. In a government-censored editorial the foremost Catholic newspaper *XX Amžius* (Twentieth Century) mirrored the public frame of mind and aired its opinion and program for future political action:

> We shall be independent. We shall work, sacrifice ourselves, and shall not be daunted by any barriers. Prone to work, with a sense of intense devotion, [and] the love of independence, we continue in the new confines of our state until death. But we must without delay review all the blunders in our foreign and domestic policies, lest new blows come our way. We have already reiterated thousands of times how to manage our domestic affairs. There is only one road to the future—to come to terms [with the parties of opposition], to rally all, all![4]

An almost identical Populist appeal, obviously the consequence of previous consultations by the members of the opposition,[5] was published the following day by the party organ *Lietuvos Žinios* (News of Lithuania).[6]

Lesser journals throughout the land similarly registered exasperation and resolve: "This awful wrong," resounded a provincial paper, "must not deject us. Let us not cease to believe in the independence and freedom of our nation. The determination to defend our beautiful farmsteads, our sacred fatherland, must attend our moves. May the spirit of the first volunteers[7] be revived within us! Let us maintain unity, let us put aside all quarrels! . . . It is better to die than to be a slave!"[8]

The Nationalist media, expressing government views, sought to rationalize Lithuania's defeat. They termed the surrender "a harsh necessity . . . which we have no strength to fight. Germany's demand is a demand of force. We must heroically bear the pain inflicted upon us."[9] The Nationalist rhetoric was distinctly terse, detached, imperious, and frequently ostentatious.

As popular distress mounted in breadth and intensity, during the next several days, the press abounded with patriotic banners, such as: "Not a foot of our land to the enemy!" "A nation's greatest treasure is its freedom and independence!" "Never has a healthy nation perished, once it firmly resolved to defend its independence!" "Never have Lithuanians allowed themselves to be subdued by force. Our enemies have succeeded in subjugating us only by deceit!" Neither deterred nor encouraged by the government, the views of the press represented a truly spontaneous reaction.

To the strain of animated and martial demonstrations among old and young alike, the popular and influential commander of the army made his ponderous contribution. General Stasys Raštikis, the munificently bemedalled personification of the nation's military, advised his countrymen to adapt themselves to the new circumstances. He suggested the need for reorganization of the government on a broader basis, and he vowed to fight for the country's independence should it be threatened in the future.[10] His advice was superfluous, his pledge intemperate; but his veiled admonition to the Nationalist government was an intervention into the civilian domain that could not be disregarded.[11]

On March 23 leaders of fourteen military, political, youth, and professional organizations published their "sacred hope" that in this "serious hour" every Lithuanian would perform his duty to his country.[12] The duty all nationals were expected to honor was the display of sobriety and restraint, top civic virtues which the regime was eager to cultivate.

Finally, on March 28 the venerable veterans of revolutionary wars published their wrathful appeal: "We shall not bear disgrace. Our descendants would curse us if we did not show that we value the Freedom of our Country more than our lives. We must defend ourselves by all means! Not a single foot of our land without a fight!"[13] Such was the nation's reaction to the loss of Klaipėda.

Economic Consequences of the Loss of Klaipėda

THE GERMAN ANNEXATION of the western slice of Lithuania necessitated the internal resettlement of some 12,000 refugees,[14] which further disrupted the national economy. The impact of this situation, however, produced different effects upon individual branches of the economy.

In March and April 1939, customer withdrawals caused banking and credit institutions to lose as much as 42.25 million lits, or 19 per cent of their total deposits. Of these, only 10.5 million lits were returned to the banks before the eruption of hostilities in September. Uncertainty about the nation's future retarded financial recovery.[15] The surrender of the country's sole seaport also inflicted severe losses on industry and trade. The manufacturing concerns of Klaipėda, grouped in Table 19, whose output in 1937 had stood at 116 million lits, accounted for approximately 30.7 per cent of Lithuania's total industrial production.[16] Furthermore, as much as 75.5 per cent of the nation's exports

116

and 68.2 per cent of its imports passed through the Baltic port.

The loss of Klaipėda impaired the interests of neighboring farmers who in the past had relied heavily on their commercial ties with the city. Their agricultural goods which were set aside for home consumption supplied the needs of the urban market. Since these provisions ordinarily were inferior to those reserved for export, a leading economist suggested that the disappearance of this ready outlet for inferior farm produce would benefit agriculture in western Lithuania by compelling local farmers to raise the quality of their yield.[17] In view of the fact that the detached area was but a minor producer of export farm commodities and that, on the whole, it served only as a limited market for agricultural goods, the losses to the rural economy did not amount to very much.

Demands for Coalition Government

WIDESPREAD DEMANDS for a more representative government were voiced at once. From two quarters, pressure was brought to bear on the Presidential residence. After a prior interchange of views among Catholics, Populists, and followers of former Prime Minister Augustinas Voldemaras, the opposition suggested to the outgoing Nationalist Prime Minister Vladas Mironas that the next administration include representatives of other parties.[18] Simultaneously, however, a more efficacious counsel than this political demarche accomplished a Nationalist reverse.

Amid general discontent and traces of Communist agitation,[19] army commander Raštikis made several appearances before the President and told him in private what he had been broadcasting in public, namely, that the army favored the formation of a coalition government. But President Smetona was loath to yield to "public psychosis" and thus furnish the opposition with an opportunity to claim political victory. Instead, he suggested the resort to police measures and added that he would think about the formation of a new government only after things had quieted

TABLE 19

THE KLAIPĖDA INDUSTRIES, 1939

Industry	Number of Firms	Per Cent of National Total	Number of Employees	Per Cent of National Total	Production in lits (000's)	Per Cent of National Total
Peat-cutting	1	6.3	35	3.1	1,271.6	13.3
Stone, clay products	22	16.9	520	13.3	—	—
Metals and machinery	24	20.0	660	17.5	2,376.6	10.6
Chemicals	10	20.8	404	21.6	7,747.5	36.6
Leather and fur	7	12.1	82	6.9	764.0	4.2
Textiles	10	12.3	3,149	41.5	28,256.9	44.2
Timber	36	13.6	2,161	39.7	20,899.0	53.9
Paper and printing	9	10.7	1,266	42.7	20,743.7	57.6
Foodstuffs	47	11.9	1,475	17.9	27,250.0	21.5
Clothing	11	6.0	253	7.1	1,495.4	6.6
Electricity and gas works	5	15.2	252	28.8	4,937.8	28.6

Source: Tarulis, "Klaipėdos krašto pramonės netekus" p. 293.

down.[20] The general persisted in his efforts. He was apprehensive lest police measures fail and the army be called upon to restore public order. This possibility apparently impressed the Nationalist President, who agreed to the idea of a new cabinet but remained adamant against the proposed participation of opposition candidates. Nevertheless, the general prevailed on President Smetona to share political responsibility with the Catholics and the Populists. In deference to his army chief's persistence, the President named General Černius to head the new Council of Ministers.[21]

This cabinet of joint action, as it was popularly known, came into being on March 27. It made history when it unveiled for the first time in more than a decade the names of four eminent opposition leaders as members of the cabinet. Because of the broad powers which the constitution vested in the President, the control of the government still rested with Smetona; but the fact that such a change had taken place at all was overlooked by none.

The admission into the Černius cabinet of Populists and Christian Democrats was not without awkward effects. Formally, there was no such thing as a Christian Democratic or a Populist party, for all opposition movements and their regional organizations had been banned. Their curtailed existence was nevertheless real. Formally, the outlawed parties did not delegate their representatives to the new government. There had not been any lengthy talks between the Premier-designate and the opposition, but in actuality their backing of the new government was evident to all.

Both parties adopted the position that their ministers had consented to serve in the government not as party functionaries but as private citizens, even though their association with the administration had been sanctioned by their central committees. For this reason both the Nationalists and the Catholic-Populist opposition were disinclined to call the Černius government a coalition government and instead employed ambiguous phrases to describe it. A new power relationship had resulted from the momentary triumph of public will over political realism. The forces of the three major political movements in the country had come together, for a duration that no one could predict and with consequences no one could foresee, to advance a common cause. The man in the street made no mistake about it.

In their immediate reaction to the retreat, the Nationalists hoped to tone down the fundamental change that had occurred by placing excessive emphasis on the four army generals who sat on the new Council of Ministers. This, they insisted, was designed to cement closer ties between the general public and the army. Unity, in their opinion, was real only when it was sustained by discipline, when a nation led by one will pursued one goal. The army supplied individuals well qualified to serve a government of national unity, and its graduates knew best how to command and how to obey.[22]

Catholics, Populists, and Social Democrats, on the other hand, were unanimous in their generous endorsement of the new administration. Their press carried a great number of reports registering nation-wide support for the new cabinet of joint action. The Nationalists' and the opposition's divergent attitudes toward this government were indicative of latent discontent which was momentarily drowned out by a flurry of public rejoicing in the new "unity."

The Lithuanian Patriotic Front

AT THE SAME TIME that the coalition government was being assembled, a venture of a different nature vied for attention in Kaunas. Hoping to rally Lithuanians of all convictions behind the government, the veterans of revolutionary wars suggested the formation of a Lithuanian Patriotic Front. The plan would have substantially altered the entire political setting. Not only did it foresee the extension of the ban on the activities of opposition parties, but it envisaged the dissolution of the privileged Nationalist Union as well.

The would-be reformers wasted no time in implementing their ideas. On March 29 some three thousand college students

120

founded an academic chapter of the Patriotic Front.[23] The following day *Lietuvos Aidas* (Echo of Lithuania), an organ of the Lithuanian Nationalist Union and the Nationalist administration, carried the veterans' appeal, entreating all citizens to back this "universal movement" which pledged to promote political tolerance, to bring about a reconciliation of the quarreling factions, to mobilize all available means in order to reactivate national, social, and economic development, and to make use of the talents of the younger generation.[24]

The Nationalists predictably wanted none of this unsolicited initiative. They published the veterans' appeal, but refrained from taking an unequivocal stand until the government ruled one way or another. They judged that the idea of a Patriotic Front amounted to an inclination, on the part of some individuals, to look for new means to realize the ideal of national unity. The Nationalists declined to venture beyond that until more information became available.[25] This inconclusive reaction is indicative of the uncertainty which penetrated the Nationalist ranks in the immediate aftermath of governmental reorganization.

The proposed formation of the Patriotic Front was vetoed by the new cabinet on April 3. The current state of affairs, Interior Minister Kazys Skučas asserted, called for discipline and sobriety, attributes which the program of the Patriotic Front would not bring into being.[26] The Council of Ministers, which advised the citizens to join the ranks of the national guard instead of the Patriotic Front, secured the endorsement of the army commander for its decision. Raštikis' interest in politics became apparent once again.[27] Government disavowal of the veterans' services gave the new administration a green light to proceed with its work.

THE NEW DEAL

THE DECLARATION which Prime Minister Černius read to the Diet on April 5 was anticlimactic. It averred that no effort would be spared to prepare the nation for self-defense, that Lithuania would continue to be neutral in foreign affairs, that all who provoked unrest at home would be repressed, that the government would welcome the cooperation of the Church, and that the value of the currency would be upheld.[1] However, in the light of future interparty rivalry, Černius' remarks on the political changes that had taken place are more significant than his formal program. They appear in the following passages:

> The new administration came into being not to ruin what had been accomplished up to now, but to carry on the work begun [by its predecessors]. . . . To be able to do that successfully, it is necessary that the government remain united, that work in all sectors of the nation's economy be done harmoniously.
>
> It is for this reason that the government, in accordance with the policies laid down by the President of the Republic and in strict adherence to the form of government established by the Constitution, will function in close contact with the Diet and will [in turn] greatly appreciate its cooperation.
>
> The moment we are going through today, and its responsibilities, demand a united effort not only on the part of the organs established by the Constitution but also on the part of the public at large. . . .
> The administration, making every effort to consolidate for that

purpose all the nation's energies, will not side with any single group, will not yield to the influence of any single trend.[2]

A Crack in the Wall

THE ADDRESS was essentially Nationalist in tone. It underscored the continuity of orthodox politics and hushed up the implications and the importance of recent changes. This conspicuous omission was given immediate publicity by the Catholics and the Populists. Without violating the constitution, commenced the widely-read *XX Amžius*, "the administration is determined nonetheless to ascribe to it a new ... content. Namely, the affairs of state are conceived in this declaration in a wider and deeper sense [than before]. The state is set free from any single group. Not one of them may claim monopolistic rights to speak in the name of the state or the nation. . . . Being above [political] parties, [the new administration] 'will not side with any single group, will not yield to the influence of any single trend, but will rather seek to assemble the creative forces of the entire nation.' "[3] The Catholic daily reached the conclusion that the principle of representative government, an aspiration the Nationalists had discarded, had been "solemnly sanctioned" by the government.[4] Politics of the coming weeks would corroborate opposition hopes, but only in part.

Meanwhile, with the exception of the Communists, who charged the new administration with pro-German and generally reactionary policies,[5] ample support rallied to the Černius cabinet. Publicly endorsed by such prestigious personalities as the elder statesman Mykolas Sleževičius,[6] assisted by a ceaseless outpour of elated editorial comment, the coalition cabinet had an enviable beginning.

Public Rallies and Voices of Dissent

DESPITE THE INTRINSIC CONSERVATISM behind the Nationalist declaration of purposes, which prepared for the new but hoped for the old, the dynamics of the coalition government soon burst into the open. Thus, it was not the Prime Minister's message to the Seimas but rather the cabinet's overt alliance with the aspirations of the man in the street that enlivened the coming weeks and supplied the key to the understanding of the days ahead.

In an unprecedented effort to narrow the distance that had severed the authorities from the public, a wave of public meetings swept the country during the next month and a half.[7] Formally, these sessions were sponsored by the regional opposition parties. Actually, however, it appears that recourse to such action had previously been adopted at opposition headquarters in Kaunas, from whence instructions were sent to the provinces.[8]

Public rallies were convened in nearly every leading town. Top government officials, as well as prominent civic leaders, appeared to promote administration policies, to learn the popular sentiment, and to receive numerous resolutions. Specifically, the travelling ministers apprised their eager audiences of such government developments as the projected aid to small landholders and the establishment of the Council of National Economy;[9] they urged their countrymen to enlist in the national guard; and they promised to provide urban and rural workers with low-cost housing. The listeners, in turn, liberally rewarded the visitors with the "greatest enthusiasm," "very violent applause," "great approval," and "thunderous ovations."

Assemblies everywhere responded in much the same way. They hurled many a bitter word at the Nationalists, who for over a decade had defied the public will and who were largely responsible for the lack of national unity. They reproached government leaders for being secretive about impending perils which menaced all, they warmly applauded the new administration and the army, and called on their fellow citizens to stand ready to defend the fatherland. The following excerpts from a speech by a Catholic member of the opposition are illustrative:

> Today we must begin to work together, but we must [also] tell you just who concealed from the nation its tragic state of affairs and who allowed the catastrophes to overtake us by surprise, who lulled the

124

nation to sleep and pacified it, when it felt instinctively that dangers were coming. . . . Let us hail this dawn of freedom and let us resolve to work together with the new consolidated government, which unites all large [political] groups in the nation. . . . We shall not retreat a single foot any more; we shall either successfully defend our liberty or we shall perish in the crusade for freedom.[10]

The resolutions acclaimed at such rallies reflected what was being said. Furthermore, they called for the restoration of civil liberties, suggested amnesty for political prisoners, asked that farmers be free to assemble and to talk over their problems, demanded a wider franchise in local government, urged a return to democracy, and, in an unmistakable reference to the Nationalist Union, favored a ban on political organizations blocking national unity.[11]

Such an insolent revolt of the masses was more than the Nationalists could endure. By the end of April and the beginning of May their campaign against these weekend excursions into the country began to mount. Words of caution, addressed by Nationalist ministers to the restive demonstrators,[12] intimated that the Council of Ministers was divided on the matter. According to Kazys Musteikis, the Nationalists and the army officers, who were generally cool to the idea, had at first yielded to the opposition, especially the Catholics, fearing that failure to do so would jeopardize the coalition. However, some of the ministers themselves became disillusioned with the practice, because occasionally the sessions would extend to unintended extremes.[13]

Conservative opposition outside the government was even more pungent, as the following observations by a Nationalist functionary reveal:

It appears that public inclination toward joint action was at once upset by those speeches and that spirit which became manifest . . . at public meetings or rallies. Due either to the lack of authority on the part of the sponsors of these meetings and their leading speakers, or their veiled partisan aims, the meetings were generating and disseminating attitudes incompatible either with the gravity of the situation, or the intentions which accompanied the formation of the present government, or the assurances which the administration offered in its declaration. ... In many instances it was not clear any more just what was black and what was white.[14]

The vigorous Nationalist paper *Vairas* (Helm) proffered its support to the Prime Minister, who threatened to put an end to all future meetings.[15]

Early in May Interior Minister Skučas addressed a circular to the heads of local government in which he ruled that all future resolutions to be placed before such meetings had to be cleared first with the district executive and that their publication had to be sanctioned by the government. In addition, this circular paved the way for police intervention in the affairs of the meetings themselves.[16]

The Nationalists emerged victorious from this skirmish, as by mid-May that particular form of public protest was a thing of the past.

Censorship and Freedom of the Press

"TO BRING TO LIGHT new ideals and to uncover the true sources of vitality, a free and courageous word is needed. All the Lithuanians are responsible for the destiny of their nation. ... All carry on their civil obligations. And all must be allowed to have a free say—. .." This was the reaction of a cultural weekly to government censorship of the press during the years of Antanas Smetona.[17] The editorial echoed the views of the political opposition and the estranged leftist intellectuals.[18]

The scourge of the Lithuanian information media was a law passed on November 16, 1935, which granted the government unlimited powers in all matters concerning the press. Under the provisions of this law the editor of a periodical could be constrained, and often was, to publicize in a favorable light those aspects of life which the government selected. Further, editors were to mention with approbation the administration's policies and theories, to promote the acceptance of unilaterally interpreted national-mindedness, and to refrain from commenting on what in the eyes of the censors might be detrimental to the national interest. Moreover, a publisher was required to print government-prepared texts on the first two pages and to do so in a way that would not deflate their value. In effect, this encroachment provided the government with a part-time job as contributing editor to opposition newspapers. If the editor-in-chief were reluctant to print all such news, as some were,[19] the law authorized the government to discipline him or his publication.[20] A series of specific government instructions to editors barred many developments abroad from critical review at home. To avoid any undesirable repercussions, news commentators were advised to confine their foreign affairs columns to factual rather than interpretive reporting.[21]

The authorities exercised their censoring powers with a certain standard of fairness. Now and then they silenced top Nationalists and the army command, as when Jonas Statkus, Secretary-General of the Nationalist Union, attempted to rally the nation for a march on Vilnius at the outbreak of World War II.[22] He planned to publish his appeal as an editorial in *Vairas*. However, after a policy clash between the young politician and the President, the journal, which as a result came out one week late, carried a front page appeal—to subscribe to *Vairas*.[23] On still another occasion the same Nationalist periodical, having first promised "to let the facts speak" in answer to "insinuations" from the opposition, had to admit that it could not do so for reasons beyond its control, presumably because of orders from above.[24]

A celebrated encounter between the censor and the army commander astounded Kaunas early in 1940 when General Raštikis in an officers' journal recapitulated his views on such issues as Lithuanian-Soviet relations, lack of national unity, and peasant welfare. In a matter of hours the copies which could still be found on the newsstands were confiscated by the police.[25]

An agency of press censorship rich in derogatory epithets, the Department of Public Affairs, conceived of originally as the nucleus of a ministry of propaganda,[26] passed from view in the initial weeks of the new administration. Formerly directly responsible to the Prime Minister, on April 12 it was demoted to the jurisdiction of the Minister of the Interior, and it soon vanished altogether.[27]

The disappearance of the unpopular Department of Public Affairs did not herald the dawn of freedom of the press, for the government swiftly created other offices of a similar nature within the Ministry of the Interior.[28] But some real changes were undeniable. Circumspect editorials, even if censored, frequently commented on major developments of the day; lengthy reports on news and views of town and country circulated daily; and some inconspicuous periodicals continued their critical opinions about foreign governments and policies.[29] There is no doubt that the press had wrested from the new administration a measure of freedom.

The Nationalists opposed the relaxation of censorship just as they opposed all the other concessions to the public will which the Černius administration was inclined to make. By the end of 1939 the Nationalists concluded to their dismay that they no longer monopolized the formation of public opinion. A partisan press was now aspiring to interpret government policies.[30] Indeed, the Nationalists and the opposition could not agree on the meaning of progress.

Velvet Glove and Iron Fist

PREPARING TO QUELL the incipient mass dissatisfaction caused by the German thrust and encouraged by the administration's liberal reforms, Prime Minister Černius assured the Seimas on April 5 that his government would exhaust all available means to inspire public confidence in the nation's future. It would also adopt a hard line against all agitators who might take advantage of the precarious situation by pitting one segment of society against another. It was not long before he did both.

In a gesture of magnanimity in the summer of 1939, President

128

Smetona relieved the country's prisons[31] of a number of inmates. In June, presidential acts of clemency of varying degrees affected some 168 delinquents; in July, 20 political prisoners regained their freedom.[92] Former Defense Minister Musteikis recalled that some such action had been planned by the old administration, but that the President was apprehensive lest such leniency undermine the authority of the military tribunal,[33] which administered justice in many of these cases. With the new administration such qualms had dissipated.

Though there was widespread popular support for recent government changes, negative reactions were not lacking either. Liberalization of the regime, experiments with new policies, and infrequent acts of clemency failed to do away with a ground swell of rumors, fears, and discontent which the press published daily. According to one report from western Lithuania, a rumor that 25 lits were being offered for an American dollar made the farmers panicky. Many flocked to the markets to purchase livestock and other goods, at prices substantially higher than usual.[34] The rush injured both the nation's morale and its economy. Those who originated rumors and disturbed the peace filled the nation's jails and institutions of forced labor. Week after week newspapers carried lists of such transgressors.

The chief legal instrument to combat actual and potential breaches of public order was disclosed by the President on May 10. This emergency law[35] was to function either during a state of vigilance, when reinforced measures to preserve domestic peace were needed, or during a state of national defense. The law was also subject to a Presidential decree, with a prior recommendation by the Council of Ministers. In the event of a state of vigilance, district leaders were to be armed with extraordinary powers. In the event of a state of national defense, such powers were to be delegated to military commandants. Moreover, if reinforced measures were needed, the Minister of the Interior was authorized to suspend all organized activities and organizations. Under the provisions of this law the district leader could do the following: impose severe restrictions on the freedom of press and radio; restrain the movement of those individuals whom he considered dangerous to public order or state security; hinder or prohibit the right to assemble; and take all necessary steps to assure proper functioning of public institutions.

This legislation was soon translated into language that the man in the street could not fail to understand. By the end of June the chairman of the Kaunas district let it be known how he thought the public ought to behave. In an executive order the district chief found it imperative to put an end to all rumors tending to offend and to humiliate the government and its members; to admonish the population not to incite one Lithuanian against another; to deal sternly with all that he considered would jeopardize the national interest; to forestall demonstrations, strikes, and all other forms of public excess; and to sound a warning to each and every individual to comply with police demands to leave any public meeting when told to do so.[36] The citizen was expected to accept this legislation as a requirement of state security. The government felt obliged to barricade itself against all eventualities. The law seemed both necessary and, for the time being, sufficient.

XII

THE NATION PREPARES FOR THE WORST

THE TIDES OF MARCH had stirred the Lithuanian people to adopt additional defense measures which were both expansive and expensive. In preparing to face future contingencies, the anxious citizens had done three things: they had made monetary contributions to an Arms Fund to purchase more military equipment; they had enrolled more men for service in the national guard; and they had stepped up military training for young persons. In all three undertakings genuine public initiative from below and government inducement from above had culminated in an impressive effort to do everything possible to be ready.

Fund Raising for Defense

LIKE PEOPLE ELSEWHERE, the Lithuanians contributed most when they thought that danger was clear and present. While it took them only several days to collect the first one million lits,[1] it took several months to raise the second million. They persistently pledged their lives and their honor, but not their fortunes, to their country.

As early as March 27 army commander Raštikis commended his radio listeners for their generous contributions to the Arms Fund. At the same time, however, he berated wealthier citizens for their alleged failure to give according to their abilities. Unless they put their ardor for the common cause into concrete form, the General went on, the government would have no alternative but to abandon its hands-off policy.[2] The reprimand anticipated murmurings by the average wage earners that did not subside for months. An editorial in *Karys* (Warrior) complimented the openhanded poor and chided the closefisted rich who failed to support this "loftiest cause" sufficiently. By the middle of May the Supreme Committee of the fund raising campaign threatened to review the lists of donors in order to see to it that those who earned millions would not continue to hand out pennies.[3] There is reason to suspect, however, that the reproof was motivated in part by a deep-seated bias against private enterprise and the liberal professions.

By mid-April 25,000 people throughout the land were engaged in organizing the campaign fund.[4] Despite the lack of enthusiasm by the prosperous citizens for this sort of progressive taxation, in the weeks immediately following the crisis the Fund quickly became rich in cash and valuables. Backed by true public concern and by government mandate, it appealed to every Lithuanian at home and abroad. In the spring of 1939 many citizens had peremptorily demanded that the country become a "fortress," that "the entire nation become an army"; a casual observer might have been pardoned for thinking that it was getting ready to do just that. All metropolitan and regional newspapers carried frequent reports about the inflow of this crisis money and about the moving circumstances that accompanied it. Stories appeared about a poor old woman who gave up all her savings and valuables; a father who yielded savings which he had reserved for his daughter's christening; a smoker and a drinker who resolved to swear off and to aid the Fund instead; and stories about soldiers who refused their salaries. Gold watches, rings, and tsarist rubles supplemented cash contributions. Laborers, small landholders, new land settlers, the clergy, government officials, and business concerns hastened to contribute.

The campaign extended not only to the adult population but also to the children. Many grade school pupils got along without movies, candies, cakes, and other things they loved, so that they could contribute their share, usually one lit or less. Encouraged by their teachers, the children applied to their parents for additional aid. They composed letters, such as:

> Dear parents! I know that our beloved Country Lithuania is in danger, because there are many enemies who wish to smother its free prosperity. [Because] you love me more than anything else, it is your ardent desire that I never be a slave. I love the country where I was born, I love the tombs of our ancestors, and I do not want our heroes' eternal rest to be in a subjugated Fatherland.[5]

The nationwide campaign was probably more successful politically than financially.[6] It spurred the citizens to invest in the future of their country and to vitalize their community interest.

The National Guard Grows

A PART of the nation's armed forces, the Union of *Šauliai*, as the national guard was known officially, was an all-Lithuanian institution as old as the republic itself. Summoned by its founders to serve the country in war and peace, this popular superorganization conditioned the citizens for war by instructing them in matters of defense against enemy air attack and in military discipline, by boosting public morale, and by teaching proper behavior in times of emergency. Originally a democratic institution, the national guard succumbed in time to triumphant authoritarianism. As a result, it was transformed into an instrument of the President, who had the power to appoint and to dismiss the organization's top command.

In addition to their military responsibilities, members of the guard were engaged in diverse cultural activities. The Union disclosed the following information indicating the nature and range of its achievements: it owned 85 homes; had a newspaper with 30,000 subscribers; numbered 139 choirs, 126 orchestras, 300 libraries, and 200 theatrical clubs among its assets; and took credit for some 500,000 publications in the previous two decades.[7] Old and young, town and country, all had a place in the guard's conglomerate activities.

The March events stimulated the Union to step up its military program. More than any other civic organization, the national guard helped bring about that degree of alertness which the Prime Minister sought: "[Our] independence can be preserved only when the entire Lithuanian nation is ready for self-defense, when in every village, every home, grove, and swamp there is a gun pointed at the aggressor. . . . Do we have any other alternative? Unfortunately, we do not."[8] New responsibilities which the government expected the national guard to assume were accompanied by a concerted propaganda effort and an increase in total membership. One commentator observed in May that all public information media were at the disposal of military propaganda. Radio, press, and public meetings were said to have been active in soliciting the citizens' assistance in the defense build-up.[9]

Not only adults but also high school students were urged by the government to enlist as *šauliai*. In mid-June the Minister of Education issued a set of regulations which permitted youth enlistments. All boys over sixteen whose conduct at school was irreproachable could hope to become members of the organization. The new instructions authorized the Union commander, with the consent of gymnasium directors, to form national guard units composed solely of students.[10] The beginning of the new academic year witnessed a rapid growth of student guard formations.[11] Led in most cases by reserve lieutenants, many boys received their basic military training. The national guard reported an increase of 10,000 in its ranks for 1939.[12] Lithuania was gradually becoming a nation at arms.

Increased Militarization and Indoctrination of Youth

THE NATIONAL GUARD'S INCURSION into the nation's schools did not originate the military training of students but only augmented it. Military studies were offered to Lithuanian boys and girls even before the spring crisis. If the entire population were to bear arms, as the authorities asserted, then the children would also have to endure rigors normally reserved for adults. One educator put it bluntly: "Storms baffle Europe. The existence of small states is left in their own hands. . . . There is no doubt that military training in primary schools is indispensable. The teaching of the basic soldierly virtues—bravery, perseverance, discipline, national aspirations, devotion, and patriotism—must not be neglected. . . . The teacher is not a blandishing, gentle nurse but a tutor of a future warrior. When on trips, let the children endure hunger, rain, fatigue."[13] It was hoped that such martial qualities taught to old and young alike would transform the country into an "iron hedgehog" and would fortify its will to survive with invincible pertinacity.[14]

An imaginative civic leader once beseeched Lithuanians to become three million spiritual tanks.[15] Tanks or tankettes, the junior citizens were being armed to do their part. The simplicity of the military indoctrination which a boy received must have made the course easy to pass. In a few succinct sentences he was told that Lithuania was one brave, disciplined, and united army on the march, and that he ought to aspire to be a good soldier. The actual practice the student had to undergo was intended to make him one. Military instruction, occasionally in army barracks, but principally in secondary schools, was offered for youths fifteen to twenty years old. In April and May 1939 many schools acquired rifles and trained their students in their use. On maneuvers and lengthy trips, sometimes in full military outfit, the young men were taught how to execute a planned attack or retreat, how to stand guard or go on patrol, and how to handle explosives. Available reports from different parts of the country point to a considerable activity of this nature.

It would be an exaggeration to imply that every citizen liked what he saw happening. There were dissenters who ventured to suggest that military discipline belonged to the trenches and not to the benches. Not so!—the decision makers would retort, implying moreover that some at home had not yet learned to respect authority sufficiently. It was hoped that military training would remedy this deficiency.[16]

In addition to intensified military curricula in schools, the

Lithuanian Scout Association accelerated its field programs. The eruption of the Klaipėda crisis prompted the seventy-nine leaders of Girl Scouts to volunteer their services and their lives for the nation's defense. Supplying their addresses and qualifications, they placed themselves at the disposal of the Ministry of Defense.[17] Moreover, they hoped to arrange courses on sanitary service and anti-chemical defense for their rural organizations[18] without delay.

The boys did not lag far behind the girls. They promptly formulated new courses. Their program, totalling forty-eight hours of theory and practice for members over fourteen, was designed to instruct boys on how to organize sanitary service in time of war, how to build anti-chemical and anti-aircraft defenses, and how to provide the wounded with medical aid. The courses had to be completed in all scout units before the summer vacation.[19] In the summer, the boys were given a general instruction to travel extensively and to know their country as a good farmer would know his farm. Only then would they be able, in time of need, to do their utmost for the fatherland.[20] Before the year was out, further programs in military training, generously backed by the army, were established.[21] True to their pledge, the scouts were prepared.

XIII

THE NATIONALIST COUNTERDRIVE

THE NATIONALISTS viewed the inclusion of Catholic and Populist ministers in the Černius administration as a blow to their prodigious efforts to cement a monolithic commonwealth.[1] They publicly belittled the essential character of the change by claiming that it was the only natural thing to do in time of enemy pressure, while they simultaneously determined to restore de facto their monopoly of political control. Their strenuous countermeasures, which continued to the time of the Bolshevik intrusion in mid-1940, were channelled in two directions. First, they carried on protracted political debates with the joint opposition. Second, they set out to rejuvenate their own ranks.

The Young Turks to the Defense

IN THE FOREFRONT of the Nationalist counterdrive stood a group of angry young men associated with the weekly *Vairas* (The Helm). Notable among them was Domas Cesevičius, to some insiders the Nationalist heir apparent.[2] After the death of the elder statesman Juozas Tūbelis, Cesevičius became Chairman of the Nationalist Union on December 2, 1939. The group also included Bronius Dirmeikis, editor in chief of *Lietuvos Aidas*; Vytautas Alantas, editor of *Lietuvos Aidas*; and Jonas Statkus, Secretary-General of the Nationalist Union. All under forty, they made their presence felt in party circles and the party press.

The spirited defense of the Nationalist method of government which these *vairininkai* (men of *Vairas*) directed against the liberal breakthroughs was based on the Nationalists' appraisal of the place of authoritarianism in contemporary political theory. They believed that there were no eternal forms of government and no eternal doctrines but only modes of political organization which answered best the different needs of different epochs.[3] These *vairininkai* agreed that as feudalism, absolutism, and liberalism had come and gone, so presumably authoritarianism would fade away in due time. But, having conceded this eventuality, the Nationalists asserted that such a time had not yet arrived. In practically every issue of *Vairas* they unleashed their resources against their adversaries.

Eager to muzzle the vexatious opposition, the Nationalists frequently resorted to political blackmail by insisting that the Catholics and the Populists forgo their criticism of the government in face of recurrent foreign and domestic threats. Whether it was the German seizure of Klaipėda, the subsequent rise of popular discontent, the outbreak of World War II, the Soviet bases, or some invented crisis such as the return of Vilnius, the Nationalists regularly upbraided their foes for censuring the regime at this or that critical moment. They called on the opposition to help maintain order and sobriety by unconditional surrender to the will of the Leader. The "critical moment" or "serious hour" was a constant factor in Lithuanian politics. Crisis politics worked, however, against both the Nationalists, who were constrained to show moderation toward the critics, and the opposition, which had to tone down its demands.

To plead in favor of some other form of government, the Nationalists believed, was to flirt with treason. They boldly threatened dire consequences to all who failed to desist from undermining tendencies. Jonas Statkus, who had concluded that authoritarianism was the way of all nations, threatened with immediate purge all critics of the administration who questioned his interpretation of events.[4] The entire *Vairas* collective appears to have concurred in the Secretary-General's review of the situation and in the need to adopt strong measures against the opposition. For the preservation of unity and order, the *vairinin-kai* vowed to carry on an unrelenting campaign against all who refused to close ranks.[5]

Invariably ready to substantiate their proud submissiveness, the young Nationalists prided themselves on having embraced authoritarianism in time, and often paraded their loyalty to the Leader. One proper occasion to reiterate their affirmation of faith came with the outbreak of World War II, when in a typically somber tone the Nationalists issued this declaration: "Current events in Europe demand of our state vigilance, discipline, and strong union. In the belief that joint action, discipline of words and thoughts, and a lasting understanding of the future are possible only upon the realization of unity of views and undivided will, the Lithuanian Nationalist Union expresses in this serious hour its absolute confidence in and unconditional obedience to the Nation's Leader, President of the Republic Antanas Smetona."[6] To the bitter end the Nationalists persisted in magnifying the prescience and the competence of their helmsman, their supreme authority, their Leader.

Conflict in the Ranks

THE NATIONALIST RENAISSANCE was not limited to the reemphasis on unity. The setback which they suffered in March 1939 spurred the Nationalists to reexamine their intraparty affairs, too. To the extent that the *Vairas* contributors' diagnosis and prescription differed from those of their senior party colleagues, they constituted an "opposition of good will." This term, coined by party secretary Statkus, meant that younger Nationalists were eager to unearth and to amend real shortcomings. However, the authority of President Smetona was not at stake.[7]

Aside from fleeting controversy in matters of foreign policy,[8] the wellspring of internal revisionism was twofold, theoretical and organizational. One possible explanation of the Nationalist failure to mold a monolithic society was their unwillingness to resort to excessive force. Now the *vairininkai* determined to be rid of this fastidiousness, and in the process they pushed to extremes all the fundamental assumptions on which Smetona's edifice rested. Smetona and his senior followers had said in the past that Lithuania had to discover her own road to the future. In a far-reaching proposal for change the *vairininkai* advocated an exclusively Lithuanian way of life. Remnants of humanism, not an entirely Lithuanian commodity, were to be removed from the country. As the flamboyant Alantas put it, "national egoism, founded in national solidarity, is the basis for the nation's survival."[9] To President Smetona, Nationalist recourse to pedagogic and propagandistic efforts to spread his ideas was a necessary and frequently sufficient means. To the *vairininkai*, however, it was necessary, but clearly insufficient. Education was too slow and out of pace with the times. The extraordinary age in which we live, argued the *Vairas* contributors, necessitates equally exceptional means, including more stringent laws to facilitate Nationalist construction.[10] Finally, Smetona's totalitarianism was not sufficiently inclusive for their taste. The *vairininkai* found it deplorable that the "national conception" in social and cultural fields had not been substantiated, rendering it impossible for the Nationalists to expound their "absolute will" in these areas of human endeavor.[11] Consequently, to further the transformation of the country into a cohesive monolith, they proposed the creation of a Chamber of Culture which would rectify this deficiency.[12] Indeed, the "opposition of good will" had every intention of closing the gap that separated Nationalist practice from theory.

Revival of Party Spirit

THE ORGANIZATIONAL disagreement between the younger generation and the senior party members resulted in two developments. First, the countercampaign attempted to alter the nature of the Nationalist Union; and, second, the party hoped to regenerate party spirit from below. In the President's design the

140

Nationalist party did not constitute a source of political power but only a bridge between the supreme authority and the general public. The *vairininkai* were not entirely pleased with this. Domas Ceseviċius was known to have complained that the Nationalists seemed to forget that they belonged to a political organization.[13]

Curiously enough, a "misinterpretation" of the leadership principle was thought to have been a barrier to the enthusiastic participation in party activities by the rank and file. The "erroneous" comprehension, to be discarded, had left the party members with nothing else to do but to carry out orders from above. Now it was asserted that a free and businesslike discussion of many matters of interest was in complete accord with the inner logic of authoritarianism.[14]

The culmination of Nationalist revival occurred at the party conference on January 5 and 6, 1940, where the *vairininkai* voiced their sentiments and then incorporated them into resolutions. By that time the Nationalists had reason to be optimistic about the future: the fears generated by the German-Polish campaign of 1939 had subsided, and at home resurgent authoritarianism had accomplished the downfall of the Černius administration.[15] The "public psychosis" which had brought about the March reorganization of the government had disappeared. The Nationalists looked toward and prepared for the future with an air of confidence. An intimation of great expectations and future evolution of the authoritarian political model were outlined by President Smetona in his last major address:

National orientation must depict the life of the state as an organism all of whose parts, all of whose members do not struggle among themselves but [rather] work, or should work, together in solidarity toward one end, namely, that the entire nation be vigorous and healthy, that it grow and become ever stronger. . . . It follows from such an organic conception of the nation that if the existence of [social] classes is not a necessary evil but a benefit, there is therefore no need to destroy them; on the contrary, their growth must be facilitated, so that one can grow into another, that they can unite and become solid, in other words, become more powerful and become conscious of their functions in the nation as a whole. . . . When the tides of war subside and [nations] prepare for a lasting order, society will have to be organized anew—it will be necessary to give it more freedom but also to impose more obligations. The basis of order is an organized society, not a mechanical one, not governed by the equality of men but emanating from their functional . . . status. Such a view tends toward a corporate system founded on a professional basis. Because the nation is a living organism, and not a mechanical one, the groundwork in the reconstruction of society . . . will have to be done with a view to national unity. Being administered in that manner, [Lithuania], as a monolithic body, will cooperate freely with other nations, having one ideal in whose name class distinctions and differences become reconciled.[16]

The Nationalist reanimation accomplished by the *Vairas* coterie was not based on new or original thought; it was a step toward the logical conclusions implicit in Smetona's general conceptions. Had it been successful, it would have eliminated the breach that had developed between Nationalist politics and Nationalist theory, a breach that guaranteed a measure of freedom.

PART FIVE

Political Repercussions of the Outbreak of World War II

XIV

THE DECISION TO REMAIN NEUTRAL

Prologue

THE GERMAN INVASION of Poland commenced on September 1, 1939. The eruption of hostilities between its next door neighbors brought about a perilous interlude in Lithuania's domestic politics. Bent on a policy of neutrality, the Lithuanian government hoped to avoid involvement in the German-Polish conflict. In a broadcast to the nation, President Smetona called on the sons and daughters of Lithuania to have confidence in their government, and to entrust it with the power of determining if neutrality were in jeopardy. For about two weeks the government did not take any precautionary measures. Army commander Raštikis recalled that he could not obtain any instructions either from the President or from the Ministry of Defense concerning the army's role in the face of new developments. However, by mid-September, when military necessities had been reconciled with budgetary limitations, the economy-minded administration finally ordered a partial mobilization and some 10,000 men were called to the colors.[1] The emergency did not last long. By the beginning of October some of the men were on their way home.

Apart from purely military considerations, the war affected Lithuania in three major ways: (1) the perennial Polish-Lithuanian dispute over the possession of Vilnius required immediate attention in view of continual Polish retreats before the Nazi

145

onslaught: (2) Soviet pressure on Kaunas resulted in the establishment in Lithuania of Russian military bases: and (3) the new events precipitated a government crisis prejudicial to the Catholic-Populist opposition.

Beginning with the Polish seizure of Vilnius in 1920, the cardinal objective of the Kaunas government was that city's reunification with Lithuania. It was therefore natural that as the German-Polish tension mounted, so did Lithuania's concern with the fate of the city and the surrounding area which they tenaciously claimed as its own. Immediately before and during the initial days of World War II Lithuania's neutrality was seriously challenged, not by enemies abroad but by impassioned citizens at home. The pressure on the Kaunas government to intervene militarily in order to recapture the medieval capital originated from two sources, the influential Nationalist circles in Kaunas, and the Lithuanian Legation in Berlin. Their respective spokesmen were the Nationalist Secretary-General Jonas Statkus and the Minister to the Reich government, Colonel Kazys Škirpa.

Questioning a Policy of Neutrality

THE GERMAN-SOVIET NONAGGRESSION PACT of August 23, 1939, was correctly interpreted by Lithuanian political commentators as a turning point in Great Power diplomacy, pregnant with the possibilities of a European war, a Polish breakdown before the German assault, and an ensuing Russian intervention.[2] In view of such potential exigencies, party secretary Statkus proceeded to question the judiciousness of the policy of neutrality. On August 24 he published a searching article in *Vairas* in which he ably proved the obvious, that neutrality, like any other policy, was subject to the ever-changing national interest. Yesterday's sagacious course of conduct could prove to be inexpedient today. Second, he was apprehensive lest the existing policy fail to satisfy all national aspirations, a clear reference to Vilnius. Statkus was alarmed that a hands-off policy might be viewed by the general public as a betrayal of one of its most cherished beliefs. To many, the protracted struggle for reunification of Vilnius with Lithuania proper was a crusade for the liberation of the very soul of the nation.[9] A week later Statkus was even more explicit when he elaborated further: "The Nationalists are determined not to neglect any of those areas in which Lithuanians live. If we failed to say this, we would be insincere. On the other hand, however, national expansion must not contradict a realistic policy. To be more specific, our national problems beyond our state borders must not jeopardize our independent country. But we would not be Lithuanians if we failed to be concerned about Lithuanians living elsewhere. Both the nation and the state must show that concern. Indifference here would be interpreted as weakness and a lack of national ambition."[4] Consequently, upon the outbreak of war, Statkus had argued privately, and by means of his stillborn editorial[5] had hoped to say publicly, that now was the time to march on Vilnius.

Vilnius Between Scylla and Charybdis

QUITE INDEPENDENTLY of the initiative from Nationalist head-quarters, the assiduous Škirpa, Minister in Berlin, plied his home office with advice to adopt a flexible foreign policy. Proceeding from a premise that in any limited war between Germany and Poland the former would be the victor, ex-staff officer Škirpa as early as May 8, 1939 had counseled his government to follow future military operations with a view to finding the most opportune moment to order the army to occupy the Vilnius territory before either the Germans or the Russians did. Once the war began, the Minister communicated his advice to cross the Polish-Lithuanian border not before September 8, when the Polish high command had completed the evacuation of its forces from the Vilnius sector, but not later than September 15, in order to enter the city before the Russian incursion into Poland. In a memorandum of September 8, insisting that the army be instructed to move immediately after the collapse of the Polish Vistula defenses, Colonel Škirpa suggested that the government issue a communiqué stating that it had not altered its policy of neutrality, that it did not consider itself at war with Poland, but only sought to right a wrong inflicted in 1920.[6] The extent of German influence in prompting Lithuanian action against Poland is a matter of some uncertainty. Minister Škirpa testified that the Reich government merely advised action by Lithuania. On the other hand, there appears to be some evidence that Berlin, through its Minister and military attaché in Kaunas, had pressed the government for immediate intervention. It volunteered to assist the campaign with aircraft, tanks, and heavy artillery. German solicitations were evinced both before the start of the war and during its early stage, when Vilnius had not yet fallen into Russian hands. As late as September 14, German Minister Erich Wilhelm Zechlin informed Berlin that he would continue his "efforts to influence the [Lithuanian] Government" with a view to its participation in the anti-Polish operations. That same day, however, Reich Foreign Minister Joachim von Ribbentrop decided to discontinue conversations with the Lithuanians, and two days later Minister Zechlin was apprised of the change.[7]

The proponents of armed intervention in the German-Polish war found considerable support in the army and the national guard.[8] Especially insistent in their demands to seize the prized city were the followers of Voldemaras, who even went so far as to threaten the government with an insurrection if it failed to take forceful measures against the Poles.[9] And in the administration itself, both the Prime Minister and the Minister of the Interior sided with the interventionists.[10]

Opposition to Armed Attack

THE COUNCIL OF MINISTERS reasoned differently, and on September 5 ruled out any armed attack. There were two principal motives: (1) to enter the war, the cabinet judged, would ipso facto make Lithuania a German ally, a role it was not particularly eager to play; and (2) to fall upon Poland at a time when it was already bearing the full brunt of German arms was considered immoral.[11]

The Catholic representation in the government was against any military action to capture the city. At a party conference shortly before the cabinet session the Catholics were hopelessly split on the issue, and the decisive vote against intervention seems to have been cast by the Deputy Prime Minister Bizauskas. Allegedly, he even threatened to quit the government if his colleagues failed to concur in his judgment.[12] The position of Prime Minister Černius appears to have been contradictory. On the one hand, he did favor some sort of action to regain Vilnius. Yet, on the other, as early as May 8 he instructed General Raštikis, on his way to Warsaw at the time, to assure the Poles that they need not be concerned with any military move by the Lithuanians, that they could safely concentrate all their forces against Germany. Moreover, he imparted the guarantee through the Polish Military Attaché in Kaunas.[13]

The decision for nonintervention once made, backers of political "realism" were indiscriminately gagged. Statkus never reached the public, and Škirpa, who had no knowledge of the September 5 decision by the Council of Ministers, was sternly reprimanded for the conversations he had had with the Germans. He was further told to display more temperance in the future.[14] However, the opponents of armed intervention suffered minor setbacks. To be sure, President Smetona seconded the cabinet decision, but only reluctantly. When Colonel Škirpa reproached him on September 21 for the failure to act, the President burst into tears, said he was insufficiently informed about the course of events, and ordered Catholic officials to stay away from his office.[15]

The seizure of Vilnius by the Red Army (September 19, 1939) prompted the government to reexamine its attitude once more. It did so on September 22. In a five-point document the administration said it hoped to have very friendly relations with the Reich government; that it was determined to remain free

149

and neutral; that it intended to be on good terms with all countries, especially the neighboring powers; that it would continue to work toward the realization of Lithuanian aspirations by peaceful means; and that it was appreciative of the recent German offers of help.[16]

ARRIVAL OF RUSSIAN TROOPS AND THE

RETURN OF VILNIUS

THE TREATIES which Germany and the Soviet Union made with each other in August and September 1939 effected a mutual division of interests in Eastern Europe. Among other things, the two powers agreed that the Baltic states should stay within the Soviet zone of action. At the time, the exact nature of this trade in the fate of nations was not generally known.

Russia Moves West

THE NEWS the Lithuanian Minister in Moscow brought home on September 30 was received in Kaunas with a cautious optimism. Ladas Natkevičius presented his Foreign Minister with an invitation from the Chairman of the Council of People's Commissars to visit the Kremlin to discuss matters of mutual interest that had arisen as a result of recent events in eastern Europe. The government complied, and by October 3 Foreign Minister Juozas Urbšys was on his way to Moscow.

Reluctant to predict what lay ahead, *Lietuvos Aidas* merely observed in general terms that conditions in eastern Europe had changed during the preceding month. Consequently, it had become necessary to review the new situation.[1] The Catholic organ similarly declined to speculate on the sum and substance of talks with the "new Russia." It expressed assurances that the

151

Lithuanian delegation would do everything humanly possible to guard the nation's liberty and hoped for the best:

> Russia today is no longer the same. Perhaps it wanted nothing so much as to be different. . . . We are talking today with this new Russia. Having entered upon a different course, she will not repeat in regard to us the mistakes of the old Russia, so gravely recorded in the history of our [country] and of old Russia. The new Russia can face the world with nobility, [and it can] disdain the actions of imperialistic . . . states.[2] We are waiting for this.[3]

Populist reaction was not devoid of optimism. Their political commentator was inclined to believe that new developments in this part of Europe did not give sufficient ground for alarm.[4] Press dispatches from the Soviet capital, which described a "very friendly spirit" and a "very good atmosphere" among the conferees, did nothing to abate the guarded optimism of the general public.

At the conference table, however, the Lithuanians did not fare as well as the man in the street was led to believe. The Soviet position was that they were willing to hand over to the Lithuanians only a part of the Vilnius territory outlined by the Soviet-Lithuanian Peace Treaty of July 12, 1920. They demanded that the Kaunas government conclude a treaty of mutual assistance with Moscow, which would authorize the stationing on Lithuanian soil of some 75,000 Soviet troops. Their refusal to return all areas set forth in the Peace Treaty was allegedly motivated by serious objections from the Byelorussian Soviet Socialist Republic, and by Moscow's inability to prevail on that republic to alter its stand. Furthermore, the bases were a matter of military necessity.[5] Irrespective of the several alternatives they had suggested, the Lithuanians, like the Estonians and Latvians before them, failed to dissuade Soviet authorities from their insistence on stationing military garrisons in the Baltic republic. But they succeeded in reducing the number of troops to 20,000 men. On October 10, after a week of Russian "demands," "dictates," "threats," and "reproaches,"[6] the treaty, with a secret supplement concerning the bases, was signed.

From Optimism to Euphoria

KAUNAS RADIO broadcast the news of the return of Vilnius on October 11. The instantaneous outburst of enthusiasm which attended the announcement defies description. Any foreboding the government had had about the admission of foreign troops was drowned amid public rejoicing. As a matter of fact, the press hardly even mentioned the articles authorizing Russian bases. While the *Te Deum* was being sung in churches throughout the land, effusive editorials and demonstrations accurately reflected the popular sentiment in mid-October. The prestige of the Soviet Union soared.

The press applauded the Kremlin for its consummation of "traditional friendship," a term frequently used by both sides to describe Lithuanian-Soviet relations between the wars. The usually reserved *Lietuvos Aidas* beamed that, "one of the most constant and positive factors in our foreign policy always has been and still is our friendly relations with Soviet Russia, which have been raised to the highest degree by the treaty that came into force today."[7] Catholic, Populist, and Nationalist periodicals, too, showered the Soviet Union with praise. The following passages are indicative of the nonpartisan encomia:

> The day the agreement is signed Lithuania [and] the Lithuanian nation will have an historic wrong righted. That is a fact which permits us to say: an imperialistic power had deprived us of all this and a peaceful state, which understands the interests of another nation, gives it back to us. So, the profession of good will on the part of the USSR is enormously impressive.[8] The Soviet Union respects a nation's right to an independent existence, and in regard to the Lithuanian nation—in the solution of the Vilnius problem— it has repeatedly honored and implemented both this right of the Lithuanian nation and its own commitments. In view of this additional event, so obvious and convincing, all compliments on our part seem to be superfluous.[9]

153

Amid toasts to the Russians, some went so far as to welcome the treaty in its entirety as a sure safeguard against the eventual wrath of *Polonia restituta*. They re-echoed former Prime Minister Voldemaras' sentiments of more than a decade past, that the savior of Lithuania from the designs of her Polish neighbor was none other than the Soviet Union.[10] Such thinking persisted among some political commentators throughout the months ahead. Weeks before the Soviet occupation one commentator was still insisting that the situation in which the Baltic states found themselves was the best possible in time of war. The outcome of the Finnish-Soviet war of 1939-1940 later emboldened a Catholic author to conclude that the Soviet Union did not harbor any aggressive designs in the Baltic and that, therefore, its military protection of the three republics was quite congenial.[11]

The impending arrival of the Red Army was discussed as a footnote to the acquisition of the eastern territory. The proportion of news space allotted to the two topics is fairly illustrated by a Populist weekly which devoted its first two pages to the coverage of the agreeable news and only several lines, somewhere on page four, to a dispatch from Finland to the effect that Russia intended to keep some five hundred military aircraft and a thousand tanks in the Baltic states. But this is not to say that sober appraisal of the situation escaped the Lithuanians entirely. A Catholic editorial was fearful of a "foreign soldier on our soil" and asserted that his presence would not relieve Lithuanians of their duty to defend the country; a Populist commentator was sufficiently keen to point out that the treaty was concluded between two partners of vastly unequal strength and that it mattered less what the terms said than what the more powerful cosignatory intended to do.[12] However, the ineradicable byproduct of the October days, important in the light of future developments, was that not only had the military incursion failed to destroy Soviet-Lithuanian amity, but that, on the contrary, the restoration of the ancient city had strengthened it. The profound impression that the realization of the Vilnius idée fixe had made obscured the fact that Lithuania's independence

154

was seriously impaired, that it in fact had become a Soviet satellite.

Klaipėda had provoked a virulent popular protest in March, when danger to national independence was largely a product of "public psychosis." Vilnius fostered a grand delusion in October, when the threat was real. The Lithuanian press absolved Moscow from any impropriety by adducing a variety of "understandable" Soviet interests and aspirations. It talked itself into believing that Russia harbored no harmful designs against its Baltic neighbor. Indeed, it confidently proclaimed the opinion that Lithuania's future remained in its own hands!

On October 11 and 12 both Lithuanian nationalists and pro-Communists demonstrated in Kaunas. The former group, who heavily outnumbered the leftists, lauded the administration for its course in regard to Vilnius; the latter group voiced its gratitude to the USSR in front of the Soviet Legation. Outstanding among the leftists was Justas Paleckis, the future front man in Soviet Lithuania. Some twenty-six pro-Communists, including Paleckis, who interrupted the festivities by demanding freedom for political prisoners and the overthrow of the Smetona regime, were put behind bars.[13] To counter the Communists, the Union of Christian Workers called a series of meetings in Kaunas and elsewhere. The well-attended rallies, organized in the later part of October, expressed satisfaction over the cession of Vilnius, condemned "demagogic agitators" and "provocateurs," and recommended land and social reforms favored by the Catholic-Populist representation in the government.[14]

The administration did not lag far behind the public in its praise for the Kremlin. Foreign Minister Urbšys declared his satisfaction to Joseph Stalin for the Soviet leader's understanding of Lithuanian interests and for his contribution to mutual confidence and the traditional friendship, which, the Minister affirmed, was unalterable.[15] Privately, however, as German Minister Zechlin disclosed on October 14, "Urbšys did not hide his concern about future developments but he also emphasized that Lithuania would still work to the utmost in the future for her

155

independence."[16] On the occasion of the entrance of Lithuanian troops into Vilnius, Prime Minister Černius expressed his appreciation of Moscow's unremitting aid to Lithuania by the conclusion of the treaty.[17] And Owen C. Norem, the United States Minister at Kaunas, informed Washington on October 13 that Deputy Premier Bizauskas, a member of the Lithuanian delegation to Moscow, "seemed quite happy over the whole affair."[18] However, judging from the correspondence of former Minister of Defense Musteikis, as well as from the precautionary measures taken after the arrival of Soviet garrisons on November 14, 1939, the professed satisfaction of top officials was exaggerated and not representative of the true situation, as perceived in government quarters. If not alarmed, these officials were nonetheless concerned.[19]

The Seimas scrutinized the Moscow settlement even less. The treaty was brought before it on October 14, and Foreign Minister Urbšys took the floor to say:

> Abroad and perhaps at home in Lithuania, too, some people might think that the presence of the Soviet army on Lithuanian territory might affect Lithuania's internal order and even her independence. These problems were discussed in great detail with Soviet statesmen who, for their part, have accentuated in categoric and clear terms that the Soviet Union does not under any circumstances and in any way intend to interfere either in Lithuania's domestic affairs, or in Lithuania's political, economic, and social order, or in her military matters. These Soviet assurances are included in the treaty, too.
>
> It is noteworthy that these questions affecting Lithuania's domestic policies were thoroughly discussed with . . . Stalin himself, who has shown much consideration for and sympathy with Lithuanian national interests and who has guaranteed that under no circumstances would the Soviet Union interfere in any way in Lithuanian internal affairs. . . .
>
> [Besides the return of Vilnius], the government is convinced that the treaty . . . will be advantageous to Lithuania also by its terms of mutual assistance. In the disquieting times in international life, when law and justice, the moral side of international relations, are

but little adhered to, the assistance of the powerful Soviet Union
... will help Lithuania to come out of these difficult ... times
intact, unharmed, and united with its historical capital Vilnius.[20]

The Seimas thought so, too. Its speakers shared the public joy
over the "event of historic significance," meaning Vilnius, and
were hopeful that Moscow would not betray their trust. To
fortify their confidence, the representatives leaned on many years
of advantageous Lithuanian-Soviet cooperation and concluded
that they had no reason to doubt Soviet good will.[21] And at least
one Catholic newspaper went so far as to suggest that Russia's
presence would encourage social justice in Lithuania's neighboring states. It reasoned that since the Soviet Union acquired
eastern Poland in October of 1939, Hungary had introduced
social reforms. Hence, the provincial publication hastened to
point out, all Soviet neighbors would be well advised to imitate
the Hungarians.[22] Kaunas pondered the timely exhortation.

Riding on the wave of popular rejoicing, the Nationalists
reaped some political profit by ascribing the fortuitous feat to
their long-range Vilnius policies. In addition, they again called
for national unity—*especially in this serious hour.*

A Shadow Falls

THE OCTOBER TREATY had stipulated that the location of Russian
troops in Lithuania, as well as attendant matters of an economic,
administrative, and legal nature, would be determined by a
separate agreement between the contracting parties. To implement these treaty provisions, a Soviet military mission arrived
in Kaunas on October 21. In the ensuing negotiations the Russians insisted on a liberal interpretation of the treaty terms and,
consequently, modified the original agreement in two respects.
First, the secret supplement had authorized the Russians to
station a maximum of 20,000 soldiers in the country, with
Lithuanians retaining the right of control. However, from the
very start the Soviet authorities had insisted on the right to bring

157

in auxiliary personnel, and they proceeded to bring them in, evading any control. Second, the treaty had provided for a bilateral determination of the exact location of the Russian bases, but it had excluded both Kaunas and Vilnius as possible areas for Soviet garrisons. Contrary to the above, the Russians ruled that their troops would stay in Vilnius, if only temporarily.[23]

In matters which were not detailed in Moscow the Soviet delegation proved to be exacting. It asked for the best barracks the Lithuanians had, demanded strategic areas, and in some instances even wanted to surround the Lithuanian army with Russian troops.[24] These illustrate some of the difficulties which arose between the cosignatories. There were others, too. The Russians interpreted the treaty provisions in a manner which benefited them most, while the Lithuanians, for fear of consequences, scrupulously abided by the contract.[25] Administrative questions, however, caused no undue difficulties; and the behavior of the Russian soldier, who was to avoid both the native population and local Communist activities, was "most correct."[26]

For their part, the Lithuanians intensified their alertness and constantly watched what the Russians were doing. The State Security Department looked into the equipment of Soviet troops, military construction, the life inside the bases, the attitude of Russian soldiers, the conversations between the soldiers and the local population, how the officers lived, where they purchased their food, and how they spent their leisure hours.[27] Moreover, the government decided to strengthen the national guard. In a circular addressed by the Secretary-General of the Council of Ministers to all government departments, the administration stated that in view of the need for all citizens to be ready more than ever before to protect the country against all eventualities, it was necessary for all civil servants and employees of private firms which received government assistance to join the ranks of the national guard. The enlisted men and women were to perform exceptional functions during their regular work hours and were to be paid for the time spent.[28]

158

Finally, there is reasonable ground for thinking that by the end of 1939 the three Baltic governments of Lithuania, Latvia, and Estonia were agreed on the need to coordinate their defenses against the possible Russian threat.[29] In earlier years the possibility of military collaboration was stillborn largely because of fear on the part of Latvia and Estonia of becoming entangled in Lithuania's quarrels with Germany or with Poland over Klaipėda and Vilnius. In the winter of 1939-1940 these particular quarrels and fears were a thing of the past.

In the meantime, all things considered, coexistence was relatively unperturbed. On January 5, 1940, Foreign Minister Urbšys disclosed before a Nationalist convention that Soviet garrisons so far had not interfered in Lithuania's domestic affairs, that the Lithuanian administration continued to go about its business just as it had before October 10, and that in general the Soviet soldiers were behaving well.[30] On April 17 Prime Minister Antanas Merkys himself reverted to the subject in order to reply to those who distrusted the foreign troops. Addressing a conference of economists, the Nationalist Premier pointed out that by reason of a twenty-year experience in dealing with the Russians and by virtue of the fact that the government had no cause for complaint about the conduct of the Russian garrisons, the administration saw no reasonable ground for regarding the Soviet Union as a threat to national security.[31] As late as June 9 a high cabinet member assured a veterans' convention that there was no cause for misgivings about the nation's future. Rumors to the contrary, originated by those who did not understand the political situation, were to be discounted as so much "unsubstantiated wild talk."[32]

Such categoric public assertions were not fully representative of government thinking. Former Finance Minister Ernestas Galvanauskas testified that in an extraordinary session "several months" before the occupation, the Council of Ministers had agreed that the Soviet Union was Lithuania's "enemy number one," a phrase attributed to the Prime Minister himself.[33] Thus the months of Lithuania's semi-independence were imbued with a sense of baffling dualism. On the one hand, the "foreign soldier on our soil" had impressed most citizens with the need to adopt additional safeguards. On the other, there is ample evidence for concluding that the nature of the peril had eluded both the leaders and the led. Until the climactic days of the Communist takeover beguiling optimism was an unrelenting rival of sober analysis.

Land Reform in Vilnius

THE ACQUISITION of the ancient capital appeased Lithuania's national aspirations but it proliferated its troubles, too. The interaction of such complexities as the depressed state of the region's economy, the losses it incurred from Bolshevik pillage,[34] its strikingly unequal distribution of land, and the spasmodically colliding national interests of its heterogeneous population,[35] confronted the Kaunas authorities with a formidable challenge which was further complicated by the European conflagration. However, in the months before Soviet occupation, the jubilant Lithuanian administrators set to work upon these problems with an ardor equalled only by their impetuous chauvinism.

One of the first enactments of the Nationalist administration was to put into effect in this eastern district the land laws which were in force in Lithuania proper. This meant that large proprietors who had been favored by the Polish authorities would be dispossessed of most of their land, which would be divided, subject to redemption dues payable in 36 years, among the area's small landholders and its landless peasants. The policy of expropriation proved to be remunerative to the expropriators in more ways than one. The Vilnius landholders were known to have been inimical to Lithuanian interests. Their large estates, those "fortresses of foreign leaven," had enabled them to give effect to their policies. By the seizure of the bulk of these lands the Lithuanians hoped to extirpate these pockets of opposition.[36] Moreover, the Lithuanian lawmakers believed, and not without reason, that expropriation decrees would win the favor of the peasant reci-

160

pients of the land. From a bleak, servile past the peasant had preserved a deep-seated resentment against working the lord's land, an aversion which the Lithuanians were eager to turn to their own immediate advantage.[37] Implementation of land reforms had its economic considerations, for as in Lithuania proper, the administration favored medium sized farms. It was reported that by the middle of March 1940, the expeditious Nationalists had disappropriated 90 country estates with some 23,000 hectares of land, and planned to expropriate a total of 110 estates covering 30,000 hectares.[38] Additional projects were planned, such as converting the 146,660 hectares of land controlled by peasant communities into individual farms. It is next to impossible to determine whether any progress was made, however.

The manufacturing establishments the Lithuanians regained in October approximated the number of firms they were deprived of in Klaipėda in March. In terms of quality, however, the gain did not make up for the earlier losses. Industrial shops in Vilnius were smaller, less mechanized, employed fewer people, and produced inferior goods. With a view toward reinforcing its urban economy, burdened with 15,000 jobless workers and a throng of war refugees, the government set a high rate of exchange for Polish currency, reserved 45 per cent of its public works appropriations for the area, floated a special aid loan which by May of 1940 totalled 28 million lits, and redirected large quantities of surplus food originally set aside for export.[39]

The Lithuanianization of Vilnius

ON THE WHOLE, the brief encounter between the fervid Kaunas nationals and the ethnically diverse Vilnius population was not overly amicable. The avowed intention of the former to Lithuanianize the estranged districts augured bitter repercussions. Lithuanian Nationalism in the ceded area promised to be irascible, intolerant, discriminatory, and unsparingly thorough. The new leaders paraded their contemptuous dislike of the area's pervasive Polish culture. Prime Minister Merkys himself told

161

members of his party that from the moment his administration set foot in the contested territory it tried "to make everybody think like Lithuanians. First of all, it was and still is necessary to comb out the foreign element from the Vilnius region. In this sense we have already done much."[40]

The theoretical basis for freeing the society from its "foreign element" had been rationalized years in advance. It belonged to the essential nature of nationalism, in Lithuania as elsewhere. "Members of the old state were citizens," postulated Antanas Maceina, a resourceful Catholic writer.

> The new [nation] state rests its existence not on the citizen but on the *national*. . . . The state, the embodiment of the nation cannot treat equally both nationals and citizens of foreign nationalities, or the so-called national minorities. Nationals are the true members of the new state, while all the rest are merely the state's *residents*. They are entitled to all the rights of nationals, but they cannot have the same privileges as nationals. Their participation in the life of national culture, in science, art, public institutions, economy is undesirable and in some cases even inadmissible.[41]

The passage summarized the distinction, in theory, between the "true members" of a nation and the "undesirables." In practice, this Catholic intellectual, who demanded that treasures of Polish culture be locked up in museums, insisted upon the following policy of liberation:

> The Vilnius resident must be liberated from that Polish nightmare which originates from Polish surroundings, Polish language, Polish art, Polish literature, Polish schools. . . . Any toleration of Polish institutions in fields of civil affairs, science, art or religion is a crime against the re-Lithuanianization of the Vilnius territory. . . . But we are not vandals. . . . We do not want to destroy all this wealth, only to eliminate it from life.[42]

While the repudiation of vandalism may have been problematical, the all but unanimous intention to monopolize community life is illustrated by such sentiments as:

All that serves as a cultural medium and is not reserved exclusively for the minority must be in the hands of the Lithuanians themselves. Therefore, all publishing houses of Lithuanian books and newspapers, all distributors of the Lithuanian and foreign press, the screen and stage, offices of film distribution, concert agencies, and radio . . . must belong exclusively to the Lithuanians.[43]

Fragmentary news reports from the capital bear witness to outbursts of Lithuanian jingoism. On March 13, 1940, an influential newspaper denounced an alien who had addressed a Vilnius civil servant in his native tongue and a Lithuanian national who, failing to see anything wrong, not only had responded in that language but also had paused for a social chat. The Catholic daily found these frequent trivial incidents to be evidences of disrespect to the official language.[44]

There seems to be some indication that discrimination against the "foreign element" marred labor relations, too. In certain cases the nationals enjoyed priorities in obtaining jobs, and non-Lithuanian businessmen were burdened with various restrictions.[45] Amid occasional clashes between contending interests, a group of leftist intellectuals publicly cautioned the militant extremists against using disgraceful means to pursue national objectives.[46] But this did not appreciably reduce the bitterness of rampant antagonism. It, too, was to be buried beneath the imminent Soviet invasion.

XVI

END OF JOINT ACTION

COOPERATION between the Nationalists and the Catholic-Populist opposition failed to outlast the period of crisis produced by the German seizure of Klaipėda in March 1939. No sooner had the popular uproar over Klaipėda waned than indications of political strife reappeared. In truth, the Nationalists had never seriously envisioned even a partial return to democracy, while the opposition had not intended to surrender to the will of the Leader. This innate incompatibility produced a government crisis.

In the ensuing summer months relations between President Smetona on the one side and opposition Ministers Leonas Bistras and Jurgis Krikščiūnas on the other became strained. The situation ultimately deteriorated to a point where the President refused to receive his Catholic Minister of Education, Bistras, who, nevertheless, declined to resign.[1] The Prime Minister had attempted a reconciliation but failed. Moreover, only vaguely comprehending the true meaning of the discord, Černius forfeited the confidence of the President, who considered the Prime Minister too weak under the circumstances.

The divergence of opinion between the President and the two opposition leaders encompassed two major domestic issues: (1) the Catholic Bistras took exception to Smetona's educational policies, and (2) the Populist Krikščiūnas questioned his social and economic policies.

164

Trouble in Education

THE NATIONALIST PRESIDENT, who attached much importance to pedagogy, did not try to conceal his displeasure with the adroit Minister of Education. The President's allegation that the coalition government was inimical to the monolithic nature of his administration was valid. Essentially their dispute concerned the efforts of the new Minister of Education to equate the rights of teachers and employees at private secondary schools with those of public school teachers, and to include the former group in the pension fund. The number of schools and teachers involved in the controversy was not small. However, a law passed in 1936 had deprived the Minister of Education of the power to decree any such changes. In order to award these benefits to more than one thousand teachers and an undisclosed number of auxiliary personnel, Bistras introduced a bill in the Seimas, asking for authority to do so. The motion, which won the approval of the Council of Ministers and thus intimated the extent of opposition influence in that body, was brought before the Diet on June 13, 1939. There the ostensibly minor proposal, which, in fact, reawakened the issue of Church-State relations, touched off a brisk debate as Nationalist members rallied in support of State priority in education. The Minister pleaded to no avail that his measure was in accord with the prevailing tendency to protect as many citizens as possible through the social security system. The Nationalists retorted that, if passed, the bill would be a blow to their long-range objective of abolishing private schools altogether. By a vote of 31 to 11 the Nationalist Seimas refused even to put the bill on the agenda.[2] Ironically, the clash between the Council of Ministers and the legislature, one dominated by the opposition, the other packed with Nationalists, projected the image of the Seimas as an adamant opponent of the administrative branch of government, a phenomenon long absent from Lithuanian politics.

Quarrels Over Social and Land Reforms

MORE NOTEWORTHY than the feud over educational policies was
the quarrel regarding social and land reforms. In 1922 the lawmakers had decreed that 80 hectares was the maximum amount
of land an individual farmer might own. In 1929 the ceiling was
raised to 150 hectares. To a number of people the increase in
the maximum limit proved to be highly objectionable both
economically and socially. Hoping to reverse the trend, they set
about to demonstrate that a medium sized farm was more efficient
than a large one. They also directed attention to the growing
number of citizens who were in need of land.[3] The acquisition
of the eastern Vilnius districts only aggravated the land issue
and constrained the administration to act.

The core of the problem was the existence of a wide gulf
between the landlord and the peasant in the newly transferred
areas, where some 0.6 per cent of owners with 50 hectares or
more held approximately 23 per cent of the land.[4] In addition,
there was a political factor present which goaded some agrarian
reformers to adopt a radical course; a majority of the large landowners were Poles who expressed hostility toward the Lithuanians. The circumstances were not without precedent. Owing in
part to extensive land reforms after World War I, the Kaunas
authorities had succeeded in their plans of making the common
man a loyal citizen. The Lithuanians hoped to repeat this
accomplishment by their overt alliance with the underprivileged
peoples in the new territory. Since the number of landless peasants and small landholders far exceeded the available land, a
drastic agrarian reform seemed to be one solution. At the end of
October 1939 the hitherto shrouded discussions by the government burst into the open when the draft of a new reform law
was made public. The radical proposals, sketched by the Populist
Minister of Agriculture and backed by the entire cabinet, envisaged 60 hectares as the new maximum applicable to the entire
country.

The Catholics and the Populists favored the proposals, but

the Nationalists, if half-heartedly, lined up against them. The Catholic journal *XX Amžius* was so heartened by the government's "bold steps" that it urged the administration to make another leap forward by adding far-flung amendments guaranteeing every citizen the right to work.[5] The opposition's intent to render workers and peasants immune to Communist ideas accounted, in part, for its support of such comprehensive actions.[6]

The Breakdown of Coalition Government

THESE HOPES AND FEARS were dispelled by President Smetona. In a speech before the Seimas on November 19 he deprecated all economic and social experiments detrimental to the existing organization of the national economy.[7] The President was known to have defended the inviolability of private property and to have remarked, on another occasion, that he had had enough of land reforms which caused embarrassment to him and to his country.[8] There is reasonable ground for supposing that the Nationalist opposition to reforms in truth reflected Smetona's personal opposition. It can be assumed that the proposals had the support of a majority of political leaders of all parties. However reluctantly, the Nationalist Party stood by the President. At a conference on January 6, Nationalist Chairman Cesevičius confided that at that moment he was against the radical solution. However, if future studies were to prove the value of the proposed legislation, he would be inclined to change his mind.[9] Furthermore, former party secretary Vincas Rastenis recalled that the idea of reforms was especially well received by the Nationalist organization in Vilnius.[10] But, as on a number of other issues, the internal Nationalist "opposition of good will" failed to deflect the obdurate President from his course and instead acquiesced in his conservatism. By mid-November the reforms were out of the question, and the Černius cabinet was out of office.

As attested to by some participants[11] in the political developments of that time, the resignation of the Černius cabinet was a veiled protest against the USSR for the imposition of the October treaty. However, the evidence does not vindicate such an explanation. The presence of Soviet troops had toned down the attitude of some opposition members during the formation of the new government, but it was not responsible for the collapse of the old. The breakdown of the coalition cabinet must be attributed to domestic factors: the inconsistency of representative government with authoritarianism in general, and the divergence of opinions between the President and the two opposition ministers in particular.

A Last Chance at Independent Government

THE PRESIDENT designated Antanas Merkys to shape what would become the last cabinet of independent Lithuania. The former mayor of Kaunas was expected to add strength to the Nationalist regime by repressing all opposition, both military and civilian. The new government was to consist solely of Nationalist supporters, with Merkys serving also as the Minister of Defense. Once more, however, Nationalist plans were frustrated by the well-timed interposition of army commander Raštikis. The encounter between the President and the General occurred on November 16. After tense talks, first with the President and then with the opposition leaders, Raštikis induced Smetona to shelve the idea of an administration congenial only to the President and persuaded the Catholics and the Populists to enter the government under the leadership of the objectionable Merkys.[12] The formation of the "foundling" cabinet, so dubbed because it failed to appease any of the three parties, was made known on November 21. The Nationalists were installed in all key ministries and opposition influence underwent a decided diminution.

The editorial pages predictably echoed the partisan sentiment. Nationalist writers censured the previous coalition for its deviation from the rules of authoritarianism. They placed their confidence in Merkys, who was believed to have fully understood the nature of the form of government and who was attached to the

President in thought and deed.[13] The despondent opposition, on the other hand, greeted the new team with a bare vote of confidence, trusting that it would succeed in keeping Lithuania free.[14] To be sure, the new government had the tacit consent of the public at large, but, unlike the Černius cabinet of joint action, its reception was anything but boisterous. In contrast to the momentous transition in March, the November reshuffling was a vapid affair.

The new arrangement was more in line with political realities than the old. For eight months many entertained the illusion that the three-power collaboration in the administrative branch of government implied a trend toward representative government. Now all such hopeful impressions vanished. Even if some ministries remained in Catholic and Populist hands, the Merkys cabinet could not in truth be styled a coalition government.

On December 6, in a trite declaration, Merkys pledged that his administration would pursue national unity, keep the budget balanced, integrate the Vilnius districts into Lithuania proper, and continue the old social and economic policies. The conciliatory *XX Amžius* responded not unfavorably, deferring its conclusive judgment until such time as it would be able to assess the cabinet by its accomplishments.[15] But the accomplishments, when they came, disappointed Catholic-Populist expectations. The Nationalists chose to be most active in areas least desired by the opposition.

During the first half of 1940 four events aided the Nationalists to complete supremacy and to quell any resistance. These were: the dismissal of General Raštikis; the occurrence of new developments in Church-State relations; the success of the Nationalists in local elections; and their attempt to gain a firmer hold on the country. The results of these efforts were many, the intention was one.

The Dismissal of General Raštikis

GENERAL STASYS RAŠTIKIS was a thorn in the Nationalists' side. This officer's perception of his duty had repeatedly ensnared him

169

in political rivalry with the Nationalists. When, early in January, Raštikis took the liberty of sharing his views on a number of issues with the reading public,[16] the Kaunas authorities decided that this time the General had gone too far, and they banned the officers' journal which he had used as his vehicle. Raštikis thereupon tendered his resignation. Instead, he was given a leave of absence, "for reasons of health," effective January 20. The irate Smetona called the outgoing commander a Bolshevik, and appointed as his successor General Vincas Vitkauskas. Following the Soviet incursion, the latter claimed that he was a Bolshevik, too.[17]

Despite the former commander's public denial that any ulterior motives were responsible for his abrupt departure from the top army post, the true story soon leaked out, provoking some disenchanted officers to contemplate recourse to forceful action in order to reinstate Raštikis. This came to naught, however, as the deposed General counseled against a military coup.[18] In this manner the Catholic-Populist opposition was dealt a severe blow, as one of its champions succumbed to the political dexterity of the Nationalist President as well as to his own blundering attempt to meddle in spheres beyond his professional competence.

Pressure on the Church

CONCURRENTLY with the degradation of the army chief the *tautininkai* turned directly against the Catholics. In a slap at the Church, the Nationalist convention of January 5 and 6 arrived at the impious conclusion that freedom of conscience would be better served if the state were to assume prime responsibility in matters of civil registry and civil marriage, then within the domain of the Church. The emboldened Nationalists resolved that they would no longer tolerate any Church activities which impeded the preponderance of the nation-state. The clergy was told to confine its attention to matters of faith and to avoid politics.[19] Pointing out that the disappearance of Poland left

Lithuania the only state in Europe which did not yet have civil registry for marriage, the Nationalists decided to put an end to this unwanted uniqueness.

A vigorous Catholic campaign to forestall the impending action had been initiated in 1939. Vincentas Brizgys, a Catholic spokesman who likened civil marriage to concubinage, charged that Nationalist proposals would further "atheism and profligacy" and appealed to the faithful to save the country from committing an "inglorious blunder" by opposing the "obsolete institution."[20] Even the urbane *XX Amžius*, identifying Catholic and national traditions, pleaded with the Nationalists, in effect, to leave things as they were.[21]

In order to get a comprehensive Catholic response to the secular challenge, the Church entrusted a Bishops' commission with the problem. In April 1940 it produced a stiff memorandum which would have affected 85 per cent of Lithuania's total population. It stated that civil marriage should not be permitted; that, as a matter of principle, marriages ought to be indissoluble; and that should there be an exceptional possibility of divorce, the exclusive jurisdiction of ecclesiastical courts in regard to marriages performed in church ought to be recognized by the state.[22] The document was followed by an even more categoric pastoral letter, which warned the laity of a heavy burden of sin if they ventured to defy the divine will. It concluded by exclaiming that a greater misfortune to the Church and to the State than the institution of the proposed reforms was inconceivable.[23] The upshot of this Nationalist-Catholic controversy remained inconclusive. As it turned out, a greater misfortune, in the form of the Bolshevik occupation, was not only conceivable but imminent.

Local Elections

THE ELECTIONS to the local government which, with the exception of the Vilnius districts, were held from February 22 to 24, 1940, were another aspect of the Nationalist counterdrive. Under the terms of the law then in force, the President of the Republic was chosen by a certain number of electors named by members of district, municipal, and county councils. Although the nature of Nationalist politics had made any similarity between the election returns and a genuine popular consensus an accidental rarity, these local bodies did merit some attention. The Nationalists conveniently neglected to announce the February elections in the usual way. Instead, the fact that elections were to take place was given only limited public notice through local officials, with the result that a significant part of the electorate knew nothing of them. When the Populist Minister of Agriculture questioned the action, the Nationalist Minister of the Interior replied that he had not considered the elections important enough either to apprise the cabinet of them or to make them known through the press.[24]

The outcome of the February elections brought to the county councils some 2,545 members, who, in turn, selected in the following month 290 representatives to serve on district councils.[25] Aside from the fact that most of the winners were listed as farmers, 2,329 on county councils and 228 on district councils, the lack of statistical data is a deterrent to analyzing the social and political implications of these elections.

Proposed New Law

ONE OF THE LAST ATTEMPTS of the Nationalists to contrive the fullest possible consolidation of power was the Prime Minister's project of passing a new law defining the rights of the district executive. The principal features of the proposed legislation, published on April 18 by the *Lietuvos Žinios*, envisioned the delegation to the district executives of virtually unlimited powers. However, after objections from the Catholics and the Populists inside the government and out, in the course of which they charged that the new law would confer upon the district leaders powers considerably greater than those accorded to cabinet members, the proposals were put off indefinitely.[26]

172

Summary

THESE DEVELOPMENTS justify the inference that in the final months of the republic the political cycle was complete. Before the outburst of the German-made crisis in 1939 the Nationalists were supreme. The unconditional consent of the Catholic and Populist leaders to participate in what was tantamount to a coalition government turned out to be capitulation to mass psychology. Because of fortuitous circumstances and not because of any genuine restructuring of internal political and social forces, the fragile alliance barely survived the crisis psychosis which gave rise to it. Once the memories of March 1939 receded and no comparable perils perplexed either the leaders or the led, the professions of united action dwindled. And before the eruption of the Russian-made final crisis in 1940, Lithuanian politics had reverted to its habitual pattern; the *tautininkai* rallied to shape an "organic nation," while the opposition sought to prevent them. Nothing essential had changed during the year.

PART SIX

The Intervention of the Soviet Union

XVII

THE PRECIPITATE END

DURING THE SPRING of 1940 it became apparent that Moscow
resolved to do away with the partial independence of the Baltic
states by their occupation and incorporation into the USSR.
Two decades of peaceful coexistence were to be brought to a
precipitate end. As late as March 29, 1940, when Vyacheslav
Molotov addressed a plenary session of the Supreme Soviet,
interstate relations appeared to be adequate and there seemed to
be no reason to anticipate any crisis. The Chairman of the
Council of People's Commissars told the delegates that the
satisfactory implementation of treaties of mutual assistance which
the Kremlin had concluded with the three Baltic governments
in 1939 presaged a continued improvement of ties between the
cosignatories in the future.[1]

A Minor Incident

AFTER GERMANY'S DESCENT on western Europe, the Russians
changed their course. Just before the end of April, judging from
the Russian attitude toward him, the Lithuanian Minister in
Moscow suspected that all was not well in Lithuanian-Soviet
relations.[2] His presentiment was substantiated the following
month, when a high Soviet officer reproached the Kaunas authorities for the alleged abduction of Russian soldiers from Russian
military bases on Lithuanian soil. The Merkys cabinet discounted

177

the charges as a minor incident.[3] However, the "minor incident" expanded when on May 29 the Soviet news agency Tass divulged Molotov's threat—conveyed on May 25 through Minister Ladas Natkevičius—of "serious consequences" if the Kaunas government failed to desist from "provocative acts."[4] The Lithuanian government termed the Soviet move a "sudden and unexpected surprise," said that because of the absence of ill will on either side there was no reason to think that the matter could not be disposed of amicably, and assured the Soviet Union that it would not tolerate anything that might stand in the way of friendly relations between the two countries.[5] Moreover, it appointed a special commission to look into the case, tried unsuccessfully to seat a Soviet member on it, and promised to punish the offenders sternly, if any were found.[6]

The consensus of editorial opinion found the "misunderstanding" deplorable, believed that nothing of importance had taken place to mar the traditionally friendly relations between the two countries, demanded that the transgressors, if any, be disciplined, and remained optimistic about future relations with Moscow.[7] But, as the Lithuanian envoy in Berlin had feared, the Russians harbored "other designs,"[8] namely, the outright annexation of the country, which rendered ineffectual all efforts to solve the Moscow-made crisis. On June 4 Molotov summoned Minister Natkevičius and demanded to see the Lithuanian Prime Minister. Accordingly, on June 7, Merkys arrived in Moscow and commenced talks with the Russians. Three days later he was joined by Foreign Minister Urbšys, who brought a message from President Smetona to Mikhail Ivanovich Kalinin, Chairman of the Presidium of the Supreme Soviet, reiterating Lithuania's intention to abide steadfastly by its commitments. In a "bestially harsh"[9] confrontation Molotov blamed the Lithuanian Minister of the Interior and the Director of the State Security Department for endangering the security of Soviet garrisons, upbraided the Kaunas government for allegedly entering into a military alliance with Latvia and Estonia,[10] berated the press for generating anti-Soviet sentiment, but failed to put forward

178

any specific demands. Consequently, the visiting Premier set out for home, leaving his Foreign Minister in Moscow.

Uncertainty in Kaunas

LATE ON JUNE 12 the President, the cabinet, and the army command assembled to hear the Prime Minister's report. The fact that the Russians refrained from advancing any specific demands disoriented the Lithuanian leaders even at this late date. Testimony on this point, however, is not uniform. On the one hand, President Smetona recorded soon after the crisis that upon hearing the Prime Minister's account of his conversations with Molotov, all were agreed that a "terrible blow" awaited Lithuania.[11] The General Staff, too, anticipated Soviet demands "of a sweeping nature."[12] On the other hand, many thought that while the outlook seemed bleak indeed, the consequences would not be catastrophic. This expectation carried more weight in determining the Lithuanian response to Soviet pressure. According to high-ranking authorities, even the Prime Minister, upon his return from Moscow, did not comprehend the nature of the conflict and remained puzzled as to Soviet designs.[13]

This uncertainty, this belief that things were not as bad as they seemed to be, reflects in part the influence which two decades of adequate Lithuanian-Soviet relations had upon the thinking of some policy makers. Even at the moment when Prime Minister Merkys was being vigorously assailed at the Kremlin conferences, normal intercourse between the two states continued unperturbed. The Soviet Union consented to the repatriation of all Lithuanian nationals who preferred to leave those territories Russia had acquired after the fall of Poland. The first train of newcomers, some 15,000 in all, was expected any day. A leading Kaunas daily pointed out that this offered "new evidence" of Soviet deference to Lithuanian national aspirations, and it predicted that the action would be well received by the public.[14]

The administration had not seen fit to print any news concerning the deterioration of its relations with Moscow. Instead, it gulled the readers by devoting much space to such trifles as the commemoration of President Smetona's name day, the reports of the wonderful time the two Lithuanian leaders were having in Russia visiting exhibitions and the Moscow-Volga canal, and the Prime Minister's remarks, which the latter made upon coming home, to the effect that he was delighted to have had the opportunity to go to the friendly capital to talk things over with Molotov.

The Beginnings of the Lithuanian Retreat

THE LITHUANIAN retreat began with the enforced resignation on June 12 of the Minister of the Interior and the dismissal the following day of the Director of the State Security Department, both objectionable to the Kremlin. But this did not avert the impending crisis. Charging the Kaunas authorities with bad faith in implementing the October 1939 treaty, the Russians presented the Lithuanians with an ultimatum on June 14, demanding the initiation of legal action against the two ousted officials, the formation of a government acceptable to Moscow, and the admission into Lithuanian territory of an unspecified number of Soviet troops.[15] Subsequently the Communists added the accusation that the Kaunas government was inviting German occupation of Lithuania. To substantiate this allegation they referred to German sources, primarily to the Proclamation of June 22, 1941, which Reich Chancellor Adolf Hitler addressed to his nation. There the Führer alleged that "the German Reich never had any intention of occupying Lithuania and not only failed to present any such demands to the Lithuanian Government, but on the contrary refused the request of the then Lithuania to send German troops to Lithuania for that purpose as inconsistent with the aims of German policy."[16] Evidence in hand gives reasonable ground for affirming that no such request by a responsible Lithuanian functionary was either authorized or made. However, the possibility of some unofficial partisan approach to the German government cannot be excluded.

180

The Next Move Is Debated

THE CABINET, meeting to consider the rigorous terms, split into two groups. The spokesman of unconditional acquiescence to Soviet demands was the Catholic Deputy Prime Minister, Kazys Bizauskas. He reasoned that it appeared to be time to prepare the country for the future contingencies of the war by siding with the eastern neighbor. The Deputy Prime Minister had served as a member of his country's delegation to Moscow in the preceding October, when the Soviet leaders gave repeated assurances that they did not under any circumstances intend to meddle in Lithuania's domestic affairs. Bizauskas appears to have been impressed by these promises as well as by the interwar history of cordial Soviet-Lithuanian relations. He now called attention to the fact that in the preceding years Moscow generally had refrained from censuring the Kaunas government for its treatment of local Communists. He summed up his views by voicing the hope that the acceptance of the ultimatum would save the Lithuanians many lives and would enable them to preserve their mode of life until the end of the war.

President Smetona spoke for armed resistance, if only symbolic. He reminded his Ministers that one of the avowed Soviet aspirations was world revolution, and that the Communists believed in exploiting every opportunity to hasten its consummation. The present war provided them with such an opportunity. Russia's objectives in the Baltic states and, in part, in Poland foreshadowed outright occupation and sovietization of these areas. Lithuania's determination to act in one way or another would not matter. But even a token defense, pleaded the President, would reveal to the world how much Lithuanians valued freedom, and it would have high moral import for future generations of Lithuanians. Resistance would at least salvage self-respect; surrender would lose all. There would be casualties in any event, and one could not predict whether they would be heavier in combat than in submission.

181

Capitulation

DISREGARDING the President's admonitions, the majority of assembled cabinet members and army officers gave way to the Soviet threat. It was the view of the military commanders that concentration of Soviet divisions along the border, as well as Red Army garrisons inside the country, left no time for mobilization and made any resistance futile.[17] The session adjourned with the resignation of the Merkys cabinet and the designation of former army commander Raštikis as the new Prime Minister, in the hope that he would be acceptable to Moscow. But on June 15 the Kremlin made it known that the general was not the man to succeed Merkys, and that the composition of the new government would have to await the arrival in Kaunas of a Russian emissary who would assume control over the selection of candidates. The outgoing Council of Ministers convened for its last conference. Maintaining that Bolshevik occupation of Lithuania was now under way and that at home he would not be free to act, President Smetona apprised the cabinet members of his decision to leave the country.[18] In conformity with the constitution, Acting Prime Minister Merkys was empowered to relieve the President during the latter's stay abroad. That same afternoon, June 15, Russian tank columns entered Kaunas.

Compliance with Soviet demands constituted a reversal of earlier government decisions to fight for Lithuania's independence in the event of enemy attack. Until the final hours there seemed to be much evidence that the Kaunas authorities would actually do what on many occasions they had publicly vowed to do. The question of how to cope with a potential threat to the nation's independent existence had been weighed by the Černius administration, and it had been resolved to resist the aggressor militarily, even in the absence of any prospect of success. This was held to be an imperative of honor.[19] In 1940, "several months" before the ultimatum,[20] the Merkys administration considered the grim alternatives anew. Identifying the Soviet Union as the nation's enemy number one, the members of the

182

Council of Ministers were unanimous in their intention to oppose any thrust from the east.[21] Despite these resolutions, the government had not done anything to make resistance feasible.

Two important factors, in addition to military considerations, exerted considerable influence upon the cabinet members. First, the majority of government and party leaders was of the opinion that Moscow did not intend to stamp out every vestige of Lithuania's independence. Second, the crisis found the Lithuanians bitterly divided among themselves. Had it been obvious to all what the Kremlin had in store, the domestic political disputes might have been shelved. As it was, however, the Russian diplomatic thrust did not seriously interrupt the progress of political rivalries. This, in turn, had its effects on the Lithuanian response to the Soviet challenge. The renewal of Nationalist power had convinced the opposition that no fundamental change in the direction of democratic rule was possible. Consequently, disinclined to be pawns in the Nationalist counterdrive, the Catholics and the Populists prepared for a political showdown. By a momentous coincidence, both the Nationalists and the opposition prepared for an internal showdown at a time shortly before and during the hours of the Soviet ultimatum. They had not invited foreign intrusion, but neither did they inhibit their moves against each other once it had taken place.

The immediate objectives which the opposition ministers reiterated at the final cabinet meetings reportedly were formulated shortly before the ultimatum of June 14. Judging that the breach with the USSR would not be fatal to Lithuania, members of the Catholic Populist opposition proposed to dismiss the Minister of Interior and the Director of the State Security Department, both of whom were objectionable to Moscow, and to bring the protracted interparty dissension to a head by effecting a cabinet crisis.[22] Opposition spokesman Bizauskas divulged these views at a conference in the President's office on June 12 when the Prime Minister recounted his travails in the Soviet capital. The session proved to be inconclusive. Interior Minister Skučas relinquished his post, but a government crisis was averted. This prompted the members of the opposition to reexamine the situation, and having done so they concurred in their previous resolve to force Merkys to quit.[23] Amid these labors to unseat the Prime Minister news was received of the Kremlin's ultimatum.

Three members of the government did not attend the final cabinet consultations: Foreign Minister Urbšys stayed in Moscow; Finance Minister Galvanauskas was out of town; and Interior Minister Skučas out of office. At the meeting of June 12, Ernestas Galvanauskas opposed concessions to the Russians and spoke against the dismissal of the Minister of the Interior.[24] Thus, faced with overwhelming military power and weakened both by the absence of some key figures and by the opposition's insistence on the resignation of the Merkys administration, the Council of Ministers agreed to make way for a new government and entrusted the former army commander Raštikis with the task. In his final attempt to profit at the expense of the Catholics and the Populists, the President suggested to General Raštikis the composition of an all-Nationalist cabinet and handed him a list of preferred candidates. Nothing came of this, as Raštikis dismissed the idea and several hours later the Russians dismissed him.[25] However, President Smetona's action survives as an integral part of the simmering domestic discord whose severity, indeed, whose very existence, was later obscured by the Russian onset.

XVIII

COLLABORATION BY COMPULSION:

THE ALLIANCE OF THE LEFT

To MOST PEOPLE the news of Soviet occupation was so unexpected that it reached them at the same time as the Russian troops. Nearly everywhere bewildered people or deserted streets waited upon the invading force. Here and there Communists and fellow travelers greeted the Red Army with open arms. The caretaker government advised its countrymen that the need for security and the preservation of peace in this quarter of Europe necessitated the admission of additional Soviet troops, and it called upon all citizens to go about their usual business and to maintain order.[1] For the most part the man in the street did just that.

We Come to Bury Caesar...

THE SPONTANEOUS REACTION of the politically conscious citizens, other than Nationalists, appears to have been satisfaction at the downfall of the Smetona regime. This was true even of some Nationalists. Public arraignment of the thirteen-year-old dictatorship was most impetuous in leftist quarters, but it was somewhat restrained in the Catholic press. In a rancorous assault on the prostrate Nationalists, a Populist weekly vented the exasperation felt in many leftist circles:

> The Smetona regime, which for over fifteen [sic] years weighed heavily upon the Lithuanian people, has perished. After so many

185

years of unheard-of oppression we can again address ourselves properly to our readers. It is impossible to recount all at once . . . the injustice and injuries which the caricature of the Nationalist dictatorship was inflicting on all citizens of our country. From the day the "nation's leader" seized power the people, the true masters of the country, were deprived of all rights. Furthermore, by means of various so-called elections the people's will was shamelessly falsified. The district executives [and] the police did the electing, but it was said that it was done by the people. The district leaders would elect Smetona's henchmen . . . who imagined themselves to be true representatives of the people, and they would speak in the name of the people. Any attempt to resist lawlessness and harm was stifled by most detestable means. . . . Today all this nightmare has come to an end.[2]

Editorial articles published in the Catholic *XX Amžius* after the Soviet coup crystalized a position which the Catholic writers adhered to as long as they were in control of their paper. Before long the journal passed into the hands of persons sympathetic to the changes that were taking place; but during the several days it succeeded in directing editorial policies, the original staff left evidence of the subordination of its partisan proclivities to the national interest. In one leading article after another the Catholic team conveyed the dual attitude it assumed: it placed the blame on the Nationalists for causing internal discord in the past, but it also accentuated the need for all Lithuanians to unite in an effort to safeguard the national heritage. "We have no right to doubt our nation's future," exhorted the outspoken editors. "Our nation will continue to be and to work, never losing its will and its determination to live."[3] The nonpartisan Vilnius organ, too, curbed its censure of the Nationalist regime by calling on all citizens to devote themselves to their country, "much dearer to us now than in time past."[4] As frequently in the past, the Nationalist press scanned the abrupt turn of events with an air of aloofness and formality. It termed the need to admit Russian troops deplorable, pleaded with the intemperate adversaries to defer their judgment of the previous administration until some

186

future time, and urged all citizens to bear misfortunes with sobriety and equanimity.[5]

Such was the demise of a regime instituted to cement national unity. The downfall of the Nationalist leadership resulted from the intervention of a foreign power, but the funeral oration, the uncommonly harsh indictment attendant upon it, was delivered by the local population. The barrage of editorial opinion the moment restrictions disappeared gave credence to what many had been saying for years, namely, that the party in power had forfeited the consent of the governed. So intense was the denunciation that the imposition of Russian domination was obscured by a sense of liberation from the Nationalist hegemony. The brief restoration of civil liberties occurred at the same time that the nation was being deprived of its freedom. Furthermore, among people conscious of their nationality, the assertion of civil rights which heightened domestic discord even in the face of enemy invasion arose out of the past denial of individual liberties; it depended also upon the image of the aggressor. Those who had most keenly suffered the abridgment of individual freedom under Smetona and who had reason to be least averse to the nature of the Soviet threat were more prone to such intemperance than others.

Genesis of People's Government

A FACTOR of cardinal importance in comprehending the genesis of the People's Government, which succeeded the Nationalists, and its operations during the transition from independence to incorporation into the USSR on August 3, 1940, was Moscow's determination to effect changes by the seeming consent of the Lithuanian people. The monopoly of power which the Soviet Union now wielded was to be shrouded in the supposed will of popular masses, and the transformation which the Kremlin had in readiness would be seemingly accomplished by due process of law. The abrupt departure of President Smetona for Germany precluded any possibility of shaping a new government in the

187

customary way. Under the terms of the constitution, Acting Prime Minister Merkys, who now discharged the duties of the President, did not have the power to form a government until the President had either died or resigned. As the fugitive Smetona had done neither, the Soviet occupational authorities in Kaunas, Minister N. G. Pozdniakov, and the newly assigned Deputy Commissar for Foreign Affairs Vladimir G. Dekanozov[6] attempted through a delegation of military and civilian officials to persuade the President to come back. When this stratagem proved to be without effect, they proceeded to give the constitution a broad interpretation by equating the President's departure with his resignation and investing the Acting Prime Minister with powers he did not possess originally.

Early on June 17 Soviet Minister Pozdniakov called Merkys on the telephone and dictated to him the names of persons whom Moscow had designated to assume office in the People's Government. When the Lithuanian found fault with one appointee and suggested the inclusion of another candidate, the Russian retorted that any changes in the list must be sanctioned by the Kremlin and that he had no time and saw no need to contact Moscow for that purpose.[7] In consequence of the Bolshevik contrivance of making the impending reforms appear the work of the Lithuanians themselves, the Communist authorities thought it expedient to popularize the new administration by seating in it a number of prominent personalities and by playing down its radical bent. In the new Council of Ministers[8] only one member, the Minister of the Interior, was a full-fledged Communist. However, with the exception of the Finance Minister, all were avowed leftists. The retention of Ernestas Galvanauskas remains anomalous, as the financial expert happened to be neither a Communist nor a leftist. The veteran economist recalled that the original list communicated by Pozdniakov made no mention of his successor to the Ministry of Finance, but that subsequently he was prevailed upon by Merkys and Justas Paleckis, the new Prime Minister and Acting President, to continue in office. Paleckis is reported to have intimated that he consented to head the People's Government provided that the Minister of Finance keep his post.[9] There is reason to presume that initially the Communist policy makers felt the need to underscore the continuity of the nation's economic organization and believed that the retention of the stanch Minister of Finance was one way to do it.

These incompatible associates soon became differentiated into relatively independent and pro-Communist factions.[10] Made up of the Deputy Prime Minister and the Ministers of Defense[11] and Finance, the former group consulted on all important issues and then attended the cabinet sessions with their views brought into accord beforehand. Believing that Russian authorities did not intend to subvert the country's internal order and that war between Germany and the USSR was unavoidable, the pro-nationalist ministers agreed to impede Soviet actions detrimental to the general welfare and to preserve as long as possible the prevailing structure of the economy. On the other hand, the pro-Communist minority, namely, the Ministers of the Interior, Justice, and Health, attempted to implement, at times reluctantly,[12] the directives which it received from the Soviet Legation. At the beginning, the Ministers of Agriculture and Education did not commit themselves to either party. The former frequently sided with the independents, the latter with the majority. For several days the coalition of independents scored some successes by foiling Communist-sponsored changes. Probably the most palpable indicator of its influence in the first days of the transitional administration was cabinet refusal to legalize the Communist Party. However, at the end of June and the beginning of July Russian emissaries packed the Council of Ministers with Communist appointees, and the balance of power tipped in favor of the radicals. The wavering ministers, too, joined the winning side.

Besides the Council of Ministers, political power in those tempestuous weeks emanated from four other sources. First, the Communist Party of Lithuania and its Central Committee, a source of energy in the transformation of the country's life. The

189

Party coerced civil servants to pay no heed to cabinet decisions and to carry out its instructions instead. Second, the Soviet army command, whose frequent demands and claims threatened the government with consequences for failure to meet them. Third, the Soviet Legation in Kaunas, which channelled its imperative views initially through the compliant Acting President Paleckis and later directly through the demurring Council of Ministers. It constantly counselled the government which officials to dismiss, what decisions to make, and what to say to foreign representatives. However, Minister Pozdniakov usually refrained from threats and even apologized for occasional excesses on the part of Dekanozov. Instead, he endeavored to convince members of the People's Government that his demands were Moscow's demands and that the Lithuanians would be well advised to acquiesce in them. Finally, the Ministry of the Interior, which frequently snubbed the cabinet and communicated directly with the Acting President. The Ministry had undergone a thorough reorganization resulting in change of personnel; its top men, mostly of alien origin, continued to be Lithuanian subjects, but they were surrounded by Russian assistants who in fact wielded the real power.[13]

The Communist policy makers had intended in the first weeks of occupation to revolutionize the country without destroying its fundamental institutions and without superimposing the Soviet economic and political system on the Lithuanians. The People's Government, the new leaders claimed, was committed to social reforms, the Red Army remained to safeguard national freedom and not to throttle it. The impression the authorities hoped to convey to the bewildered citizens was that popular government had replaced the Nationalists. There is reasonable ground for presuming that a great many people, from the Nationalists to the Communists themselves, thought that this was the case, and they were not altogether unhappy about it. It is therefore quite understandable that both the composition of the leftist government and its first days in office allayed the fears that gripped the nation in consequence of the entry of foreign

190

troops, and heartened the people and the press to respond favorably.

From the very outset the revolutionary leaders turned violently against the Nationalist past, uniting in solidarity with citizens who under the old regime lived on the periphery of society, namely, the urban and rural laborers, craftsmen, petty white collar workers, and the impoverished peasants. In their denunciation of the administration which they superseded, the spokesmen of the new order shattered all the major tenets underlying the Nationalist establishment. They criticized Nationalist concepts and thrust out of public life those who espoused them. On June 18 Acting President Paleckis addressed the nation, stressing in general terms some of the theses the Communist decision makers wished to impress on all listeners. The former journalist first censured the arbitrary nature of Smetona's rule, which had answered the interests of the few, and then sketched the outlines of the administration he had consented to head. He assured his radio audience that, unlike the dictatorial regime they had been subjected to in the past, the new People's Government would be based upon the principles of democracy; unlike their predecessors, the new rulers would look out for the well-being of all citizens.[14] In the days and weeks following the seizure of power, every leftist speaker who occupied a platform, broadcast a message, or published an article vilified the Nationalists and their associates. Members of the government and their supporters engaged in bitter and unprecedented name-calling. The Nationalists were described as "the vile gang," "oppressors of the people," "plutocrats," "enemies of the people," and "despots turned into stinking corpses." Similarly, the new government was described by its popularizers as the "true government of the people." It was dramatically explained that "reaction had suffered a deadly blow" and that now the "wide popular masses" would enjoy "full rights" and a "bright future." In a matter of days the People's Government had accomplished in form what the year-old coalition cabinet had hoped to do in content; it brought together in a closer union the nation's leaders and the general public.

191

The repudiation of Nationalist policies, methods, and symbols proved so striking that in practically every respect the new regime did the opposite of what its predecessor had done. In times past, special events took place in presidential quarters, officers' clubs, or the State Theater in the presence of government, church, party, and military dignitaries. Now they took the form of mass meetings before political prisoners. Workers' militia supplanted the national guard; the army became the People's Army; and police turned into militia. The training vessel "President Smetona" blotted out its bourgeois affiliations by changing its name; uniforms were stripped of swords, epaulets, and other indications of rank; imported Marxist literature displaced the works of the former President; and the Communist Party, the sole political movement legalized on June 26 by order of the Minister of the Interior, established itself in Nationalist headquarters and inherited the property of the defunct Nationalist Union. Everywhere the once prevalent term "national" receded before the indispensable "popular." One of the first acts of the new administration was the liberation of political prisoners. From June 18 to June 21 some 272 inmates, mostly Communists, walked out of their cells to be feted at public rallies as "heroic fighters for the people's freedom and well-being."[15] Besides high government officials, a host of well-known leftist intellectuals and pro-Communists was at hand, some impelled by advice from above, to make the release a memorable occasion.

The Takeover Commences

THE POSITIVE PROGRAM which the People's Government adopted for the immediate future was first put together by the Communist Party. By the end of June ranking Party functionaries, augmenting resolutions already acclaimed at mass meetings, put together a platform calling for the establishment of labor unions in industry and agriculture, the provision of work and a decent living for idle laborers, the adoption of a progressive tax system, improvement in social security and medical aid with a view to greater accessibility, the reduction of rents to a minimum, the apportionment of country estates among small landholders and landless peasants, the abrogation of the Nationalist constitution, the disavowal of chauvinism, the realization of freedom of conscience by the separation of Church and State, the removal from the civil service and the army of persons inimical to "the revolution," and the arrest of all "enemies of the people."[16] These objectives imparted material form to the first stage of the revolution, which lasted from the assumption of authority in June to the convocation of the People's Diet in July. They accentuated social and political reforms and omitted any mention of the imminent radical institutional changes in the established form of government, the administrative apparatus, and the organization of the economy.

There was no readily distinguishable sequence in the organization of the civil service with the revolution. Several new establishments, such as the workers' militia and the Ministries of Health and Labor, were set up, but old institutions, with some exceptions, were not abolished. Apparently, instead of a fundamental change of institutions, the Communist decision makers originally hoped to bring the existing agencies under their control and to impregnate them with men and ideas sympathetic to the recent developments. To that end they "denationalized" the appearance of public offices and "popularized" them instead, symbolically effacing the distance which allegedly had earlier kept apart the nation's leaders and private citizens. To make the country safe for revolution, government authorities effected far-reaching changes of personnel. The elimination from public office of people affiliated with the Nationalist regime began without delay. Reports published daily in the nation's press in the first weeks of occupation afford evidence of a swift consolidation of the organs of administration. During the first month of the new administration approximately 85 per cent of the mayors, 67 per cent of the county executives, and 82 per cent of the district military commanders were replaced.[17] Eyewitnesses recall, however, that the legal capacity of the new administrators

193

was impaired by the actions of Russian officials, the Red Army's political commissars and agents of the People's Commissariat of Internal Affairs, who interfered in local affairs frequently and peremptorily. Commenting on the dismissal of 175 county leaders, the government press hastened to point out that action was being taken only against unqualified persons whose only credentials consisted of their loyalty to the Nationalist regime.[18] In the main, the great purge descended on the Nationalists, Catholics, and the conservatives in general. It raised in station individuals with liberal and radical backgrounds. The minimal requirement for officeholders in the middle ranks seems to have been evidence of a neutral, reserved attitude toward the old regime. In the upper reaches, however, leftist proclivities, a grudge against the Nationalists, present or past association with the Social Democrats or the Populists, participation in the uprisings of 1905 and 1917, studies and travels in the USSR, and a predilection for Soviet cultural and economic gains facilitated promotion to an office of responsibility.

Inquiry into the functioning of administrative organs in June and July is frustrated by the anomalous procedures commonly attendant upon social and political upheavals in their incipient stages. Executive power in the period under consideration devolved upon several centers possessing a measure of independent initiative. This inadvertent decentralization, brought about by the course of revolutionary events, engendered lawlessness and disorder.

Shortly after the June crisis all media of information were made subservient to the new government. The official publication of the Nationalist Union at once received a new editor and, in a reversal of attitude, lauded the policies of the new government. Other newspapers, however, succeeded in delaying Communist encroachment, and for a time they even contrived to insert critical comment into their leading articles. When Justas Paleckis asked the press to be unswerving in allegiance to his administration, the *Vilniaus Balsas* (Voice of Vilnius) still was at liberty to respond equivocally that it would indeed be loyal to

194

the government, if it guarded the nation's independence and well-being.[19] And on another occasion, amid mounting apprehensions of what might be coming, the same journal placed emphasis on the nation's continuity. It gave expression to a hope that in the pluralist society of European states, eternal Lithuania would be visible, as a distinct entity, to make its contribution to the cultural achievements of other peoples.[20] The *XX Amžius*, too, preserved the attitude it assumed on June 15. Again and again its undaunted editor cautioned the People's Government to bear in mind Lithuania's ancestral heritage and the nation's future, and by so doing hurried his banishment to Siberia. The typical passage excerpted below is an example of the editorial policy of the Catholic daily:

We have known how to treasure our nation's past [and] our land, and we still do. We have been taught this love by the difficult and at times tragic course of our nation's history. Preserved in the memory of all elder countrymen are all those sufferings which they themselves experienced in times of tsarist oppression. Is there a village which has no martyrs on account of a Lithuanian book, a Lithuanian word, on account of the disposition and the endeavors to study in the native language? Our fathers and forefathers put up with [severe privations], rotted in prisons, traversed the Siberian lands, but did not betray their nation. Their eloquent testament passed on to their grandchildren.[21]

At a time when demands to pay homage to Bolshevik leaders were being made by the Communists with insolent persistence, and when failure to comply sufficed to cause one to be suspected of an inimical attitude toward the government, such nationalism could not be, and was not, tolerated for long. Both these newspapers suffered the loss of their original editors, who were replaced by individuals who clearly espoused radical policies.

Even with staffs obedient to the new authorities, the three major Kaunas periodicals were obliged to discontinue publication. The *Lietuvos Aidas* passed from sight before the other two. On July 16, appearing under a different heading, the former

195

Nationalist publication concluded that even if the paper had a management committed to the reforms now under way, its "oppressive and disagreeable past" made its demise inevitable, as inevitable as the elimination of every vestige of the old order. The *Lietuvos Žinios*, long free from the control of Populist leaders, vanished on August 1. In their last issue the leftist editors said that they had accomplished their mission, to help institute a new mode of government in Lithuania. That very same day the *XX Amžius* also discontinued its operations. It also credited itself with the preparation of its reading public for the momentous social reforms, and considered its work done.[22]

Attempts to Lessen Anxieties

To ASSUAGE the concern inspired by the force, speed, and scope of the transformation, the government took great pains to assure the populace that it would not renounce the foundations of the prevailing form of government and would not tolerate high-handed acts. In frequent appeals to the nation one cabinet member after another pleaded for restoration of public order and for confidence in the future. As early as June 21 Interior Minister Mečys Gedvilas, the leading Communist in the Council of Ministers, delivered a speech, advising his radio audience to dismiss the reports of impending Sovietization as "fantastic rumors" inspired by those who either did not know what they were talking about or were outspokenly adverse to peaceful reorganization of public life. He then ventured to say that "the essential nature of the organization of government is as yet unchanged. No one is making an attempt upon rightful private property or possession. The Red Army came to our country not to change our way of life or to enforce some kind of occupation but only to protect us from the danger of war and to help us to maintain our independence."[23] The next day Agriculture Minister Matas Mickis addressed the nation's farmers, who dreaded possible collectivization of land. Upbraiding the deposed "despots" for spreading "all sorts of nonsense," he offered

196

the farmers these assurances: "The People's Government is fully aware of your vital needs and will never let you down. Every farmer for whom land is a source of livelihood and not an object of speculation is guaranteed its absolute inviolability. The land which through centuries you have soaked by your sweat and blood is yours and will remain yours."[24] An incident which occurred on July 1 revealed how sensitive were the farmers about possible loss of land and how nimble was the government in moving to calm their fears. Talking that day to a convention in Vilnius, the Director of Land Reform apprised his listeners of the land policies which the government had in readiness. The indiscreet Stasys Elsbergas made it known that the administration had plans for a radical agrarian reform which envisaged the expropriation of all church lands and all holdings in excess of 50 hectares. He said further that in the proposed reallotment faithfulness to the regime would be taken into consideration.[25] This premature disclosure of government thinking, which appeared in print the following morning, spurred the Minister of Agriculture to repudiate the speech as a fabrication of a "provocative nature" and occasioned the Director's immediate removal from office.[26] Intensifying its efforts to win the confidence of the rural population, the administration reiterated in no uncertain terms that land would forever belong to those who work it and condemned any talk to the contrary as a "malicious lie."[27]

The most conspicuous step the Kaunas authorities took to allay popular disquiet over the future course of events was the performance of national honors at the tomb of the Unknown Soldier on June 26. Here before a large crowd and the entire cabinet Acting Prime Minister Vincas Krėvė-Mickevičius vowed that his government would strive for a happy and independent Lithuania.[28]

The Tightening Circle

As "REVOLUTION" GAINED MOMENTUM, conditions throughout the land became increasingly chaotic. In town and country Com-

197

munists and their collaborators engineered huge public demonstrations where, carrying portraits of Soviet leaders, they applauded the Kremlin for toppling the Nationalist regime. The Communist Party,[29] the NKVD, the Red Army, and the militia confiscated private property, ejected tenants from their homes, publicly called for liquidation of "enemies of the people," and terrorized the population. Old organizations and publications disappeared one after another. The relative ease and calm which followed the formation of the new government dissipated amid mounting uncertainty, disorganization, and fear. By the end of June the Council of Ministers could no longer cope with internal developments. Professor Krėvė thought that the time had come to resign as Acting Prime Minister, but he was dissuaded from doing so by Minister Galvanauskas, who persisted in his opinion that they should stay in the government to the last. A conference of senior citizens, formerly prominent in public life, not only agreed with the Minister of Finance but persuaded Krėvė to go to Moscow in order to apprise the Kremlin authorities of the conditions in Lithuania. There the Acting Prime Minister was to press the Russians to desist from undermining government authority by instructing their diplomatic agents and military personnel not to interfere in Lithuania's domestic affairs and by recalling all their nationals from the Lithuanian Ministry of the Interior.[30]

The talks between Krėvė and Molotov took place the night of June 30 and lasted two and a half hours. What many had feared now occurred. Molotov told the Lithuanian visitor that his government had decided to incorporate the Baltic country into the USSR. The stunned Krėvė proposed the conclusion of a new treaty, which would have limited Lithuania's freedom in the conduct of foreign relations but would have retained a measure of internal independence. Molotov retorted that in view of Bolshevik prospects of benefiting by the war, the Russians could not very well leave in their rear a small country enjoying a form of government destined to disappear in all of Europe.[31]

Upon his return home Krėvė learned that in his absence Acting President Paleckis had dissolved the Nationalist Seimas and had abrogated the Treaty of Good Understanding and Cooperation signed by the Baltic governments in 1934. Moreover, yielding to the Minister of the Interior, the Kaunas government denounced the concordat, the "cloak of superstition, servitude, and exploitation,"[32] which it had concluded with the Vatican in 1927. Mocking the supporters of clericalism, whom it dubbed the "divine propagandists," the controlled press commended the action by saying that it would make the people free to create heaven here on earth.[33] Having concluded from his conversations in Moscow and from these arbitrary decisions in Kaunas that his services had become quite ineffective, Krėvė once more made ready to step aside but was again prevailed on by Galvanauskas to stay in office in a continuing endeavor to thwart Russian designs.

The consultations which Krėvė had with influential government leaders after his return from the Soviet capital give a reasonable ground for presuming that at the time of the formation of the People's Government the local Communists, to say nothing of their leftist collaborators, were not apprised of Moscow's plans to sovietize the country, assuming that there were such plans in the first place. After Krėvė informed Gedvilas that the Kremlin intended to annex Lithuania and inquired if he had any previous knowledge of these intentions, the Communist Minister of the Interior disclosed that when he was offered his post he received guarantees that the Red Army was to assist Lithuania to safeguard its independence and not to subvert its internal order. Pursuant to these assurances, recounted Minister Gedvilas, he had drawn up the radio message of June 21, (see p. 196) which was endorsed by the Party's Central Committee and by Dekanozov himself. He had learned of the impending merger with the USSR only during the Prime Minister's absence. The dejected Gedvilas is reported to have added that, after learning the truth, he found himself in such a mess that there remained nothing else for him to do but to go crazy, shoot himself, or wait until he was shot. He could not relinquish office for fear of being liquidated, as under the strict rules of party discipline resignation would be tantamount to treason.[34] The testimony of the Minister of the Interior was corroborated by the Acting President. He, too, with tears in his eyes, related to Krėvė that when he had consented to head the new government Deputy Commissar Dekanozov vowed that Lithuania's independence was not in danger. On the basis of these guarantees, Paleckis turned to a number of government officials and urged them to work with him. After the Kremlin's duplicity became too evident for doubt, the unfortunate President suffered a nervous breakdown; and when he recovered, he was sorry he did.[35]

Mock Coalition

THE COMMUNIST AUTHORITIES rightly claimed that the Nationalists, who obliterated Lithuanian democracy, were loath to convene a popular assembly, and that when after nearly a decade in power they finally did so in 1936, it did not in any way alter the unrepresentative nature of the regime. Emphatically claiming to have discarded the highhanded practices of their predecessors, the Communists resolved to display their solidarity with the people by summoning in the very near future a truly democratic Diet, invested with supreme authority to act in the name of the Lithuanian nation.

Soon after his visit to Moscow, the Acting Prime Minister received urgent calls for a cabinet meeting in order to consider a new electoral law. However, Krėvė informed his impatient pro-Communist colleagues that there was no need to act with undue haste. When in the course of ensuing conversations even Paleckis failed to prevail on Krėvė to change his mind, Pozdniakov and Dekanozov interceded openly. In an ill-tempered altercation with the Soviet representatives, Professor Krėvė attempted to delay the rapid progress of events by reiterating that important economic matters demanded immediate attention and that elections could wait. Suspecting not without reason that the Acting Prime Minister's recalcitrance was buoyed up in some measure by the Minister of Finance, the impassive Dekanozov upbraided Krėvė for giving ear to what Galvanauskas whispered to him and insisted that elections be held forthwith. Angrily, the Lithuanian Premier retorted that he was not a child, that he had a mind of his own, and that he and his government and not the Russians would decide which matters to take up and which to put off.[36] Krėvė certainly was no child and he did have an independent mind, but neither he nor his associates wielded enough power to govern as they saw fit. The next day, on July 5, Ernestas Galvanauskas resigned as Finance Minister, and the Council of Ministers convened to discuss the forthcoming elections. Thereupon Krėvė asked to be relieved from his post but instead received a two-week leave of absence.[37] The able Minister of the Interior now moved to assume the duties of the Acting Prime Minister.

The meeting of July 5 approved a reformed electoral law, selected a five-member Supreme Electoral Commission made up of Communists and their sympathizers, and set July 14 as the election day.[38] The new law stipulated that candidates for people's representatives were to be selected at district rallies of working people. The Electoral Commission retained the right to disqualify individual nominees and to instruct the district meetings to name other choices. To see to it that nothing forestalled a heavy turnout of voters, the Commission made it known that it would create a number of "flying squads" which, on election day, would visit and persuade the apathetic to cast their ballots. Finally, the registrars at the polls were authorized to stamp the voters' identification papers with appropriate initials, so as to be able to tell whether or not a person had performed his civic obligation.[39]

The Communist Party of Lithuania now created a mock coalition of workers, peasants, and leftist intelligentsia purporting to represent the people's interests. Known as the Lithuanian Union of Labor, the ephemeral alliance, which fragmented after the election, endowed the Communists with a greater

201

popular appeal than they would have enjoyed if they faced the electorate merely as Communists. The Union platform embodied a succinct declaration of principles on foreign and domestic issues. In view of the impending merger with the Soviet Union, a course decreed by the Kremlin and by the beginning of July known to the members of the People's Government, the platitudinous campaign pledge of having very close ties with the Russians amounted to palpable deceit. Similarly, the domestic plank neglected to apprise the voters of prospective nationalization of land and indeed much of the nation's economy, matters of utmost concern to the voting public. Instead, the sixteen articles which constituted the party program, embracing inviolability of person and of private property, democratization of the army, promises to the workers of extensive liberties to defend the interests of labor, increase in workers' pay and improvement in their conditions of employment, greater protection of the working population in the event of illness, accident, and old age, lowering of rents for apartments, proffers of land and technical aid to peasants who owned little or no land, all pictured the Union candidates as earnest social and economic reformers but not as radicals.[40]

The 79 candidates to the Seimas were selected for the Union by the Communist Party's Central Committee.[41] Their political orientation conformed to the familiar pattern: the list of nominees comprised a Communist nucleus, which included almost all veteran leaders, and a host of pro-Communist, leftist, and independent individuals adverse to Nationalist policies. To exhibit the contrast between the old and the new in an ostentatious manner, the Communist policy makers contrived to seat in the People's Diet a number of laborers, peasants, women representatives, and some 49 deputies emblazoned with records of imprisonment for their anti-Nationalist and treasonable, under the Nationalists, activities.[42] Not infrequently the appointees were nominated without prior consultation. To those who rushed to the party headquarters to protest their induction, and there were some who did, the Communist authorities conceded that, indeed, it would have been only proper to secure the candidates' consent in advance, but alas, the Central Committee had been so busy that it simply forgot to do so. The future legislators were then told that public announcement of their candidacy precluded any possibility of withdrawal and that, in general, the high honor inherent in the office made it inconceivable that a person should decline to serve. Lastly, the disgruntled recipients of special Communist consideration were cautioned against doing anything foolish, as they already had been placed under police surveillance.[43]

Bandwagon Psychology

THE PRACTICE of rallying crowds for civil action now reached its apogee: several days before the election it transformed town and country into a torrent of vituperation alien to local politics. Identifying the common interests between workers and peasants, the Communist organizers spared no effort to bring together as many people as possible. To the accompaniment of leftist performers mustered to entertain the assembled spectators by awakening ridicule toward the fallen Nationalists, speaker after speaker, a member of the Communist Party, a representative of the Communist Youth, a woman, a soldier, a worker, or a "decent" officer, painted a bright future and attacked those who might hazard to obstruct its realization. At such meetings engineered by the Communists, the Communist-selected candidates were put forward and unanimously acclaimed as best qualified to speak in behalf of the people.

Despite the appearance of popular spontaneity which the Communists fostered in order to substantiate their professions of democratic faith, the mass meetings proved to be well under control, as there is practically no evidence of departure from the prearranged course of action. The most patent example of the directing influence which the Communist authorities and the security organs exercised over the pre-election procedures is the approval by every nominating rally of the single slate of candidates drawn up by the party.[44] Thus the citizens were deprived of the possibility of choice, which even the electoral law had not foreclosed altogether.

The number of persons attending these mass gatherings voluntarily evidently fell short of Communist expectations and spurred the ruling body to make direct appeals and to admonish those who hedged. One center of latent opposition turned out to be the army.[45] The Communist Party's Central Committee felt impelled to remind the soldiers that they "cannot be indifferent to current events."[46] The civil servants made up another segment of the population averse to public demonstrations. Apparently the teachers, too, were apathetic or hostile, for the Minister of Education had to pressure them to participate in the movement toward popular emancipation without delay.[47] Throughout the campaign the Communists wanted it known that indifference to the pre-election rallies, as well as the failure to vote, was sufficient reason to be classed among the enemies of the people. And they did not hesitate to make it quite clear how such enemies would be dealt with: the first mass arrests struck the country the night of July 11-12, two days before the election. The operation, which removed from public life some 2,000 men, was carried out by the thoroughly purged State Security Department, headed by the practiced Party Secretary Antanas Sniečkus. The victims of the Communist blow included leaders of political parties, high-ranking government officials, newspaper editors, members of the clergy, educators, local public functionaries, Nationalist workers, agricultural experts, and farmers, in short persons prominent in the life of the nation and the community who might have swayed the average citizen counter to the course of the "revolution."[48] The rumbling of the trucks, the knocking at the doors, the sight of the NKVD, and the screams of women and children attendant upon the concerted night raids, unprecedented in this part of the continent, reduced the country to a state of terror.

The drive to coerce the average Lithuanian to exhibit his "revolutionary fervor" became so vigorous that by the time the election came, the risks attended upon failure to respond were obvious. The concept of guilt was broadened to include not merely the perpetrators of acts contrary to the will of the Party but also the bystanders who preferred to remain aloof from the midsummer turbulence. A person who shunned the polls declined to have anything to do with the construction of the new society. He thus unveiled his lack of concern for the welfare of the comman man. Who but an enemy of the people would harbor such unsympathetic detachment? And enemies were not to be tolerated in Lithuania. In a similar way the Communist leaders deduced the moral obligation incumbent on every progressive citizen to take part in the pre-election campaign, the preparation for the historic days ahead. Consequently, all progressive writers, musicians, actors, and painters were coerced to enliven the campaign by putting their talents at the service of the revolution.

The justification of constraint over the individual introduced little novelty in Lithuanian thought. The idea that society had every right to compel a member insusceptible to the "duties of a citizen" or the "weighty social obligations" to mend his ways was common both to the Nationalist and the Communist writers. But the Nationalists had in general refrained from behaving as dictatorially as their rhetoric threatened or implied. The events in June gave enough ground for suspecting that under the Communists this moderation would vanish, and in July there no longer was any room for doubt.

Some Scattered Opposition

THE PRE-ELECTION DAYS produced the first traces of active opposition. The columns of the official press not infrequently referred to the "dark elements," the "packs of hooligans," or the "enemies of the people who were afraid of truth." The single task which this opposition set itself was to warn their countrymen not to vote in the forthcoming elections. Strongly inclined toward Nationalist and Catholic sentiments, the leaflets which flooded many localities beseeched all citizens not to betray their freedom and their religion by casting their ballots for the People's deputies, whom they labelled as traitors, or by inviting the "return of serfdom."[49]

The pre-election propaganda culminated in renewed assurances to the rural population and in an appeal to the nation delivered by the Acting President. "Peasants," exclaimed the front pages, "in distant corners the feeble remnants of plutocracy are trying to hiss like snakes the most abominable fabrications to the effect that our land, our homes, our modest belongings, which we have paid for in blood, would be taken away from us. We retort to such calumny with indignation and contempt, for we know that in the newly formed Lithuania our land, besprinkled with our sweat, and our homes will be ours. . . ."[50] Justas Paleckis spoke on the day of the election and said that every citizen was voting for a Lithuania which many had dreamed of and fought for in the past, for education accessible to all, for peaceful coexistence of all nationalities, for freedom of conscience, for the elimination of poverty and unemployment.[51]

A Not So Popular Mandate

DESPITE GOVERNMENT PRESSURE, a great many people had the courage to abstain from voting. Because of a light turnout, which the authorities attributed to bad weather, the voting was prolonged by one day. According to official returns, 95.51 per cent of the eligible voters had done their duty, 99.19 per cent of them casting their ballots for the Union candidates.[52] Privately, however, foremost members of the administration were quoted as conceding that the total turnout had not gone beyond 32 per cent,[53] a more plausible estimate than the 18 per cent put forward by non-Communist observers.[54] The former Secretary of the Presidium of the People's Diet revealed the dissatisfaction over the light turnout which was rife among the Leftist leaders. "What the devil has gone wrong?" fumed Gedvilas on July 25 in the presence of his colleagues. "Does our propaganda falter,

206

or is it that we do not yet know [how to hold elections] . . . . Such a small percentage of voters! Now, it could have been 50 per cent, even 30 per cent: one cannot expect much from a country which only recently was Fascist. But to have in many districts only 16 per cent voting for the People's Diet—that's a scandal!"[55] Owing to deliberate falsification of information, it is well-nigh impossible to ascertain the true count. For instance, a diligent newspaperman gave an account of balloting in the Vilnius district and placed the turnout of voters at about 87 per cent. This spurred the electoral commission to respond in haste that the published returns did not conform to fact.[56] The final version credited the area with a total of 95.95 per cent. In two electoral districts the number of those who voted exceeded the number of those who had the right to vote. This was said to have resulted from changes of residence brought about by travels, the relocation of troops, and the mobility of seasonal labor, all of which had made it necessary for a number of people to vote in places where they would not have voted under normal circumstances.[57]

The Door Closes

THE MAJORITY of the People's deputies displayed high spirits. Convinced that momentous affairs of state had devolved upon them, the delegates tried to be worthy of the honor and mindful of their obligations by being attentive, sagacious, and alert participants.[58] Not unlike members of the Council of Ministers a month before, they became differentiated into relatively independent and outright Communist camps. On July 20 the two groups caucused separately to talk about and to rehearse for the opening session to be held in the State Theater the following day. Hoping to scent the views current among the independents, the Communist policy makers broached the possibility of land reform and the nationalization of private property. In response, the more independent deputies, thinking that their opinions would carry weight, offered suggestions on how to reallot the land. Their protracted consultations resulted in this consensus:

207

the conferees believed that Lithuania should benefit by Soviet experience but that it ought to conduct its affairs independently; all deprecated the collectivization of land and some proposed to keep intact the centers of country estates as experimental state farms; nearly all favored the immediate institution of civil registry and civil marriage but thought it fair to reserve for the church several hectares of land and all the inventory it possessed. This ardor in the pursuit of equitable reforms was especially noticeable among the rural delegates, who had not yet been sufficiently impressed with the controlling influence which the Russian authorities wielded over domestic matters. Moreover, it must be remembered that irrespective of the conversation between Krėvė and Molotov, whose substance had been kept secret, occasional reports indicated that Moscow had not yet decreed the definitive status of its Baltic dependency and that it would not deprive the Lithuanians of self-government in local affairs. Allegedly, even a segment of the Communist Party's ruling body demurred at the idea of sovietization and only vigorous action on the part of Dekanozov ultimately dispelled their doubts.[59]

The People's Diet opened its sessions on July 21 and soon disheartened those who had hoped for some authenticity. Intimidated by agents of the secret police, the delegates went through with the functions which the Communist Party assigned to them, and those who had no part to play were not recognized by the chair.[60] The People's deputies received no agenda and could not familiarize themselves in advance with the items of business to be brought up. One reason for this disregard of parliamentary convention, disclosed Communist Party Secretary Sniečkus, was his inability to have all of Moscow's directives translated in time. This veteran Communist functionary said further that there would not be any lengthy talks, as the days of bourgeois democracy when such practices were in vogue were at an end.[61] A member of the Party's ruling body conceded in private that "our People's Diet resembles a Fascist vinaigrette and not a popular representation."[62]

208

In a brusque departure from the previous campaign oratory the bewildered delegates proclaimed Lithuania a Soviet Socialist Republic, pleaded for admission into the USSR, resolved upon a radical land reform, and decreed the nationalization of banking and heavy industry. All declarations were passed unanimously, with spectators, party members, Communist youth, secret service, former political prisoners, and workers voting together with the representatives. No one bothered to count the raised hands, no one cared to know if anyone had voted against.

Contrary to persistent Communist affirmations, the Diet did not speak in the name of the Lithuanian people. The single slate of candidates that excluded any possibility of choice, the absence of lists of registered voters, the intimidation of voters, the falsification of election returns,[63] and the manipulation by Russian agents of every step of its proceedings unmask the People's Diet as a false pretender to representative government. The omnipresence of the aggressor's power, the heralds of the Kremlin's will, the deliberate inspiring of delusive hopes, the skill of the professional revolutionary, and the tragedy of men and women ensnared by events beyond their control—these were some of the elements which converged to allow the People's Diet to consummate the inevitable.

XIX

CONCLUSION

THE SURRENDER of Klaipėda to Germany and the imposition of the Kremlin's will upon the People's Diet underscore the extent of outside influence upon Lithuania. The immediate consequence for domestic politics of the German intrusion in March 1939 was the formation of a coalition government under Jonas Černius. The Russian thrust in July 1940 brought to a climax the transitional stage, known as the People's Democracy, which had been the result of Lithuanian submission to the Soviet ultimatum in mid-June 1940. Hence, only the Merkys administration, from November 1939 to June 1940, was relatively free from external pressure. In this context of Great Power diplomacy, the Lithuanians endeavored to administer their internal affairs and to work out their problems.

In Lithuania in 1939, as in most of continental Europe, authoritarianism was in the ascendant. Its adherents, the Nationalists, showed confidence. Since the turn of the decade at the close of the 1920's, they had become convinced that the form of government which they espoused answered best the requirements of the time, just as other modes of political organization had met the needs of other times. Liberal democracy, to them, was a fossil, and a return to it was an unthinkable anachronism. Gradually authoritarianism spread over large areas of the nation's life, crystallizing its basic tenets and, at least in theory, approaching certain Fascistic psychological and political assumptions.

Authoritarian government in Lithuania resulted from developments which were both domestic and foreign. Existing systems frequently prepare the way for systems that succeed them. The defects of Lithuanian democracy from 1918 to 1926 facilitated the spread of authoritarianism from 1927 to 1939. The constitution-makers of 1920 were relatively young men: 26 per cent of them were under thirty, and only 7 per cent were over fifty. They had little familiarity with constitution-making and virtually none with the ways of representative government. Lithuania's past was too distant to be of any practical use either to them or to the politicians of the democratic period.

Problems related to inexperience were aggravated by a pronounced ideological propensity. Dogmatic thinking tended to sharpen party differences and to lessen the chances of compromise. An experienced leadership might have succeeded in moderating the unduly rigid party attitudes, and greater practical-mindedness might have blunted the problems stemming from inexperience. But inexperience combined with dogmatism generated political instability and party strife which exceeded conventional bounds.

Politics of both the democratic and the authoritarian period was attended with a measure of inevitability, a feeling that things could not have happened any other way. Many leaders sensed that their freedom of action was limited by events beyond their control. Thus, parliamentary democracy was adopted in Lithuania because it was the vogue at the time. Postwar radicalism demanded a land reform program and political parties felt that they must promise one. The tendency to view political issues from an ideological point of view was symptomatic of continental politics in general and Lithuania could not hope to resist it. Lastly, the sweeping changes in politics and economics which distinguished the democratic period were bound to awaken a conservative opposition. The democratic leadership was disinclined to moderate the intensity of change, while the conservatives were disinclined to tolerate it. The combination of a determined radical drive and an equally determined conservative opposition to it ended democracy in Lithuania.

The fortunes of authoritarianism in Lithuania were to some extent contingent upon the course of events elsewhere on the continent. Its prestige rose and declined inversely with that of parliamentary democracy and directly with that of dictatorial experiments in the major European powers. Lithuania in this respect was a piece of the continent, a part of the main. Evidence suggests that the Nationalists had not initially intended to destroy democracy in Lithuania. To be sure, the Nationalists insisted that there could be no return to the form of government which Lithuania had before the coup d'état of 1926, but they were not at all certain about its substitute. The Nationalist take-over, then, did not ipso facto foreclose the possibility of a democratic government. Had the continental powers succeeded in devising a form of government with a strong executive authority but one which retained its democratic character, it is possible that the Kaunas Nationalists would have considered its adaptation for Lithuania. As it turned out, increase in executive power meant a decline of democracy. The growing prestige of the dictatorial states in the 1930's, together with a lack of concern for democracy on the part of the Lithuanian Nationalists, resulted in an authoritarianism whose psychological basis was akin to that of Fascism.

Over the years, the Nationalists succeeded in staining the image of Lithuanian democracy, but they failed to eradicate the democratic political elements. The proximity of foreign threats, the sense of practical moderation which the senior Nationalists were ruled by, the ethical standards by which they were guided, despite their rhetorical bombast and verbal violence, and the intimacy which characterized the small world of politics in Kaunas, all suggest why opposition to the will of the Nationalists and their leader had not in fact been eradicated. In this manner authoritarianism, dominant but not absolute, encountered an anomaly. The democratic forces continued to exist and, by virtue of the combined Catholic-Populist strength, to display their independent initiative in a political environment which in theory explicitly precluded such a possibility. Thus, the political community was

212

pregnant with contradictions implying domestic political strife.

This inconsistency was brought into sharper focus with the institution of a coalition government in March 1939. Only a severe setback, such as the Klaipėda debacle, could have forced such a retreat on the Nationalists, and only the domestic repercussions of Germany's action deterred them from their efforts to recover the ground. As soon as the crisis period passed, political controversy reemerged. Subsequent developments, namely, the politics of both the Černius and the Merkys administration, must be considered in the light of this contradiction and the intent to resolve it. Thus, the coalition government was imperiled from the day of its inception.

Initially, the Catholic and Populist ministers had the upper hand and were on the offensive. The measures to which they resorted constituted a remedy for the faults which they attributed to the Nationalists. The opposition channeled its criticism in two directions. Politically, it blamed the Nationalists for the chasm between the leaders of the state and the general public, and maintained that the Nationalists had forfeited the consent of the governed. In economic matters, the opposition censured the regime's failure to deal forcefully with the economic hardships which had become increasingly severe. Consequently, once in office, the Catholics and the Populists strove to unite in action with the public at large and adopted a number of measures to that end. In drafting their economic policies, they directed their efforts to the achievement of a higher rate of economic growth and to the improvement of the living conditions of Lithuania's fringe population. They proposed to do this by rationalizing the nation's economic life and by introducing a radical land reform, the "second land reform." In politics, the new course tended to make the regime more representative; in economics, it subordinated free enterprise to a greater direction from above.

Political disagreement came to a head in November of 1939. The ensuing cabinet crisis forced the Catholics and Populists under the strong urging of commander Raštikis to resubmit to the authoritarian Nationalists. The trend toward a more liberal

213

regime was arrested, and the possibility of a radical solution of the nation's social and economic ills aborted. Though the rejection of the radical proposals demonstrated Presidents Smetona's power over his subordinates, it could not obscure the fact that many of his Nationalist associates were agreeable to the opposition's plans. For the time being the younger Nationalists acquiesced in the decision of their Leader, but their inclination to a bolder course made the future of economic conservatism insecure.

The domestic developments of the Merkys government were already implicit in the crisis which led to its formation. Having gained a measure of success, the Nationalists rallied to strengthen the regime and tried to solve economic problems by means short of radical changes. The culmination of their economic legislation was the law of May 1940, which delegated extraordinary powers to the Minister of Finance. This law was intended to give greater direction to an economy which in essence preserved its free-market pluralism.

The experiment in coalition government calls attention to three developments. First, during the Nationalist administration the average citizen had frequently been reproached for his alleged indifference to public affairs. Popular response to the change in the government in the spring of 1939 refuted this charge; the citizens displayed their interest in civic life when the occasion called for it and when the authorities granted them liberty of action. Second, the social and economic policies of the Catholics and the Populists attested to the presence of political forces ready to grapple with the mounting discontent by resorting to drastic measures, such as the envisaged second land reform, without shattering the fabric of society. The opposition's recommendations were an alternative to the policies of the Nationalists as well as to those of the Communists. Third, political developments during the Černius administration offer sufficient evidence for deducing that the Nationalists were disinclined to liberalize the regime. Some observers perceived a trend in the last years of the interwar decades to a more representative government. Such a trend proved to be a delusion.

214

The Nationalists bowed only to superior pressure, as after the loss of Klaipėda. When the pressures on them lessened, they resumed their progress toward a more definite form of authoritarianism, emancipating themselves from the coalition's restraints as soon as it became feasible.

The last days of independent Lithuania witnessed a climactic escalation of political strife. The Catholics and the Populists realized that their hopes for a more democratic government had been dashed. Therefore, they prepared for an eventual showdown, the collapse of the Merkys cabinet. However, in June 1940, a new factor appeared. The Kremlin commenced its diplomatic offensive against the Baltic republics. The fact that internal friction continued unabated in Lithuania testifies to the partial success of Moscow's strategy, which was to annex the Baltic states gradually and with the seeming consent of their peoples. The Soviet Union never gained the Lithuanians' consent, but it did palliate the stroke inflicted in June. Hours before the ultimatum, the majority of government leaders in Kaunas concluded that the deterioration of relations with the USSR would not be disastrous for Lithuania. Consequently, domestic rivalries continued to ripen. And when the ultimatum did come, the Lithuanians still counted on the presumed continuation of limited self-government. This expectation affected their decision to comply with Soviet demands. If Russian aggression had been undisguised, it is quite probable that internal disputes would have been suspended and it is quite possible that the Lithuanians would have offered at least token resistance to the Red Army.

Events in Lithuania subsequent to the People's Diet, which opened its sessions on July 21, 1940, are a chapter in the history of the USSR. To a Russian chronicler that chapter might well have started with the actual occupation of the southernmost Baltic republic in the middle of June, for the compulsory collaboration traced in this book can justly be interpreted as a strategy of incorporation. The principal feature of this Soviet strategy was the adroit exploitation of the deep-seated domestic discord rife in Lithuania, whereby the Soviets sought to minimize the

215

chances of open resistance to their gradually unfolding designs. Certainly, the controlling influence which the Soviet troops and the Soviet officials possessed and used over every important phase of the country's public life after the occupation gives ample ground for appending the transient chapter of the People's Democracy to a book on Soviet Russian history. But then, analyzing the rapid progress of events in June and July from the point of view of the vanquished Lithuanian population, there emerges, too, a continuity of crisis in which the policies and aspirations of the People's Government form an integral part of earlier developments. The link is provided by the hopes of the "revolution," essentially understood as a reversal of Nationalist policies, but not as sovietization. It was founded in the lingering expectation that Lithuania would be conceded a semblance of independent existence. The revealing sessions of the People's Diet and the ensuing merger with the USSR bring this period of history to an end. Lithuania's demise, formalized on August 3, 1940, in the decision of the Supreme Soviet to admit its Baltic dependency into the USSR, ended the June-July transition and, with it, the remote possibility of the semi-independent survival of Lithuania.

In the weeks after the annexation the new Union Republic hastened to bring into concrete existence the resolutions which the people's deputies had acclaimed in the Diet, a legislature which according to an exuberant plaudit "has done in three days what no parliament in the world had done in hundreds of years."[1] The Communist policy makers brought forward an appropriate constitution, which was founded on Soviet basic law, and proceeded to adjust governmental institutions accordingly. They carried out a radical land reform which left the farmer a maximum of 30 hectares for his permanent use. They nationalized banking, heavy industry, and ultimately commerce. The process of sovietization, accompanied by a reign of terror and deportations, reduced internal friction and united the nation for eventual insurrection against the relentless foe. That uprising took place in the following year, when, in June 1941, German armies commenced their assault upon Soviet Russia.

216

APPENDICES

APPENDIX A

LITHUANIAN ELECTION RESULTS, 1920-1936

PARTIES	Constituent Assembly 1920-1922	1st Seimas 1922-1923	2nd Seimas 1923-1926	3rd Seimas 1926-1927	4th Seimas 1936
Christian Democrats ⎱		15	14	14	
Farmers' Union ⎰	59	12	14	11	
Federation of Labor ⎰		11	12	5	
Populists	29	19	16	22	
Social Democrats	14	11	9	15	
Communists		5			
Farmers' Party				2	
Nationalists				3	46
Minorities					
Jews	6	3	6	3	
Poles	3	2	11	4	
Russians			1		
Germans	1		2	6	3
TOTAL	112	78	85	85	49

217

APPENDIX B

MEMBERS OF THE LITHUANIAN NATIONALIST AND PEOPLE'S GOVERNMENTS AND OTHER PERSONS OF PROMINENCE

THE ČERNIUS GOVERNMENT: *March 27, 1939*

Prime Minister: General Jonas Černius
Deputy Prime Minister: Kazys Bizauskas
Minister of Foreign Affairs: Juozas Urbšys
Minister of Internal Affairs: General Kazys Skučas
Minister of Finance: General Jonas Sutkus
Minister of Defense: General Kazys Musteikis
Minister of Justice: Antanas Tamošaitis
Minister of Agriculture: Jurgis Krikščiūnas
Minister of Education: Leonas Bistras
Minister of Communications: Kazys Germanas

THE MERKYS GOVERNMENT: *November 21, 1939*

Prime Minister: Antanas Merkys
Deputy Prime Minister: Kazys Bizauskas
Minister of Foreign Affairs: Juozas Urbšys
Minister of Internal Affairs: General Kazys Skučas
Minister of Finance: Ernestas Galvanauskas
Minister of Defense: General Kazys Musteikis
Minister of Justice: Antanas Tamošaitis
Minister of Agriculture: Juozas Audėnas
Minister of Education: Kazimieras Jokantas
Minister of Communications: Jonas Masiliūnas

THE PALECKIS GOVERNMENT: *June 17 to July 1, 1940*

Prime Minister, Acting President: Justas Paleckis
Deputy Prime Minister, Minister of Foreign Affairs: Vincas Krėvė-
Mickevičius

218

Minister of Internal Affairs: Mečys Gedvilas
Minister of Finance: Ernestas Galvanauskas
Minister of Defense: General Vincas Vitkauskas
Minister of Justice: Povilas Pakarklis
Minister of Labor: Martynas Junča-Kučinskis
Minister of Agriculture: Matas Mickis
Minister of Education: Antanas Venclova
Minister of Communications: Stasys Pupeikis
Minister of Health: Leonas Koganas
State Comptroller: Liudas Adomauskas
Representative for the Vilnius District: Karolis Didžiulis-Grosmanas

OTHERS

Alantas, Vytautas. Editor of *Lietuvos Aidas*
Aleksa, Jonas. Politician and author
Bielinis, Kipras. One of the leaders of the Lithuanian Social Democratic
    Party
Brazaitis, Juozas. Catholic politician
Cesevičius, Domas. Chairman of the Lithuanian Nationalist Union
Dirmeikis, Bronius. Editor in Chief of *Lietuvos Aidas*
Kardelis, Jonas. Editor of the Populist *Lietuvos Žinios*
Krupavičius, Mykolas. Catholic statesman
Maceina, Antanas. Catholic author
Mašalaitis, Vincas. Secretary-General of the Lithuanian Council of
    Ministers
Natkevičius, Ladas. Lithuanian Minister in Moscow
Rastenis, Vincas. Secretary-General of the Lithuanian Nationalist
    Union, 1931-1935
Raštikis, Stasys. Commander of the army
Statkus, Jonas. Secretary-General of the Lithuanian Nationalist Union
Šalkauskis, Stasys. Catholic philosopher
Škirpa, Kazys. Lithuanian Minister in Berlin
Šmulkštys, Liudas. One of the leaders of the Lithuanian Peasant-
    Populist Union
Vilkaitis, Jonas. One of the leaders of the Lithuanian Social Demo-
    cratic Party

219

APPENDIX C

FOREIGN CAPITAL IN LITHUANIA'S JOINT-STOCK COMPANIES
DECEMBER 31, 1939
(in thousands of lits)

BRANCHES	Firms with Foreign Capital	Entire Capital Stock	Foreign Capital
Metals and machinery	2	6,700	2,135
Chemicals	4	6,950	6,476
Textiles	5	4,725	2,350
Paper and printing	1	280	167
Foodstuffs	3	2,500	771
Clothing and footwear	2	600	110
Electricity	2	21,000	20,851
Credit	4	9,000	2,247
Insurance	2	1,400	287
Miscellaneous	3	1,900	316
Total	28	55,055	35,710

Source: *Annuaire statistique...*, XII, 288-89.

APPENDIX D

CHRONOLOGY OF THE MOST IMPORTANT EVENTS
1918-1940

February 16, 1918	Declaration of independence
April 4, 1919	Antanas Smetona becomes the first President
May 15, 1920	Constituent Assembly meets in Kaunas
July 12, 1920	Russia and Lithuania conclude a peace treaty
October 9, 1920	Polish forces seize Vilnius
September 22, 1921	Lithuania admitted into the League of Nations
March 29, 1922	Seimas adopts the law of land reform
December 21, 1922	Aleksandras Stulginskis elected President
June 7, 1926	Kazys Grinius elected President
June 15, 1926	Mykolas Sleževičius forms a government composed of Populists and Social Democrats

September 28, 1926	Lithuania and Soviet Union conclude a treaty of nonaggression
December 17, 1926	A military coup ousts constitutional authorities, Antanas Smetona becomes the Leader of the State, and Augustinas Voldemaras forms a new Council of Ministers
September 27, 1927	Lithuania signs a concordat with the Vatican
September 12, 1934	Lithuania, Latvia, and Estonia conclude the Treaty of Good Understanding and Cooperation
September 1, 1936	Nationalist Seimas meets in Kaunas
March 17, 1938	Poland demands the establishment of diplomatic relations
March 22, 1939	Germany demands the surrender of Klaipėda
March 27, 1939	General Jonas Černius forms a coalition government
September 1, 1939	Germany invades Poland
September 2, 1939	Lithuania proclaims its neutrality
September 17, 1939	Soviet Union enters war against Poland
September 19, 1939	The Red Army occupies Vilnius
October 10, 1939	Lithuania and Soviet Union conclude a treaty of mutual assistance
October 28, 1939	Lithuanian troops enter Vilnius
November 21, 1939	Antanas Merkys forms the last government of independent Lithuania
June 14, 1940	Soviet Union presents Lithuania with an ultimatum
June 15, 1940	President Smetona departs from Lithuania
June 17, 1940	Justas Paleckis heads a government dictated by the Kremlin
July 11-12, 1940	First mass arrests in Lithuania
July 14-15, 1940	Elections to the People's Diet
July 21, 1940	The People's Diet proclaims Lithuania a Soviet Socialist Republic
August 3, 1940	Lithuania incorporated into the USSR

NOTE ON SOURCES

THIS STUDY is based primarily on Lithuanian periodicals published in 1939-1940. International tensions make it difficult for the foreign researcher to have access to source materials in Soviet-occupied Lithuania. It is necessary to rely on collections found outside Lithuania.

Most of the principal newspapers and journals of the period under consideration can be located in the United States. Unfortunately, they are dispersed among many individuals and institutions, and as a result are not easily available to those who may want to use them.

In New York City, three institutions preserve valuable materials. Columbia University keeps *Vyriausybės Žinios* (Government News) and the *Yearbooks of Lithuanian Statistics*. The New York Public Library possesses *Statistikos Biuletenis* (Bulletin of Statistics), *Lietuvos Banko Biuletenis* (Bulletin of the Bank of Lithuania), and *Lietuvos Ūkininkas* (The Lithuanian Farmer). Lastly, the Consulate General of Lithuania preserves *Talka* (Collective Action), *Tautos Ūkis* (National Economy), and *Vairas* (The Helm). Every one of these volumes lacks some issues; but on the whole, the collections are fairly complete.

Other possessors of numerous publications include the Sisters of the Crucified Jesus in Brockton, Massachusetts, the Marianapolis Preparatory School in Thompson, Connecticut, the Lithuanian Legation in Washington, and, in Chicago, the Lithuanian Consulate, the publishers of *Margutis*, and the Sisters of St. Casimir. Together, these institutions contain nearly complete volumes of Lithuania's major newspapers: *Lietuvos Aidas* (Echo of Lithuania), *XX Amžius* (Twentieth Century), *Lietuvos Žinios* (News of Lithuania, only for 1940), *Mūsų Laikraštis* (Our Newspaper), *Darbo Lietuva* (Labor Lithuania),

222

Tautos Mokykla (The Nation's School), *Naujoji Romuva* (The New *Romuva*). In addition, they have several provincial publications, such as *Panevėžio Garsas* (The Sound of Penevėžys), *Žemaičių Prietelius* (The Friend of *Žemaičiai*), and *Šaltinis* (The Fountainhead), and a number of specialized periodicals. The Sisters of the Crucified Jesus, the Sisters of St. Casimir, and the Marianapolis Preparatory School are particularly rich in Catholic sources.

Unfortunately, *Vilniaus Balsas* (Voice of Vilnius), *Kardas* (The Sword), and *Mūsų Žinynas* (Our Record), the capital daily and two journals of military affairs, are available only in single copies.

Books that deal with the events of 1939-1940 are few. Here are some which were especially useful:

Balčiūnas, J[uozas] (ed.). *Lietuvių archyvas: bolševizmo metai*. Lithuanian Archives: The Bolshevik Years. 2d ed. Kaunas: Studijų biuras, 1942. A series of articles depicting the events in Lithuania during the Soviet occupation (June 1940 to June 1941). Especially illustrative are the contributions by Liudas Dovydėnas, Antanas Garmus, and Vincas Krėvė-Mickevičius.

Balčiūnas, V[alerionas]. *Lietuvos kaimų žemės tvarkymas istorijos, ūkio ir statistikos šviesoje*. The Organization of Lithuanian Rural Land in the Light of History, Economy, and Statistics. Kaunas: Žemės reformos valdyba, 1938. The work is a comprehensive study of the organization of rural land. It surveys the administration of land under the tsars and outlines the changes effected after 1918.

Daulius, Juozas [Stasys Yla]. *Komunizmas Lietuvoje*. Communism in Lithuania. Kaunas: Šviesa, 1937. The book is based on Communist sources.

Dovydėnas, Liudas. *Užrašai*. Diary. 2d ed. Kaunas: Br. Daunoro leidykla, 1944. Former member of the People's Diet writes about the policies of the Communist government and the men who made them.

Krikščiūnas, Jurgis. *Agriculture in Lithuania*. Translated by Vikt. Kamantauskas. Kaunas: The Lithuanian Chamber of Agriculture, 1938. One of the nation's leading economists examines the rural economy.

Raštikis, Stasys. *Kovose dėl Lietuvos: kario atsiminimai.* In the Struggles for Lithuania: Memoirs of a Soldier. 2 vols. Los Angeles: Lietuvių Dienos, 1956-1957. Even if occasionally trifling, these voluminous memoirs contain a wealth of information relative to the military and political developments in Lithuania before and after World War II.

Smetona, Antanas. *Pasakyta parašyta, 1927-1934.* Spoken Written, 1927-1934. Kaunas: Pažanga, 1935. This work embodies the President's views on nearly every aspect of the country's life. According to the author himself, it elucidates his "national ideology."

X. Y. [Mykolas Römeris]. *Lietuvos sovietizacija, 1940-1941 m.* The Sovietization of Lithuania, 1940-1941. Augsburg: Lietuvos teisininkų tremtinių draugija, 1949. A noted professor of international law gives a succinct account of Lithuania's occupation and Sovietization.

Žiugžda, J[uozas] (ed.). *Lietuvos TSR istorijos šaltiniai.* Sources for the History of the Lithuanian SSR. Vol. IV. Vilnius: Lietuvos TSR mokslų akademija, 1961. This is a collection of laws, resolutions, decrees, and information about independent Lithuania published by the Communists. Although the selection of materials is tendentious, it is nevertheless an instructive source.

BIBLIOGRAPHY

DOCUMENTS

Appeal by Representatives of the Baltic Nations to the General Assembly of the United Nations. Presented November 24, 1947.

Feigelsonas, G., and Others (eds.). *Lietuvos komunistų partijos atsišaukimai*. Appeals of the Communist Party of Lithuania. 4 vols. Vilnius: Valstybinė politinės ir mokslinės literatūros leidykla, 1963.

Gantenbein, James W. (ed.). *Documentary Background of World War II, 1931 to 1941*. New York: Columbia University Press, 1948.

International Institute of Agriculture. *International Yearbook of Agricultural Statistics, 1939-1940*. Rome, 1940.

International Labour Office. *Year-Book of Labour Statistics, 1940*. Geneva, 1940.

————. *Year Book of Labour Statistics, 1941*. Montreal, 1942.

Jacovskis, E., and Others (eds.). *Tarybų valdžios atkūrimas Lietuvoje 1940-1941 metais: dokumentų rinkinys*. Restoration of Soviet Power in Lithuania, 1940-1941: Collection of Documents. Vilnius: Mintis, 1965.

League of Nations. Economic Intelligence Service. *Statistical Year-Book of the League of Nations, 1939-40*. Geneva, 1940.

Liet. komunistų partijos V konferencijos rezoliucijos. Resolutions of the Fifth Conference of the Communist Party of Lithuania. N.p.: LKP CK, 1934.

Lithuania. Central Bureau of Statistics. *Recensement agricole en Lithuanie*. Vol. I. Kaunas, n.d.

————. Central Bureau of Statistics. *Résultats de l'enquête organisée*

225

en Lithuanie durant les années 1936-1937, sur les budgets de 297 familles ouvrières, d'employés et de fonctionnaires. Kaunas, 1939.

————. Central Bureau of Statistics. *Annuaire statistique de la Lithuanie, 1939.* Vol. XII. Vilnius, 1940.

————. Ministry of Agriculture. *Žemės ūkio ministerijos metraštis, 1918-1938.* Yearbook of the Ministry of Agriculture, 1918-1938. [Kaunas], n.d.

Sontag, Raymond James, and Beddie, James Stuart eds. *Nazi-Soviet Relations, 1939-1941.* Department of State Publication No. 3023. Washington, 1948.

Šaulių sąjungos įstatymas ir statutas. The Law and Statute of the Union of Šauliai. Kaunas: Šaulių sąjungos leidinys, 1936.

U.S. House of Representatives, Select Committee to Investigate Communist Aggression and the Forced Incorporation of the Baltic States into the U.S.S.R. *Third Interim Report.* 83rd Congress, 2nd Session, Washington, 1954.

————. House of Representatives, Select Committee to Investigate the Incorporation of the Baltic States into the U.S.S.R. *Hearings, Baltic States Investigation.* Part 1, 83rd Congress, 1st Session, Washington, 1954.

————. Department of State. *Documents on German Foreign Policy, 1918-1945.* Series D, Vols. V, VIII, IX. Washington, 1953-1954.

————. Department of State. *Foreign Relations of the United States: Diplomatic Papers. The Soviet Union, 1933-1939.* Washington, 1952.

————. Department of State. *Foreign Relations of the United States: Diplomatic Papers, 1939.* Vol. I. Washington, 1956.

————. Department of State. *Foreign Relations of the United States: Diplomatic Papers, 1940.* Vol. I. Washington, 1959.

Vyriausybės Žinios (Government News, Kaunas), 1939-1940.

Woodward, E. L., and Butler, Rohan eds. *Documents on British Foreign Policy, 1919-1939* (3rd series). Vol. IV. London: His Majesty's Stationery Office, 1951.

Žiugžda, J[uozas] ed. *Lietuvos TSR istorijos šaltiniai.* Sources for the History of the Lithuanian SSR. Vol. IV. Vilnius: Lietuvos TSR mokslų akademija, 1961.

BOOKS

Aleksa, Jonas. *Lietuviškų gyvenimo kelių beieškant.* In Quest of Lithuanian Ways of Life. Vol. II. Kaunas: By the author, 1933.

Ambrazevičius, Juozas. *Lietuvių rašytojai: literaturiniai straipsniai.* Lithuanian Writers: Literary Essays. N.p.: Šv. Kazimiero Draugija, n.d.

Atamukas, S. *LKP kova prieš fašizmą, uš tarybų valdžią Lietuvoje 1935-1940 metais.* The Struggle of the CPL Against Fascism, for the Soviet Government in Lithuania, 1935-1940. Vilnius: Valstybinė politinės ir mokslinės literatūros leidykla, 1958.

Audrūnas, Jonas [Bronius Dirmeikis], and Svyrius, Petras [Vincas Rastenis]. *Lietuva tironų pančiuose.* Lithuania in Chains of Tyrants. Vol. I. Cleveland: Lietuvai vaduoti sąjunga, 1946.

Augustaitis, J. *Antanas Smetona ir jo veikla.* Antanas Smetona and His Activities. Chicago: Chicagos lietuvių litcratūros draugija, 1966.

Balčiūnas, J[uozas], ed. *Lietuvių archyvas: bolševizmo metai.* Lithuanian Archives: The Bolshevik Years. 2nd ed. Kaunas: Studijų biuras, 1942.

Balčiūnas, V[alerionas]. *Lietuvos kaimų žemės tvarkymas istorijos, ūkio ir statistikos šviesoje.* The Organization of Lithuanian Rural Land in the Light of History, Economy, and Statistics. Kaunas: Žemės reformos valdyba, 1938.

Baltramaitis, Casimer V. ed. *Lithuanian Affairs.* New York: Lithuanian Press Club, 1945.

Baranauskas, B[oleslovas]. *Devyniolika metų pogrindyje.* Nineteen Years in the Underground. Vilnius: Vaga, 1965.

Beržinskaitė, A. *LKP veikla auklėjant Lietuvos darbo žmones proletarinio internacionalizmo dvasia, 1927-1940.* The Activities of the CPL in Educating the Working People of Lithuania in the Spirit of Proletarian Internationalism, 1927-1940. Vilnius: Valstybinė politinės ir mokslinės literatūros leidykla, 1962.

Bimba, Antanas. *Naujoji Lietuva faktų ir dokumentų šviesoje.* The New Lithuania in the Light of Facts and Documents. N.p.: Lietuvos draugų komitetas, 1940.

Biržiška, Vaclovas, and Others (eds.). *Lietuvių enciklopedija.* Lithuanian Encyclopedia. Vols. I-XXVII. So. Boston, Mass.: Lietuvių enciklopedijos leidykla, 1953-1962.

Bulavas, Juozas. *Rinkimai ir "tautos atstovavimas" buržuazinėje Lietu-*

227

voje. Elections and "National Representation" in Bourgeois Lithuania. Vilnius: Valstybinė politinės ir mokslinės literatūros leidykla, 1956.

Butkutė-Ramelienė, A. *Lietuvos komunistų partijos kova už tarybų valdžios įtvirtinimą respublikoje, 1940-1941 m.* The Struggle of the Communist Party of Lithuania for the Consolidation of Soviet Power in the Republic, 1940-1941. Vilnius: Valstybinė politinės ir mokslinės literatūros leidykla, 1958.

Cimbolenka, P. ed. *20 metų Tarybų Lietuvos liaudies ūkiui.* 20 Years of People's Economy in Soviet Lithuania. Vilnius: Lietuvos TSR mokslų akademija, 1960.

Dallin, David J. *Soviet Russia's Foreign Policy, 1939-1942.* Translated by Leon Dennen. New Haven: Yale University Press, 1942.

Daulius, Juozas [Stasys Yla]. *Komunizmas Lietuvoje.* Communism in Lithuania. Kaunas: Šviesa, 1937.

Dirvelė, E., and Others (eds.). *Lietuvos komjaunimas.* The Communist Youth of Lithuania. Vilnius: Valstybinė politinės ir mokslinės literatūros leidykla, 1962.

Dominas, K. *Spalio aidai.* Echoes of October. Vilnius: Valstybinė grožinės literatūros leidykla, 1961.

Dovydėnas, Liudas. "Mano kelias į Liaudies Seimą" (My Road to the People's Diet), in J. Balčiūnas ed., *Lietuvių archyvas: bolševizmo metai.* Lithuanian Archives: The Bolshevik Years. Vol. III. Kaunas: Studijų biuras, 1942.

———. *Užrašai.* Diary. 2nd ed. Kaunas: Br. Daunoro leidykla, 1944.

Eretas, Juozas. *Stasys Šalkauskis, 1886-1941.* Brooklyn, N.Y.: Ateitininkų Federacija, 1960.

Gaigalaitė, A., and Others (eds.). *Lietuvos TSR istorija.* History of the Lithuanian SSR. Vol. III. Vilnius: Mintis, 1965.

Garmus, A[ntanas]. "Lietuvos įjungimas į SSSR—Maskvos diktatas" (Lithuania's Incorporation into the USSR—Moscow's Dictate), in J. Prunskis ed., *Lietuvių archyvas: bolševizmo metai.* Lithuanian Archives: The Bolshevik Years. Brooklyn, N.Y.: Tėvų Pranciškonų spaustuvė, 1952.

Gregorauskas, M[arijonas]. *Tarybų Lietuvos žemės ūkis, 1940-1960.* Agriculture of Soviet Lithuania, 1940-1960. Vilnius: Valstybinė politinės ir mokslinės literatūros leidykla, 1960.

Jablonskis, K[onstantinas], and Others (eds.). *Lietuvos TSR istorija.* History of the Lithuanian SSR. Vilnius: Lietuvos TSR mokslų akademija, 1958.

Jacovskis, E. *Uždangą nuplėšus.* After Tearing off the Cover. Vilnius: Valstybinė politinės ir mokslinės literatūros leidykla, 1959.

Kačinskas, Henrikas. "Liaudies Seimas—jėgos įvykių uždanga" (The People's Diet—a Cover for Acts of Force), in J. Balčiūnas ed., *Lietuvių archyvas: bolševizmo metai.* Vol. III. Kaunas: Studijų biuras, 1942.

Kapsukas, V[incas]. *Buržuazinė Lietuva.* Bourgeois Lithuania. Vilnius: Valstybinė politinės ir mokslinės literatūros leidykla, 1961.

Kazlauskas, B. *L'entente baltique.* Paris: Libraire Du Recueil Sircy, 1939.

Krėvė-Mickevičius, V[incas]. "Bolševikų invazija ir Liaudies vyriausybė" (The Bolshevik Invasion and the People's Government), in J. Balčiūnas ed., *Lietuvių archyvas: bolševizmo metai.* Vol. III. Kaunas: Studijų biuras, 1942.

Krikščiūnas, Jurgis. *Agriculture in Lithuania.* Translated by Vikt[oras] Kamantauskas. Kaunas: The Lithuanian Chamber of Agriculture, 1938.

League of Nations. European Conference on Rural Life, 1939. *Lithuania.* Geneva, 1939.

———. Economic, Financial and Transit Department. *Europe's Population in the Interwar Years.* Written for the League of Nations by Dudley Kirk. Princeton, N. J., 1946.

———. Economic, Financial and Transit Department. *Economic Demography of Eastern and Southern Europe.* Written for the League of Nations by Wilbert E. Moore. Geneva, 1945.

Lopajevas, S. *Lietuvos komunistų partijos idėjinis ir organizacinis stiprėjimas, 1919-1924.* Increase in Ideological and Organizational Strength of the Communist Party of Lithuania, 1919-1924. Vilnius: Valstybinė politinės ir mokslinės literatūros leidykla, 1964.

Maceina, Antanas. "Krikščioniškasis turinys ir lietuviškoji forma" (The Christian Content and the Lithuanian Form), in [P. Mantvydas ed.], *Krikščionybė Lietuvoje: praeitis, dabartis, ateitis.* Christianity in Lithuania: The Past, the Present, the Future. Kaunas. Šv. Kazimiero Draugija, 1938.

Mačiuika, Benedict V. ed. *Lithuania in the Last 30 Years.* New Haven: Human Relations Area Files, Inc., 1955.

Mačiulis, Petras. *Trys ultimatumai.* The Three Ultimata. Brooklyn, N. Y.: Darbininkas, 1962.

Mantas, Jurgis. *Lietuva bolševikų okupacijoj.* Lithuania Under Bolshevik Occupation. Buenos Aires: Liet. Inform. Centras P. Amerikoje, 1948.

229

[Mantvydas, P. ed.] *Krikščionybė Lietuvoje: praeitis, dabartis, ateitis.* Christianity in Lithuania: The Past, the Present, the Future. Kaunas: Šv. Kazimiero Draugija, 1938.

Matusas, Jonas. *Šaulių sąjungos istorija.* History of the Union of *Šauliai.* Kaunas: Šauliu sąjunga, 1939.

Meissner, Boris. *Die Sowjetunion, die Baltischen Staaten und das Völkerrecht.* The Soviet Union, the Baltic States and the International Law. Köln: Verlag für Politik und Wirtschaft, 1956.

Merkelis, Aleksandras. *Antanas Smetona: jo visuomeninė, kultūrinė ir politinė veikla.* Antanas Smetona: His Civic, Cultural, and Political Activities. New York: Amerikos lietuvių tautinė sąjunga, 1964.

Meškauskas, K. *Tarybų Lietuvos industrializavimas.* The Industrialization of Soviet Lithuania. Vilnius: Lietuvos TSR mokslų akademija, 1960.

Mickus, Pranas. "Liaudies Seimo rinkimų duomenų klastojimas" (The Falsification of Returns of Elections to the People's Diet), in J. Balčiūnas ed., *Lietuvių archyvas: bolševizmo metai.* Vol. III. Kaunas: Studijų biuras, 1942.

Musteikis, A. ed. *Lietuvos žemės ūkis ir statistika.* Lithuanian Agriculture and Statistics. Dillingen: Žemės ūkio darbuotojų sąjunga, 1948.

Musteikis, Kazys. *Prisiminimų fragmentai.* Fragments of Reminiscences. London: Nida, 1970.

Paleckis, J[ustas]. *Das Sowjetische Litauen.* Soviet Lithuania. Berlin: SWA-Verlag, 1948.

———. *Gyvenimas prasideda.* Life Begins. Vilnius: Vaga, 1967.

Potemkin, V. P. ed. *Istoriia diplomatii.* History of Diplomacy. Vol. III. Moskva: Gosudarstvennoe izdatel'stvo politicheskoi literatury, 1945.

Pranckūnas, J. *Pavasario vėjas gaivus.* Brisk is the Wind of Spring. Vilnius: Valstybinė grožinės literatūros leidykla, 1960.

Prunskis, J[uozas] ed. *Lietuvių archyvas: bolševizmo metai.* Lithuanian Archives: The Bolshevik Years. Brooklyn, N. Y.: Tėvų Pranciškonų spaustuvė, 1952.

Purickis, J[uozas]. "Seimų laikai" (The Period of the *Seimas*), in *Pirmasis nepriklausomos Lietuvos dešimtmetis, 1918-1928.* The First Decade of Independent Lithuania, 1918-1928. 2nd ed. London: Nida, 1955, Vol. I, pp. 128-173.

Raštikis, Stasys. *Kovose dėl Lietuvos: kario atsiminimai.* In the Struggles for Lithuania: Memoirs of a Soldier. 2 vols. Los Angeles: Lietuvių Dienos, 1956-1957.

Raud, V. *The Smaller Nations in World's Economic Life.* London: P. S. King and Staples, Limited, n.d.

Rūkas, Antanas ed. *Mykolas Sleževičius.* Chicago: Terra, 1954.

Šalkauskis, Stasys. "Katalikiškosios pasaulėžiūros reikšmė Lietuvos ateičiai" (The Significance of the Catholic World View for Lithuania's Future), in *Krikščionybė Lietuvoje: praeitis, dabartis, ateitis.* Kaunas: Šv. Kazimiero draugija, 1938.

Šapoka, Adolfas. *Vilnius in the Life of Lithuania.* Translated by E. J. Harrison. Toronto: Lithuanian Association of the Vilnius Region, 1962.

Šarmaitis, R. ed. *Revoliucinis judėjimas Lietuvoje.* Revolutionary Movement in Lithuania. Vilnius: Partijos istorijos institutas prie LKP CK 1957.

————. *Karolis Požela: Raštai.* Karolis Požela: Writings. Vilnius: Mintis, 1966.

Senn, Alfred Erich. *The Emergence of Modern Lithuania.* New York: Columbia University Press, 1959.

————. *The Great Powers, Lithuania, and the Vilna Question: 1920-1928.* Leiden: E. J. Brill, 1966.

Simutis, Anicetas. *The Economic Reconstruction of Lithuania After 1918.* New York: Columbia University Press, 1942.

Skipitis, Rapolas. *Nepriklausoma Lietuva: atsiminimai.* Independent Lithuania: Memoirs. Chicago: Privately printed, 1967.

Škirpa, Kazys. "Pakeliui su Mykolu Sleževičium" (On the Road with Mykolas Sleževičius), in Antanas Rūkas ed., *Mykolas Sleževičius.* Chicago: Terra, 1954.

Šliogeris, Vaclovas. *Antanas Smetona: žmogus ir valstybininkas.* Antanas Smetona: Man and Statesman. Sodus, Mich.: Juozas J. Bachunas, 1966.

Smetona, Antanas. *Vienybės gairėmis.* For Unity. Kaunas: Spindulio b-vė, 1930.

————. *Šviesos takais.* On the Paths of Light. Kaunas: Spindulio b-vė, 1930.

————. *Pasakyta parašyta, 1927-1934.* Spoken Written, 1927-1934. Kaunas: Pažanga, 1935.

Šopa, E. "Buržuazinės diktatūros nuvertimas ir Lietuvos įstojimas į Tarybų Sąjungą" (The Downfall of the Bourgeois Dictatorship and Lithuania's Entrance into the Soviet Union), in J. Jurginis ed., *Lietuvos TSR istorijos bruožai.* Aspects of the History of the Lithuanian SSR. Kaunas: Šviesa, 1965.

Stimburys, J. *Kito gyvenimo neturiu.* I Have No Other Life. Vilnius: Valstybinė grožinės literatūros leidykla, 1960.

Sudavičius, B. *LKP kova už darbininkų klasės vienybę, 1934-1937.* The Struggle of the CPL for the Unity of the Working Class, 1934-1937. Vilnius: Valstybinė politinės ir mokslinės literatūros leidykla, 1961.

Tarulis, Albert N. *Soviet Policy Toward the Baltic States, 1918-1940.* Notre Dame, Indiana: University of Notre Dame Press, 1959.

Ten Years of Lithuanian Economy. A Report Prepared by the Chamber of Commerce, Industry and Crafts. Kaunas, 1938.

Tiškevičius, K. "Fašistinės santvarkos krizė Lietuvoje tarybų valdžios atkūrimo išvakarėse, 1938-1940 m." (The Crisis of the Fascist Regime in Lithuania on the Eve of the Restoration of Soviet Government, 1938-1940), in J[uozas] Jurginis, R[omas] Šarmaitis, and J[uozas] Žiugžda eds., *Už socialistinę Lietuvą.* For a Socialist Lithuania. Vilnius: Valstybinė politinės ir mokslinės literatūros leidykla, 1960.

Valuckas, Andrius. *Kolektyvinė tironija.* Collective Tyranny. Kaunas: Valstybinė leidykla, 1943.

Vardys, V. Stanley ed. *Lithuania Under the Soviets: A Portrait of a Nation, 1940-1965.* New York: Frederick A. Praeger, 1965.

X. Y. [Mykolas Römeris]. *Lietuvos sovietizacija, 1940-1941 m.* The Sovietization of Lithuania, 1940-1941. Augsburg: Lietuvos teisininkų tremtinių draugija, 1949.

Žiugžda, J[uozas]. *Lietuvos kaimo darbo žmonių kova dėl žemės buržuazijos viešpatavimo metais.* The Struggle for Land by the Working People of the Lithuanian Village in Years of Bourgeois Domination. Vilnius: Lietuvos TSR mokslų akademija, 1952.

ARTICLES

A., V. "Žvilgsnis į ateitį" (A Look into the Future), *Vairas* (Helm), December 21, 1939, pp. 942-43.

Akminis, A. "Ūkininko balsas" (Voice of a Farmer), *Šaltinis* (The Fountainhead), January 27, 1940, p. 71.

Alantas, Vyt[autas]. "Nacionalizmo baimė" (Fear of Nationalism), *Vairas*, September 21, 1939, pp. 718-20.

———. "Politinė tautos vienybė" (The Nation's Political Unity), *Vairas*, December 14, 1939, pp. 927-30.

232

————. "Tautinės kultūros problemos" (Problems of National Culture), *Vairas*, October 12, 1939, pp. 781-89.

————. "Vieningos tautos keliu" (On the Way of a United Nation), *Vairas*, June 1, 1939, pp. 389-90.

————. "Žygiuojanti tauta" (A Nation on the March), *Vairas*, June 8, 1939, pp. 430-37.

Ancevičius, Pranas. "Istorija be pagražinimų" (History Without Trimmings), *Naujienos* (News), September 14, 1960, p. 3.

Andrašiūnas, A. "Planingas tautos ūkis" (Planned National Economy), *Naujoji Romuva* (The New *Romuva*), May 28, 1939, pp. 468-74.

Angarietis, Z[igmas Antanas]. "Kaip Lietuvos komunistai taiko bendro fronto taktiką" (How the Lithuanian Communists Apply the Tactics of the United Front), *Priekalas* (Anvil), no. 3 (March, 1936), pp. 129-37.

————. "Lietuvos komunistų partijos darbas VII kongreso tarimų šviesoj" (The Work of the Lithuanian Communist Party in the Light of the Decisions of the Seventh Congress), *Priekalas*, no. 10 (October, 1935), pp. 593-605.

Apanavičius, M. "Kariniai teismai—buržuazijos įrankis kovoje prieš revoliucinį judėjimą Lietuvoje fašistinio režimo metais" (Military Courts—the Instruments of the Bourgeoisie in the Struggle against the Revolutionary Movement in Lithuania During the Years of Fascist Rule), in *Lietuvos TSR Aukštųjų Mokyklų Mokslo Darbai: Teisė* (Scientific Works of the Higher Schools of the Lithuanian SSR: Law), IV (1964), 119-134.

————. "Buržuazinės Lietuvos karinių teismų klasinė prigimtis, 1926-1940" (Class Nature of Bourgeois Lithuania's Military Courts, 1926-1940), in *Lietuvos TSR Aukštųjų Mokyklų Mokslo Darbai: Teisė* (Scientific Works of the Higher Schools of the Lithuanian SSR: Law), V (1965), 155-164.

Augaitis, V. "Tiesiu keliu" (On a Straight Road), *Vairas*, August 10, 1939, pp. 625-26.

Aurimas, A. "Mūsų ekonominės aktualijos" (Our Economic Topics of the Day), *Tautos Ūkis* (National Economy), April 27, 1940, pp. 299-301.

B., R. "Priežastys ir priemonės" (Causes and Means), *Lietuvos Aidas* (Echo of Lithuania), February 8, 1940, p. 3.

Balsys, Vl[adas]. "Dėl priemonių, kovojant su darbininkų bėgimu iš kaimo" (Concerning the Means in Combating Labor Flight from the Village), *Tautos Ūkis*, June 3, 1939, pp. 487-88.

Baranauskas, P. "Reikalinga žemės ūkio priežiūra" (The Need for Supervision of Agriculture), *Tautos Ūkis*, February 3, 1940, pp. 81-82.

Bartkus, K. "Privatinė ir visuomeninė iniciatyva" (Private and Public Initiative), *Talka* (Collective Action), September 1, 1939, pp. 352-54.

————. "Tiesos beieškant" (In Quest of Truth), *Talka*, June 15, 1939, pp. 244-45.

Barzda, P. P. "Konsolidacijos reikalas lietuvių ūkinėje veikloje" (The Question of Consolidation in Lithuanian Economic Activities), *Talka*, May 20, 1940, pp. 281-82.

Barzdukas, St[asys]. Letter to the Editor, *Naujoji Romuva*, April 30, 1939, pp. 371-72.

Bilevičius, E. "Vienu Lietuvos KP istorijos klausimu" (Concerning one Question in the History of the CP of Lithuania), *Komunistas* (The Communist), no. 11 (November, 1965), pp. 51-54.

"Birželio 13" (June 13), *Vairas*, June 8, 1939, p. 401.

Biržys, Jonas. "Gamybinė ir kita Raseinių kooperacija" (Production and Other Cooperatives in Raseiniai), *Talka*, April 15, 1939, pp. 159-60.

————. "Kooperatinio dinamizmo siekiant" (In Quest of Cooperative Dynamism), *Talka*, June 1, 1939, pp. 222-23.

Brizgys, V[incentas]. "Katalikai pasenusiojo pavojaus akyvaizdoje" (The Catholics in the Presence of an Antiquated Danger), *Šaltinis*, June 10, 1939, p. 389.

————. "Neužtraukime Lietuvai gėdos!" (Let Us Not Put Lithuania to Shame!), *Šaltinis*, June 17, 1939, pp. 405-406.

Bulvičius, Vyt[autas]. "Mažosios valstybės pasaulio arenoje" (The Small States in World Arena), *Karys* (The Warrior), June 8, 1939, pp. 675-78.

Cesevičius, D[omas]. "Kalbos ir nuotaikos" (Speeches and Tempers), *Vairas*, May 4, 1939, pp. 321-22.

————. "Moderninė tautinė valstybė" (The Modern Nation-State), *Lietuvos Aidas*, January 11, 1940, pp. 1, 6-7.

————. "Mūsų politinės sąmonės evoliucija" (The Evolution of Our Political Thought), *Vairas*, June 8, 1939, pp. 402-409.

————. "Po deklaracijos" (After the Declaration), *Vairas*, April 14, 1939, pp. 273-74.

————. "Rūpesčiai ir viltys" (Worries and Hopes), *Vairas*, March 30, 1939, pp. 237-38.

———. "Tautiškumo perspektyvos" (The Perspectives of National-Mindedness), *Vairas*, November 30, 1939, pp. 895-97.
———. "Vienybė" (Unity), *Vairas*, April 6, 1939, pp. 257-58.
Česnavičius, V. "Z. Angarietis apie buržuazinės Lietuvos ekonominį vystymąsi" (Z. Angarietis on the Economic Development of Bourgeois Lithuania), in *Lietuvos TSR Aukštųjų Mokyklų Mokslo Darbai: Ekonomika* (Scientific Works of the Higher Schools of the Lithuanian SSR: Economics), VI, Part 1 (1965), 5-16.
Cieska, Ip. "Darbo inteligentija" (The Labor Intelligentsia), *Vilniaus Balsas* (Voice of Vilnius), July 2, 1940, p. 3.
Cylius, A. "Tautos ūkio uždaviniai gyvenamuoju momentu" (The Tasks of National Economy at the Present Moment), *Tautos Ūkis*, June 29, 1940, p. 457.
Dagilis, A. "Jaunime, suprask senuosius" (Young People, Understand the Elders), *Talka*, June 1, 1939, pp. 223-24.
Dagys, J. "Žemės ūkių skaidymasis buržuazinėje Lietuvoje" (Fragmentation of Farms in Bourgeois Lithuania), in *Lietuvos TSR Aukštųjų Mokyklų Mokslo Darbai: Ekonomika* (Scientific Works of the Higher Schools of the Lithuanian SSR: Economics), V (1965), 127-133.
Darbėnas, Alb. "Visuomeninio aktyvumo versmės" (The Sources of Public Activity), *Naujoji Romuva*, June 25, 1939, pp. 505-508.
Daugaila, A. "Pramonės priežiūra" (The Supervision of Industry), *Vairas*, December 14, 1939, pp. 931-33.
Dauguvietis, B. "Įspūdžiai ir pastabos" (Impressions and Comments), *Jaunoji Karta* (Younger Generation), March 24, 1939, p. 282.
Daunys, A. "Kaimas ir kooperatyvai" (The Village and the Cooperatives), *Talka*, January 21, 1940, p. 33.
"Deklaracija" (Declaration), *Bendras Žygis* (Joint Action), January 8, 1939, pp. 1-2.
Dirmeikis, B[ronius] T[omas]. "Būtinos sąlygos dabarčiai" (Indispensable Conditions for the Present Time), *Vairas*, May 18, 1939, pp. 353-55.
———. "Entuziazmas ar blaškymasis" (Enthusiasm or Vacillation), *Vairas*, April 14, 1939, pp. 277-79.
———. "Gyvenimas be pasaulėžiūros" (Life Without a World View), *Vairas*, June 22, 1939, pp. 468-71.
———. "Pakilo kaip sakalas" (Took off Like a Falcon), *Vairas*, August 17, 1939, pp. 341-42.

―――. "Seimas 1938 m. konstitucijoj" (The Diet in the Constitution of 1938), *Vairas*, May 11, 1939, pp. 339-42.

―――. "Stiprybės beieškant" (In Quest of Strength), *Vairas*, April 20, 1939, pp. 289-91.

―――. "Tarp dviejų klausimų (Between Two Problems), *Vairas*, July 6, 1939, pp. 497-502.

―――. "Tautos atstovybė" (National Representation), *Vairas*, April 27, 1939, pp. 305-07.

―――. " 'Vėl nereali teorija' " (Again an Unreal Theory), *Vairas*, June 1, 1939, pp. 387-89.

―――. "Vyriausybė 1938 m. konstitucijoj" (The Executive in the Constitution of 1938), *Vairas*, May 4, 1939, pp. 324-26.

Dominas, St. "Organizacijų reikalai" (The Affairs of Organizations), *Vairas*, March 30, 1939, pp. 252-53.

Elsbergas, St[asys]. "Žemės reforma Lietuvoje" (Land Reform in Lithuania), *Židinys* (Hearth), no. 2 (February, 1940), pp. 193-206.

G., P. "Tarnautojų darbo sąlygos" (The Employees' Conditions of Work), *Talka*, April 15, 1939, pp. 152-53.

Galinis, K. [Kazimieras Nausėdas]. "Reikia apsispręsti" (It Is Necessary to Make Up Our Minds), *Vairas*, August 24, 1939, pp. 671-72.

Galvanauskas, Gediminas. "Steigtinas ūkiui tirti institutas" (The Case for an Institute of Economic Research), *Tautos Ūkis*, September 2 to September 23, 1939 (serialized in a weekly journal).

Gdr. Alg. "Išganymas ir gundymai" (Salvation and Temptations), *Karys*, December 14, 1939, pp. 1453-55.

Giedrimas, R. "Tautinė bazė" (The National Base), *Vairas*, October 5, 1939, pp. 746-48.

Giedrys, V. K. "Įvykių atmosferoje" (In the Atmosphere of Events), *Vairas*, September 28, 1939, pp. 730-32.

―――. "Režimų pastovumas" (The Stability of Regimes), *Vairas*, August 3, 1939, pp. 617-19.

Girbinis, A. "Steponas Kairys," *Mintis* (The Thought), no. 1 (February, 1939), pp. 5-12.

Girnius, Juozas. "A Glimpse Into Polish-Lithuanian Relations," *Lituanus*, no. 3 (September, 1957), pp. 9-14.

Glemža, J[onas]. "Kooperatyvų uždaviniai gyvenamuoju momentu" (The Tasks of the Cooperatives at the Present Time), *Talka*, November 15, 1939, pp. 473-76.

236

G-nas, A. "Suvažiavimą prisiminus" (Recollections of the Convention), *Talka*, April 1, 1939, pp. 127-28.

Gobis, J[uozas]. "Apie patriotizmą" (On Patriotism), *Draugija* (Society), May 15, 1939, pp. 507-512.

———. "Apie savos valstybės laisvės vertę" (On the Worth of Freedom of One's Own State), *Draugija*, March 30, 1939, pp. 361-65.

———. "Mažosios tautos dabartinio karo akivaizdoje" (The Small Nations in the Presence of the Current War), *Draugija*, May 5, 1940, pp. 437-40.

———. "Tauta ir jos likimas" (The Nation and its Fate), *Draugija*, April 15, 1939, pp. 409-414.

———. "Vilnius, Lietuva ir SSSR" (Vilnius, Lithuania, and the USSR), *Draugija*, December 21, 1939, pp. 1224-25.

Gruodis, D. "Sąlygos darbo kultūrai kelti" (Conditions for Promoting the Culture of Labor), *Vairas*, May 18, 1939, pp. 361-62.

Institute of Party History. "Lietuvos komunistų partijos istorijos apybraiža" (A Sketch of the History of the Communist Party of Lithuania), *Komunistas*, January, 1967, to April, 1968 (serialized in a monthly journal).

Jablonskis, S. "Linų prekybą nauju keliu pasukus" (After the Flax Trade Was Turned in a New Direction), *Talka*, December 15, 1939, pp. 522-23.

Jakubauskas, S[tasys]. "Dėl žemės reformos gilinimo" (Concerning the Intensification of Land Reform), *Vairas*, May 4, 1939, pp. 323-24.

———. "Žemės ūkio politika" (Farm Policies), *Vairas*, November 9, 1939, pp. 846-47.

"Jaunosios Lietuvos Sąjungos ateities darbo gairės, priimtos rajonų, apylinkių ir skyrių vadų suvažiavime kovo 19" (Outlines of Future Work of the Union of Young Lithuania, Adopted on March 19 at the Convention of Regional, District, and Chapter Leaders), *Jaunoji Karta*, March 24, 1939, pp. 280-81.

Juodikis, J. "Kai kurie bruožai iš finansų politikos" (Some Features from the Fiscal Policies), *Vairas*, December 21, 1939, pp. 943-45.

K., J. "Klaipėdos krašto netekus" (After the Loss of the Klaipėda Territory), *Talka*, April 1, 1939, pp. 123-24.

K[aralius], Pr. "Nacionalinės lietuvių bendruomenės ugdymas" (Promoting the Growth of a Lithuanian National Community) *Tautos Mokykla* (The Nation's School), June 1, 1939, pp. 246-50.

Karvelis, P[etras]. "Aktualieji mūsų politikos ir ūkio reikalai" (Our

Political and Economic Topics of the Day), *XX Amžius* (Twentieth Century), July 7, 1939, p. 3.

Katilius, J. "Ką naujo davė 1939 metai socialinėj srity" (What New [Accomplishments] Has the Year 1939 Brought About in the Social Field), *XX Amžius*, December 30, 1939, p. 4.

———. "Viešoji pagalba" (Public Aid), *XX Amžius*, December 19, 1939, p. 3.

Keliuotis, J[uozas]. "Šiandieninė epocha ir jaunuomenės misija" (The Contemporary Epoch and the Mission of the Young People), *Naujoji Romuva*, November 12, 1939, pp. 797-800.

Kondrotas, A. "Žemės ūkis ir bedarbiai" (Agriculture and the Unemployed), *Lietuvos Aidas*, February 22, 1940, p. 3.

Kr., B. "Į tikrovę pažvelgus" (After Looking at Reality), *Talka*, December 1, 1939, pp. 508-10.

Krėvė, Vincas. "Pasikalbėjimas Maskvoje su V. Molotovu" (Conversation with V. Molotov in Moscow), *Aidai* (Echoes), no. 3 (March, 1953), pp. 122-31.

Krikščiūnas, J[urgis]. "Dabartinė žemės ūkio šakų padėtis ir artimiausieji uždaviniai" (The Present Condition of the Branches of Agriculture and the Immediate Tasks), *Tautos Ūkis*, May 6, 1939, pp. 393-94.

———. "Kaip reikėtų vykdyti Vilniaus krašte žemės reformą" (How the Land Reform Should be Carried Out in the Vilnius Territory), *Tautos Ūkis*, March 23, 1940, pp. 219-21.

———. "Kiek nukentėjo mūsų žemės ūkis, atskyrus Klaipėdos kraštą" (What Losses Has Our Agriculture Sustained After the Detachment of the Klaipėda Area), *Tautos Ūkis*, April 1, 1939, pp. 291-93.

———. "Kokio didumo ūkiai—stambūs, vidutiniai ar smulkūs—našiausi" (What Size Farms—Large, Medium, or Small—Are Most Productive), *Tautos Ūkis*, January 27, 1940, pp. 59-61.

Kulvičius, V. "LKP gimimas" (The Birth of the CPL), *Tiesa* (Truth), October 1, 1968, p. 2.

Kulvis, P. "Kooperacija, spauda ir visuomenė" (The Cooperation, the Press, and the Public), *Talka*, May 15, 1939, pp. 196-97.

Kupraitis, P. "Kokia Lietuva?" (What Sort of Lithuania?), *Studentų Žodis* (The Students' Word), no. 3 (March, 1939), pp. 51-53.

"Lietuvos ateities santvarkos pagrindai" (The Bases of Lithuania's Future Form of Government), *Žygis* (Action), December 17, 1938, pp. 7, 10-11.

"Lietuvos bažnytinės provincijos vyskupų laiškas" (Letter by the Bishops of the Lithuanian Ecclesiastical Province), *Tiesos Kelias* (The Road of Truth), no. 6 (June, 1940), pp. 23-28.

"Lietuvos vyskupų komisijos memorandumas dėl santuokos įstatymo projekto" (A Memorandum by a Commission of Lithuanian Bishops Concerning the Bill on Marriage), *Draugija*, April 20, 1940, pp. 45-49.

"LKP atstovo drg. Adomo kalba KJS VI kongrese" (Speech by the CPL Representative Comrade Adomas Before the Sixth Congress of the Union of Communist Youth), *Priekalas*, no. 1 (January, 1936), pp. 13-20.

Lipčius, M[ikalojus]. "Nepaprastų valstybės išlaidų vaidmuo tautos ūkyje" (The Role of the Extraordinary State Expenditures in the Nation's Economy), *Tautos Ūkis*, March 9, 1940, pp. 183-85.

Lukošaitis, A. "Kokio dydžio žemės ūkiai mums naudingiausi?" (What Size Farms Are Most Beneficial to Us?), *Tautos Ūkis*, January 20, 1940, pp. 39-40.

M., V. "Nueitas kelias" (The Road Traversed), *Vairas*, April 6, 1939, pp. 259-60.

Maceina, A[ntanas]. "Tauta ir valstybė" (The Nation and the State), *Naujoji Romuva*, March 19, 1939, pp. 227-30.

————. "Tautinis auklėjimas nutautintoje Vilniaus aplinkoje" (National Upbringing in Denationalized Vilnius Surroundings), *Lietuvos Mokykla* (The Lithuanian School), no. 1 (January, 1940), pp. 3-15.

————. "Valstybė ir pasaulėžiūra" (The State and the World View), *XX Amžius*, July 20 to July 22, 1939 (serialized in a daily newspaper).

Mačys, V. "Reikalinga prekybos įmonių steigimo priežiūra" (The Need for Supervision of the Establishment of Trading Firms), *Tautos Ūkis*, May 20, 1939, pp. 438-40.

Maiminas, J. "Apie kapitalizmo vystymosi Lietuvos žemės ūkyje kelius" (On the Ways of Capitalist Development in Lithuania's Agriculture), in *Vilniaus Valstybinio V. Kapsuko Vardo Universiteto Mokslo Darbai: Ekonomika* (Scientific Works of the V. Kapsukas State University of Vilnius: Economics), I (1960), 99-110.

Marcelis, A. "Dėl padėties Lietuvos komunistų partijoje po fašistinio perversmo" (On the State of the Communist Party of Lithuania After the Fascist Coup), *Komunistas*, no. 8 (August, 1966), pp. 68-71.

————. "Kovoje prieš fašistinę diktatūrą" (In the Struggle Against the Fascist Dictatorship), *Tiesa*, December 10, 1968, p. 2.

Masiliūnas, K[azimieras]. "Menas ir valstybė" (Art and State), *Vairas*, June 8, 1939, pp. 410-13.

Medelis, R[omualdas]. "Kariškas parengimas pr. mokykloje" (Military Training in Primary Schools), *Tautos Mokykla*, May 1, 1939, p. 191.

Miknevičius, J. "Steigtinas ūkio racionalizacijos institutas" (The Case for an Institute to Rationalize the Economy), *Tautos Ūkis*, January 13, 1940, pp. 22-23.

"Mūsų vyriausybė apie kooperaciją" (Our Government on Cooperation), *Talka*, April 15, 1939, p. 147.

Nasvytis, A. "Mūsų pramonės racionalizavimas" (Rationalization of Our Industry), *Tautos Ūkis*, March 16, 1940, pp. 202-03.

Nausėdas, K[azimieras]. "Tauta 1938 metų konstitucijoj" (The Nation in the Constitution of 1938), *Vairas*, May 25, 1939, pp. 371-73.

Orintaitė, P[etronėlė]. "Liet. charakterio bruožai" (Traits of the Lithuanian Character), *Naujoji Romuva*, April 23, 1939, pp. 340-41.

P., J. "Lietuvos ūkių skaičius ir jų dydis" (The Number of Lithuanian Farms and Their Size), *Žemės Ūkis* (Agriculture), no. 7 (July, 1931), pp. 429-32.

Packevičius, J. "Mąstymas gegužės pirmajai" (Contemplation of the First of May), *Šaltinis*, May 4, 1940, pp. 257-58.

Paginevietis, A. "Tarno balsas" (Voice of a Servant), *Šaltinis*, February 10, 1940, p. 98.

Pakalnis. "Lietuvos ūkio 1939 metų apžvalginiai metmens" (A Survey of Lithuania's Economy in 1939), *XX Amžius*, December 30, 1939, p. 4.

[Paknys, Juozas]. "Lietuvos ūkio raida 1939 m." (The Course of Lithuanian Economy in 1939), *Tautos Ūkis*, March 9, 1940, pp. 179-83.

Pakštas, Kazys. "National and State Boundaries," *Lituanus*, no. 3 (September, 1959), pp. 67-72.

Palčiauskas, K. "Verslo pelno mokesčio įstatymo projektas" (The Tax Bill on Profit from Trade), *Talka*, April 1, 1939, pp. 128-29.

Paleckis, Justas. "Gimė nauja Lietuva" (A New Lithuania Was Born), *Tiesa*, July 21 and July 22, 1967, pp. 2-3.

Pauliukonis, V. "Kooperacijos įaugimas į valstybinio monopolistinio kapitalizmo sistemą buržuazinėje Lietuvoje" (Incorporation of the Cooperatives into the System of State-Monopolistic Capitalism in Bourgeois Lithuania), in *Lietuvos TSR Aukštųjų Mokyklų Mokslo*

Darhai: Ekonomika (Scientific Works of the Higher Schools of the Lithuanian SSR: Economics), II (1962), 89-110.

Pavilonis, Vl. "Buržuazinio demokratinio režimo Lietuvoje klausimu" (On the Question of the Bourgeois-Democratic Regime in Lithuania), in *Lietuvos TSR Aukštųjų Mokyklų Mokslo Darbai. Teisė* (Scientific Works of the Higher Schools of the Lithuanian SSR: Law), VI (1966), 29-42.

Pikčilingis, J[onas]. "Darbas ir dabartis" (Work and the Present Time), *Vairas*, April 27, 1939, pp. 316-17.

————. "Idėjiniai pagrindai Lietuvos socialinei politikai" (The Theoretical Bases for Lithuania's Social Policies), *Vairas*, June 8, 1939, pp. 413-16.

————. "Viešosios labdaros etika socialinės pagalbos įstatymo projekte" (Ethics of Public Charity in the Social Assistance Bill), *Vairas*, December 7, 1939, pp. 910-12.

————. "Žmoniškumo variantai" (The Variants of Humaneness), *Vairas*, November 9, 1939, pp. 851-54.

Povilavičius, St. "Politinių srovių vienybė" (The Union of Political Movements), *Vairas*, May 25, 1939, pp. 376-77.

Povilonis, J. "Moksleiviai ir 'poniškumas' " (Pupils and "Lordliness"), *Tautos Mokykla*, April 15, 1939, p. 167.

Ragevičius, M. "Kooperatyvų revizavimas-instruktavimas" (The Auditing-Instructing of Cooperatives), *Talka*, June 15, 1939, pp. 260-64.

Raila, St. "Angelaičiai" (The Little Angels), *Draugija*, March 30, 1939, pp. 406-407.

Raistys, J. "Lietuvos ūkio keliai" (The Ways of Lithuanian Economy), *Vairas*, April 20, 1939, pp. 295-97.

Ramutis, An. "Lietuvos darbininkų padėtis ir jų kova 1935 m." (The State of Lithuanian Workers and Their Struggle in 1935), *Priekalas*, no. 5 (May, 1936), pp. 284-91.

Rastenis, V[incas]. "Faktai ir norai" (Facts and Wishes), *Vairas*, May 18, 1939, pp. 355-57.

————. "Kūryba ir griovyba" (Production and Destruction), *Vairas*, June 29, 1939, pp. 483-85.

————. "Reikia, bet ir užtenka" (Necessary and Sufficient), *Vairas*, June 8, 1939, pp. 437-40.

————. "Tautininkų s-ga seimo tribūnoj" (The Nationalist Union on the Rostrum of the Diet), *Vairas*, June 22, 1939, pp. 471-74.

———. "Vingiai aiškėja" (The Sinuosities Become Clear), *Vairas*, July 27, 1939, pp. 573-75.

Razma, Just[inas]. "Nepateisinti lūkesčiai ir propaganda" (Unfulfilled Expectations and Propaganda), *Vairas*, April 27, 1939, pp. 307-309.

Razma, Pr. "Auklėjimas ir švietimas mūsų kariuomenėje" (Training and Education in Our Army), *Lietuvos Aidas*, April 17, 1940, p. 5.

Rudys, Bronius. "Klaipėdos uosto laisvoji zona" (The Free Zone of the Port of Klaipėda), *Tautos Ūkis*, April 1, 1939, pp. 295-96.

———. "Lietuvos jūrinės prekybos perspektyvos" (The Outlook of Lithuania's Sea Trade), *Tautos Ūkis*, April 8, 1939, pp. 318-19.

Ruseckas, Z. "Žemės ūkio darbininkų klausimu" (Concerning the Question of Agricultural Labor), *Vairas*, April 20, 1939, pp. 300-301.

S., J. "Kalėdos—vienybės ir sugyvenimo šventė" (Christmas—a Holiday of Unity and Harmony), *Karys*, December 21, 1939, pp. 1485-86.

———. "Kariuomenės šventė ir visuomenės pareigos" (The Armed Forces Day and the Duties of the Public), *Karys*, November 23, 1939, p. 1350.

Sabaliūnas, Leonas. "Prelude to Aggression," *Lituanus*, no. 3 (September, 1957), pp. 2-8.

———. "The Politics of the Lithuanian-Soviet Non-Aggression Treaty of 1926," *Lituanus*, no. 4 (December, 1961), pp. 97-102.

Šalčius, P[etras]. "Ar pagrįsti priekaištai?" (Are the Reproaches Well-Founded?), *Talka*, May 1, 1939, pp. 171-72.

———. "Ko mums trūksta?" (What Are We Short Of?), *Talka*, April 15, 1939, pp. 148-49.

———. "Kooperatinės talkos kelias—naujas Lietuvos ūkio istorijos posūkis" (The Way of Collective Cooperative Action—A New Turn in the History of Lithuanian Economy), *Talka*, January 28, 1940, pp. 51-52.

———. "Lietuvos kooperacijos judėjimas 1938-1939 metais" (The Lithuanian Cooperative Movement in 1938-1939), *Talka*, June 15, 1940, pp. 322-26.

———. "Vienybėje—galybė" (Union Is Strength), *Talka*, April 1, 1939, pp. 124-25.

Šalkauskis, St[asys]. "Ideologiniai dabarties krizių pagrindai ir katalikiškoji pasaulėžiūra" (The Ideological Bases of Contemporary Crises and the Catholic World View), *Draugija*, March 19, 1939, pp. 300-305.

————. "Socialinė ekonominė krizė" (The Social Economic Crisis), *Draugija*, April 15, 1939, pp. 414-19.

————. Letter to the Editor, *Naujoji Romuva*, April 9, 1939, pp. 315-16.

————. "Teigiamosios christianizacijos idėjos, sudarančios antidotum prieš krizines ideologijas" (The Positive Ideas of Christianization Which Constitute an Antidote Against Crisis-Ideologies), *Draugija*, July 20, 1939, pp. 736-40.

Senkus, J. "Karinė propaganda ir *Karys*" (Military Propaganda and *Karys*), *Karys*, May 22, 1939, pp. 598-99.

Šileikis, J. "Kooperatinių pieninių veikla 1939 m." (The Activities of Cooperative Dairies in 1939), *Talka*, February 28, 1940, pp. 129-31.

Šimaitis, Vikt[oras]. "Karinis rengimas mokyklose" (Military Training in Schools), *Ateitis*, no. 9 (April, 1940), pp. 524-25.

Simonavičius, V. "1940 m. socialistinės revoliucijos Lietuvoje socialinių-ekonominių prielaidų klausimu" (On the Question of Social-Economic Premises of the Socialist Revolution in Lithuania in 1940), in *Vilniaus Valstybinio V. Kapsuko Vardo Universiteto Mokslo Darbai: Ekonomika Teisė* (Scientific Works of the V. Kapsukas State University of Vilnius: Economics-Law), IV (1958), 5-31.

Škirpa, Kazys. "Vilnius—nepriklausomybės raktas" (Vilnius—Key to Independence), *Sėja* (Sowing), May, 1956, to June, 1957 (serialized in an intermittent journal).

Smailys, R. "Žodžio ir darbo gadynės" (The Ages of Word and Work), *Naujoji Romuva*, April 7, 1940, pp. 269-72.

Šmulkštys, Julius. "The Annexation of Lithuania by Soviet Union," *Lituanus*, no. 2 (March, 1955), pp. 7-9.

Stapulionis, K. "Pramonės racionalizavimas" (The Rationalization of Industry), *Tautos Ūkis*, May 13, 1939, pp. 411-13.

Stašaitis, M. "Gamyba negali būti sutrukdyta" (Production Cannot Be Delayed), *Tautos Ūkis*, July 12, 1940, p. 477.

Statkus, Jonas. "Gyvybinė sąlyga" (The Vital Condition), *Vairas*, October 19, 1939, pp. 797-98.

————. "Išminties ar nuotaikų politika?" (Politics of Wisdom or of Moods?), *Vairas*, May 11, 1939, pp. 337-39.

————. "Lietuvos neutralumas" (Lithuania's Neutrality), *Vairas*, August 24, 1939, pp. 657-58.

————. "Momento reikalavimai" (The Demands of the Moment), *Vairas*, August 31, 1939, pp. 673-74.

――. "Mūsų kelias" (Our Way), *Vairas*, July 20, 1939, pp. 557-59.

――. "Pervertinimų šviesoje" (In the Light of Reappraisal), *Vairas*, June 15, 1939, pp. 449-51.

――. "Reikia pastovios vienybės" (A Stable Unity is Needed), *Vairas*, March 30, 1939, pp. 245-46.

――. "Venkime dviejų frontų" (Let Us Avoid Two Fronts), *Vairas*, April 27, 1939, pp. 310-11.

Stonys, M. "Mokykla ir lietuviškumo ugdymas" (The School and the Promotion of Lithuanian-Mindedness), *Tautos Mokykla*, May 15, 1939, pp. 216-19.

Strazdas, Jurgis. "Visuomeniškumo krizė" (The Crisis of Public-Mindedness), *Naujoji Romuva*, March 24, 1940, pp. 245-49.

Sušinskas, Alfa. "Laisvą kraują Dievui ir savo kraštui" (Free Blood for God and One's Country), *Ateitis* (The Future), no. 9 (April, 1939), pp. 513-16.

[Sutkus, Jonas]. "Aktualieji ūkio klausimai" (The Economic Topics of the Day), *Tautos Ūkis*, July 22, 1939, pp. 579-80.

――. "Bus sudaromi planai gamybai suintensyvinti" (Plans Will Be Made to Intensify Production), *Tautos Ūkis*, April 22, 1939, pp. 339-41.

T., S. "Ūkiškos centralizacijos problema" (The Problem of Economic Centralization), *Tautos Ūkis*, May 4, 1940, pp. 339-40.

Tamošaitis, Pr. "Akcinės bendrovės 1939 m." (The Corporations in 1939), *Tautos Ūkis*, June 1, 1940, pp. 419-20.

Tarulis, Albertas. "Klaipėdos krašto pramonės netekus" (Having Lost the Klaipėda Industries), *Tautos Ūkis*, April 1, 1939, pp. 293-95.

――. "Lietuvių kultūrai saugoti įstatymas" (The Law to Protect Lithuanian Culture), *Naujoji Romuva*, December 10, 1939, pp. 908-909.

――. "Viešieji darbai ir pramoninės investicijos" (Public Works and Investments in Industry), *Tautos Ūkis*, April 13, 1940, pp. 260-62.

Tauginas, Ant[anas]. "Mokyklų vertinimas" (The Estimation of Schools), *Vairas*, June 22, 1939, pp. 465-67.

Toliušis, Z[igmas]. "Mykolui Sleževičiui mirus" (After Mykolas Sleževičius Had Died), *Naujoji Romuva*, November 19, 1939, pp. 828-29.

Tolutis, K. "Privatinės ar valstybinės mokyklos?" (Private or State Schools?), *Tautos Mokykla*, July 1, 1939, pp. 294-95.

Tomkus, J[uozas]. "Korporatyvizmo gadynės angoje" (At the Opening of the Age of Corporativism), *Vairas*, no. 2 (February, 1940), pp. 103-16.

———. "Sava valstybė" (Own State), *Vairas*, May 4, 1939, pp. 331-32.

———. "Tautos saviteiga" (The Nation's Self-Conviction), *Vairas*, April 6, 1939, pp. 265-67.

———. "Valstybė ir jos pasaulėžiūra" (The State and Its World View), *Vairas*, September 21, 1939, pp. 690-702.

Truska, L. "Visuomenės klasinės sudėties pakitimas Lietuvoje socializmo statybos metais" (Change in the Class Structure of the Lithuanian Society During the Years of Socialist Construction), in *Lietuvos TSR Mokslų Akademijos Darbai* (Works of the Academy of Sciences of the Lithuanian SSR), series A, no. 1 (1965), pp. 109-132.

Ubeika, Kaz. "Mokytojas, visuomenė ir vyresnybė" (The Teacher, the Public, and the Authorities), *Tautos Mokykla*, May 1, 1939, pp. 193-96.

"Ūkininko ir vartotojo teisės" (The Rights of Farmer and Consumer), *Talka*, June 1, 1939, pp. 221-22.

Unguraitis, J. "Ūkininkas turi veikliai dalyvauti tikslingoje ir taisyklingoje žemės ūkio gamyboje" (The Farmer Must Take an Active Part in a Purposeful and Correct Agricultural Production), *Tautos Ūkis*, March 16, 1940, p. 206.

V., A. "Viena ar dvi verslų kryptys" (One Direction in Trade, or Two), *Talka*, November 1, 1939, pp. 450-52.

Vainys, V. "Kooperacija ir darbininkai" (Cooperation and Labor), *Talka*, March 30, 1940, pp. 192-94.

Vaitiekūnas, L. "Auklėjimas ir švietimas 1938 m. konstitucijoje" (Upbringing and Education in the Constitution of 1938), *Vairas*, June 1, 1939, pp. 385-87.

Valiukėnas, A[ntanas]. "Privatinės mokyklos" (Private Schools), *Vairas*, May 11, 1939, pp. 342-43.

———. "Tautininkų ir jaunalietuvių suvažiavimas" (The Convention of the Nationalists and the Young Lithuanians), *Vairas*, November 30, 1939, pp. 899-900.

———. "Už vienybės uždangų" (Behind the Curtains of Unity), *Vairas*, April 14, 1939, pp. 280-81.

Valsonokas, R. "Ūkiniai padariniai, atskyrus Klaipėdos kraštą" (Economic Consequences After the Detachment of the Klaipėda Territory), *Tautos Ūkis*, April 8, 1939, pp. 317-18.

"Valstybės biudžetas seime" (State Budget in the *Seimas*), *Vairas*, June 15, 1939, pp. 451-57.

Vasinauskas, P. "Gabūs žmonės kooperacijoje" (Able People in Cooperation), *Talka*, April 1, 1939, pp. 125-26.

Vazalinskas, V. "Tautos gerovės besiekiant" (In Quest of National Well-Being), *Naujoji Romuva*, February 4, 1940, pp. 77-79.

————. "Ūkinės centralizacijos klausimu" (On the Question of Economic Centralization), *Tautos Ūkis*, May 11, 1940, pp. 363-65.

————. "Žemės reformos klausimu" (On the Question of Land Reform), *Naujoji Romuva*, November 26, 1939, pp. 845-49.

Venckus, A. "Prekybinės kooperacijos socialinis bei ekonominis vaidmuo buržuazinėje Lietuvoje" (The Social and Economic Role of the Trade Cooperatives in Bourgeois Lithuania), in *Lietuvos TSR Aukštųjų Mokyklų Mokslo Darbai: Ekonomika* (Scientific Works of the Higher Schools of the Lithuanian SSR: Economics), III, Part 2 (1963), 67-82.

Vengrys, A. "Lietuvos komunistų partija apie buržuazinės Lietuvos ekonominės raidos etapus" (The Communist Party of Lithuania on the Stages of Economic Development of Bourgeois Lithuania), in *Lietuvos TSR Aukštųjų Mokyklų Mokslo Darbai: Ekonomika* (Scientific Works of the Higher Schools of the Lithuanian SSR: Economics), IV, Part 2 (1964), 39-47.

Vileišis, V. "Ūkiniams uždaviniams ryškėjant" (While the Economic Tasks Become Clear), *Vairas*, October 19, 1939, pp. 803-805.

Vitkauskas, Vincas. "Tą neužmirštamą vasarą" (That Unforgettable Summer), *Švyturys* (Beacon), June 30 and July 15, 1960.

Ylius, K. A. "Isgirskim darbininkų balsą" (Let Us Hear the Voice of Labor), *Šaltinis*, December 16, 1939, p. 920.

Žilėnas, A. "Klasinis žemės mokesičo pobūdis Lietuvoje buržuazijos valdymo metais" (The Class Nature of the Land Tax in Lithuania During the Years of Bourgeois Rule), in *Lietuvos TSR Aukštųjų Mokyklų Mokslo Darbai: Ekonomika* (Scientific Works of the Higher Schools of the Lithuanian SSR: Economics), V, Part 1 (1964), 23-42.

SPEECHES

Cesevičius, Domas. A speech of April 14 read to Nationalist and Young Lithuanian leaders meeting in Kaunas, *Lietuvos Aidas*, April 16, 1940, pp. 1 and 3.

———. A speech of March 10 given to the Nationalist leaders of the Vilkaviškis district, *Lietuvos Aidas*, March 11, 1940, p. 3.

Gedvilas, Mečys. An address to the nation broadcast on June 21, *Lietuvos Ūkininkas* (The Lithuanian Farmer), June 27, 1940, p. 1.

Jokantas, Kazimieras. A speech of December 28 read before a teachers' convention, *Tautos Mokykla*, January 1, 1940, pp. 3-4.

Merkys, Antanas. A speech before a plenary meeting of the Chamber of Commerce, Industry, and Crafts, *Lietuvos Aidas*, May 8, 1940, pp. 1 and 10.

———. An address to the nation broadcast on June 16, *Lietuvos Žinios* (News of Lithuania), June 17, 1940, p. 10.

Mickis, Matas. A message to the nation's farmers broadcast on June 22, *Lietuvos Ūkininkas*, June 27, 1940, p. 1.

Paleckis, Justas. An address to the nation broadcast on June 18, *Lietuvos Ūkininkas*, June 20, 1940, p. 3.

———. An address to the nation broadcast on July 14, *Lietuvos Žinios*, July 15, 1940, p. 1.

Skučas, Kazys. A speech of March 7 delivered at the Officers' Club, *Lietuvos Aidas*, March 8, 1940, pp. 1-2.

Smetona, Antanas. A speech in *Seimas* read on November 29, *XX Amžius*, November 30, 1939, pp. 1 and 4.

———. A message observing the twentieth anniversary of the establishment of the Union of *Šauliai*, *Tautos Mokykla*, July 1, 1939, pp. 291-92.

———. An address of January 5 delivered before a convention of the Lithuanian Nationalist Union, *Tautos Mokykla*, January 15, 1940, pp. 35-39.

———. A radio message on the occasion of Lithuania's Independence Day, *Karys*, February 22, 1940, pp. 229-30.

———. A speech of May 18 celebrating the opening of new quarters of the Chamber of Labor, *Lietuvos Aidas*, May 20, 1940, pp. 1 and 3.

Šalčius, Petras. A speech of June 10 opening the Sixth Conference of Baltic Cooperative Societies, *Talka*, June 15, 1939, p. 247.

NEWSPAPERS AND PERIODICALS

Aidas (Echo, Vilnius), 1939.

Ateities Spinduliai (Rays of the Future, Kaunas), 1939-1940.

Ateitis (The Future, Kaunas), 1939-1940.

Balsas (Voice, Tilsit), 1929 and 1931.
Darbininkų Žodis (The Workers' Word, Kaunas), 1940.
Darbo Lietuva (Labor Lithuania, Kaunas), 1940.
Dienovidis (Midday, Kaunas), 1939.
Draugija (Society, Kaunas), 1939-1940.
XX Amžius (XX Century, Kaunas), 1939-1940.
Economic and General Bulletin (London), 1939-1940.
Ekonomika (Economics, Kaunas), 1939.
Jaunoji Karta (Younger Generation, Kaunas), 1939.
Karys (Warrior, Kaunas), 1939-1940.
Liepsnos (Flames, Marijampolė), 1939.
Lietuvos Aidas (Echo of Lithuania, Kaunas), 1939-1940.
Lietuvos Banko Biuletenis (Bulletin of the Bank of Lithuania, Kaunas),
    1939-1940.
Lietuvos Mokykla (The Lithuanian School, Kaunas), 1939-1940.
Lietuvos Statistikos Metraštis (Yearbook of Lithuanian Statistics,
    Kaunas and Vilnius), 1938-1940.
Lietuvos Ūkininkas (The Lithuanian Farmer, Kaunas), 1939-1940.
Lietuvos Žinios (News of Lithuania, Kaunas), 1940.
Mintis (Thought, Kaunas), 1939-1940.
Mūsų Laikraštis (Our Newspaper, Kaunas), 1939-1940.
Naujoji Romuva (The New *Romuva*, Kaunas and Vilnius), 1939-1940.
Naujoji Vaidilutė (The New Priestess, Kaunas), 1939-1940.
New York Times, 1939-1940.
Panevėžio Garsas (The Sound of Panevėžys, Panevėžys), 1939.
Priekalas (Anvil, Moscow), 1936.
Skautų Aidas (Echo of the Scouts, Kaunas), 1939-1940.
Statistikos Biuletenis (Bulletin of Statistics, Kaunas and Vilnius), 1939-
    1940.
Studentų Dienos (Student Days, Kaunas), 1939.
Studentų Žodis (Students' Word, Thompson, Conn.), 1939-1940.
Šaltinis (The Fountainhead, Marijampolė), 1939-1940.
Talka (Collective Action, Kaunas), 1939-1940.
Tautos Mokykla (The Nation's School, Kaunas), 1939.
Tautos Ūkis (National Economy, Kaunas), 1939-1940.
Tiesos Kelias (The Road of Truth, Kaunas), 1939-1940.
Trimitas (Trumpet, Kaunas), 1939.
Ūkininkas—Vyrų Žygiai (The Farmer—Men's Actions, Kaunas), 1939.
Vairas (The Helm, Kaunas), 1939.

Vilniaus Balsas (Voice of Vilnius, Vilnius), 1940.
Žemaičių Prietelius (The Friend of *Žemaičiai*, Telšiai), 1939.
Židinys (Hearth, Kaunas), 1939.
Žvaigždutė (Little Star, Kaunas), 1939-1940.

UNPUBLISHED MATERIAL AND OTHER SOURCES

Audėnas, Juozas. Unpublished memoirs. (Typewritten.)
———. Unpublished statement relative to Lithuanian-Soviet tension in 1939-1940. New York, N. Y., October 21, 1953.
Bielinis, Kipras. "Socialdemokratija Lietuvoje" (Social Democracy in Lithuania). Paper prepared for publication in Lithuanian Encyclopedia, So. Boston, Massachusetts.
Brazaitis, Juozas. Personal letter. October 31, 1961.
Černius, Jonas. Personal letter. November 4, 1961.
Galvanauskas, Ernestas. Personal letter. December 30, 1961.
Kardelis, Jonas. Personal letter. January 5, 1962.
Krupavičius, Mykolas. Personal letters. October 7 and November 3, 1961.
Lithuanian National Martyrological Archives. Chicago, Illinois. [This private collection preserves valuable information relative to Bolshevik terror in Lithuania.]
Mašalaitis, Vincas. Unpublished statement relative to Lithuania's occupation. Bryn Mawr, Pennsylvania, October 25, 1953.
Musteikis, Kazys. Personal letters. November 1 and November 19, 1961.
Personal interview with Juozas Audėnas. October 24, 1961.
Personal interview with Kipras Bielinis. August 31, 1961.
Personal interview with Bronius Dirmeikis. March 10, 1961.
Personal interview with Vincas Mašalaitis. October 19, 1961.
Personal interview with Vincas Rastenis. October 5, 1961.
Personal interview with Kazys Škirpa. October 10, 1961.
Personal interview with Jonas Vilkaitis. September 25, 1961.
Raštikis, Stasys. Personal letter. October 24, 1961.
Smetona, Antanas. "Pro Memoria." The President's account of the last days of his administration. July 1 to July 25, 1940. (Photostat.)

NOTES

I. DOMESTIC AFFAIRS

1. This account of events in Lithuania soon after the end of the war owes much to material contained in J[uozas] Purickis, "Seimų laikai," (The Period of the Seimas), in *Pirmasis nepriklausomos Lietuvos dešimtmetis*, 1918-1928 (The First Decade of Independent Lithuania, 1918-1928; 2nd ed., London: Nida, 1955), I, 128-173.

2. For Lithuanian election results in 1920-1936, see Appendix A.

3. Lit is the monetary unit of Lithuania. In 1939-1940 six lits equaled one United States dollar.

4. A[ntanas] Smetona, *Pasakyta parašyta, 1927-1934* (Spoken Written, 1927-1934; Kaunas: Pažanga, 1935), pp. 28-29. This source will henceforth be referred to as *Pasakyta parašyta*.

5. Ibid.

6. In 1939-1940 the individuals who sympathized with the banned Christian Democrats, the Farmers' Union, the Federation of Labor, or the nascent Lithuanian Front usually battled over interests which were common to the Catholic bloc as a whole. That is why the term "Catholic," synonymous with the aspirations of the entire bloc, rather than "Christian Democratic," associated with only one Catholic party, will be used in the succeeding chapters.

II. FOREIGN AFFAIRS

1. According to German statistics for 1911 quoted in Lithuanian documents, the area that was intended for Lithuania had 71,810 Lithu-

250

anians and 66,719 Germans. However, the town on Klaipėda had 25,000 Germans and 7,000 Lithuanians. See Lithuanian Information Bureau, *The Memel Problem* (London, n.d.), p. 4.

2. Petras Mačiulis, *Trys ultimatumai* (Three Ultimatums; New York: Darbininkas, 1962), p. 54.

3. For a detailed account of the Vilnius problem, see Alfred Erich Senn, *The Great Powers, Lithuania, and the Vilna Question: 1920-1928* (Leiden: E. J. Brill, 1966).

4. See *League of Nations Treaty Series* (Lausanne: Secretariat, 1927), LX, 152-159.

5. See *League of Nations Treaty Series* (Geneva: Secretariat, 1935), CLIV, 95-99.

6. See *Vyriausybės Žinios* (Government News), January 25, 1939, pp. 19-20.

7. See *Lietuvos Aidas* (Echo of Lithuania), January 11, 1939, p. 1.

III. THE TENETS OF MODERN LITHUANIAN NATIONALISM

1. *Vairas* (The Helm), June 8, 1939, p. 401.

2. See Antanas Smetona, *Vienybės gairėmis* (For Unity; Kaunas: Spindulio B-vė, 1930), p. x.

3. Ibid., pp. 1-2; *Tautos Mokykla* (The Nation's School), January 15, 1940, p. 37.

4. See *Pasakyta parašyta*, pp. 28-29, 65-66, 101, 280, and 323; Jonas Aleksa, *Lietuviškų gyvenimo kelių beieškant* (In Quest of Lithuanian Ways of Life; Kaunas: privately printed, 1933), p. 415; Vyt[autas] Alantas, "Politinė tautos vienybė" (The Nation's Political Unity), *Vairas*, December 14, 1939, p. 930.

5. Political independence and the urge to create, two trends intrinsic to Lithuanian nationalism of pre-World-War-I years, were sketched by a historian of political thought: "[By mid-nineteenth century] the right of the Lithuanian nation to an independent existence is being based on past traditions; the fact that the nation does exist is being strengthened by an even greater familiarity with the past and by a cultural and economic enlightenment. ... If it [that is, the nation] wants to live, it must demonstrate signs of creativity. Failing to create anything new, it would prove to be superfluous in the world and undoubtedly would have to vanish. Just as every spiritually alive

person thrusts toward a certain goal, so, too, a nation has its destiny, a historic mission." Juozas Ambrazevičius, *Lietuvių rašytojai: literatūriniai straipsniai* (Lithuanian Writers: Literary Essays; n.p.: Šv. Kazimiero Draugija, n.d.), pp. 30 and 143-144.

6. Aleksa, pp. 410 and 415.

7. *Pasakyta parašyta*, p. 315.

8. See *Tautos Mokykla*, April 15, 1939, p. 166.

9. Aleksa, pp. 159 and 398.

10. Ibid., p. 271.

11. For a discussion of the place of education in the new nation-state, see A[ntanas] Maceina, "Tauta ir valstybė" (The Nation and the State), *Naujoji Romuva* (The New *Romuva*), March 19, 1939, p. 229.

12. *Pasakyta parašyta*, p. 11.

13. Ibid., p. 327.

14. B[ronius] T[omas] Dirmeikis, "Stiprybės beieškant" (In Quest of Strength), *Vairas*, April 20, 1939, p. 291.

15. See Vyt[autas] Alantas, "Tautinės kultūros problemos" (Problems of National Culture), *Vairas*, October 12, 1939, p. 785; Maceina, p. 229.

16. Aleksa, p. 400.

17. The influence of moral factors is evidenced by the measure of moderation the Nationalists applied in domestic politics. A fact which merits attention is that not a single leading member of the Catholic-Populist opposition was liquidated during the thirteen years of Smetona's rule.

In foreign policy, the year 1939 registered two instances where morality intervened in decision-making. After the seizure of Klaipėda, Germany had offered the Lithuanians, as a partial compensation for their investments in the port town, a variety of Czechoslovak arms, including tanks and heavy artillery. Badly in need of such military equipment, the government nevertheless refused the offer on the grounds that, among other things, it would have made the Lithuanians beneficiaries in the Czechoslovak tragedy. See Kazys Škirpa, "Vilnius—nepriklausomybės raktas," (Vilnius—Key to Independence), *Sėja* (Sowing), June 1956, pp. 17-18.

Subsequent to the outbreak of the German-Polish war in September 1939 the government had considered the possibility of recapturing Vilnius from the Poles. One of two major considerations that deterred the administration from such a course was its belief that it would be immoral to attack a crushed foe. Interview with Vincas Mašalaitis, October 19, 1961.

18. Maceina, p. 229.

19. *Pasakylu parašyta*, pp. 280 281.

20. See *Lietuvos Aidas* (Echo of Lithuania), April 17, 1940, p. 5.

21. See *Tautos Mokykla*, June 1, 1939, p. 249.

22. K. Masiliūnas, "Menas ir valstybė" (Art and State), *Vairas*, June 8, 1939, p. 413.

23. B[ronius] T[omas] Dirmeikis, "Vyriausybė 1938 m. konstitucijoj" (The Executive in the Constitution of 1938), *Vairas*, May 4, 1939, p. 324.

24. *Pasakyta parašyta*, p. 116.

25. Ibid., p. 323.

26. Onetime party secretary Vincas Rastenis reminisces that, much to the dismay of many of his disciples, Antanas Smetona never produced a definitive document which could be referred to as the Nationalist creed. Instead, he was obliged to concede that Nationalists lacked a distinct set of propositions and that they had to be content with a general orientation. Interview with Vincas Rastenis, October 5, 1961; Smetona, *Pasakyta parašyta*, p. 305. One may conjecture that this was because of the President's inability to reconcile the permanence of national evolution with the conclusive nature of any statement of purposes. However, Smetona's biographer thinks that two factors deterred the President from attempting such a work: lack of time and uncertainty about the nature of Lithuania's system of government. See Aleksandras Merkelis, *Antanas Smetona: jo visuomeninė, kultūrinė ir politinė veikla* (Antanas Smetona: His Civic, Cultural, and Political Activities; New York: Amerikos lietuvių tautinė sąjunga, 1964), p. 385.

27. *Pasakyta parašyta*, pp. 101, 315, 323, and 326.

28. Stasys Šalkauskis had inferred that "modern civilization had endeavored to develop a fondness for freedom, a demand for equality, but simultaneously it was destroying that on which public order had rested, namely, authority, tradition, discipline." St[asys] Šalkauskis, "Ideologiniai dabarties krizių pagrindai ir katalikiškoji pasaulėžiūra" (The Ideological Bases of Contemporary Crises and the Catholic World View), *Draugija* (Society), March 19, 1939, p. 303. And on another occasion the Catholic writer had judged that "the modern world was unable to combine in a proper balance individual freedom and public authority, and that is why it was doomed to stagger between

anarchy and despotism." St[asys] Šalkauskis, "Teigiamosios christiani-zacijos idėjos, sudarančios antidotum prieš krizines ideologijas" (The Positive Ideas of Christianization Which Constitute an Antidote Against Crisis-Ideologies), *Draugija*, July 20, 1939, p. 739.

29. *Pasakyta parašyta*, pp. 35, 117, and 304; *Karys* (Warrior), September 7, 1939, p. 1045.

30. See *Pasakyta parašyta*, pp. 38-39, 45-46, and 323.

31. Vyt[autas] Alantas, "Žygiuojanti tauta" (A Nation on the March), *Vairas*, June 8, 1939, p. 437.

32. See letter in *Naujoji Romuva*, April 9, 1939, p. 315.

33. See letter by Stasys Barzdukas in *Naujoji Romuva*, April 30, 1939, p. 371; P[etronėlė] Orintaitė, "Liet. charakterio bruožai" (Traits of Lithuanian Character), *Naujoji Romuva*, April 23, 1939, p. 340.

34. See Šalkauskis, "Ideologiniai dabarties . . ." p. 304.

35. See *Pasakyta parašyta*, pp. 66, 323, and 326.

36. Ibid., pp. 65-66, 254, 323, 328-329.

37. Dirmeikis, "Stiprybės beieškant" p. 290.

38. *Pasakyta parašyta*, p. 39.

39. Ibid., p. 328.

40. *Lietuvos Aidas*, January 6, 1938, quoted in A. Gaigalaitė and others (eds.), *Lietuvos TSR istorija* (History of the Lithuanian SSR; Vilnius: Mintis, 1965), III, 233.

41. See Smetona *Pasakyta parašyta*, pp. 304 and 331.

42. Ibid., p. 308; see also Merkelis, p. 399.

43. The enrollment in the nation's schools for the 1939-1940 academic year was:

Schools of higher education . .	3,990
Secondary schools	40,713
Primary schools	338,460
Total	383,163

See Lithuanie, Centralinis statistikos biuras, *Annuaire statistique de la Lithuanie: 1939*, XII, 72.

44. See *Pasakyta parašyta*, pp. 328-329.

45. See Alantas, "Tautinės kultūros problemos" p. 787.

46. See *Tautos Mokykla*, May 1, 1939, p. 189.

47. See discussions of Kaunas educators in *Tautos Mokykla*, June 1, 1939, pp. 246-250; ibid., May 15, 1939, p. 214.

48. See *Jaunoji Karta* (Younger Generation), March 24, 1939, pp. 280-281.

49. Ibid., April 7, 1939, p. 322.

50. Ibid., May 19, 1939, p. 451.

51. *Lietuvos Aidas*, March 13, 1940, p. 4.

52. Antanas Maceina, "Krikščioniškasis turinys ir lietuviškoji forma" (The Christian Content and the Lithuanian Form), in *Krikščionybė Lietuvoje: praeitis, dabartis, ateitis* (Christianity in Lithuania: The Past, the Present, the Future [ed. Pranas Mantvydas] Kaunas: Šv. Kazimiero Draugija, 1938), p. 100.

53. Šalkauskis, "Teigiamosios christianizacijos . . ." p. 739.

54. See *XX Amžius* (XX Century), July 7, 1939, p. 3.

55. See Jonas Statkus, "Mūsų kelias" (Our Way), *Vairas*, July 20, 1939, p. 557. There is reason to think that one factor responsible for the Social Democrats' refusal to associate with the Catholic-Populist anti-Nationalist front was their distrust of Catholic fidelity to democracy. Interview with Jonas Vilkaitis, September 25, 1961.

56. An epithet derived from the chief export commodity.

57. See J[uozas] Keliuotis, "Šiandieninė epocha ir jaunuomenės misija" (The Contemporary Epoch and the Mission of the Young People), *Naujoji Romuva*, November 12, 1939, pp. 797-798; Jurgis Strazdas, "Visuomeniškumo krizė" (The Crisis of Public-Mindedness), *Naujoji Romuva*, March 24, 1940, p. 245; *Lietuvos Žinios* (News of Lithuania), April 4, 1940, p. 1; *Tautos Mokykla*, January 1, 1940, p. 2; *Naujoji Romuva*, April 7, 1940, p. 285; Justinas Rasma, "Nepateisinti lūkesčiai ir propaganda" (Unfulfilled Hopes and Propaganda), *Vairas*, April 27, 1939, p. 307.

58. Letter in *Naujoji Romuva*, April 9, 1939, p. 316.

59. For two poems documenting the ardor of a latent intellectual revolt, see *Kultūra* (Culture), no. 10 (1939), p. 588; *Lietuvos Žinios*, March 2, 1940, p. 12.

60. D[omas] Cesevičius, "Mūsų politinės sąmonės evoliucija" (The Evolution of Our Political Thought), *Vairas*, June 8, 1939, p. 409; V. M., "Nueitas kelias" (The Road Traversed), *Vairas*, April 6, 1939, p. 260.

61. See Domas Cesevičius, "Rūpesčiai ir viltys" (Worries and Hopes), *Vairas*, March 30, 1939, p. 238.

62. See Jonas Statkus, "Reikia pastovios vienybės" (A Stable Unity is Needed), *Vairas*, March 30, 1939, p. 246; Bronius Tomas Dirmeikis,

"Entuziazmas ar blaškymasis" (Enthusiasm or Vacillation), *Vairas*, April 14, 1939, p. 279; V. M., "Nueitas kelias," p. 260.

63. Interview with Vincas Rastenis; Kazys Škirpa, "Pakeliui su Mykolu Sleževičium" (On the Road with Mykolas Sleževičius), Antanas Rūkas, ed. *Mykolas Sleževičius*, (Chicago: Terra, 1954), p. 294; Merkelis, p. 346.

IV. THE CENTERS OF OPPOSITION

1. At this point a word of caution is in order. In the discussion of "Catholic," "Populist," or "Social Democratic" attitudes under dictatorial conditions there is danger that what is attributed to the whole may in fact characterize only a part. Furthermore, for the same reason the leading men of the several centers of opposition might at times also find it difficult to determine conclusively what constituted or conformed to their party's "general line" and what merely multiplied inconsequential deviations.

2. Vytautas Alantas, "Politinė tautos vienybė" (The Nation's Political Unity), *Vairas*, December 14, 1939, p. 929; Nationalist chairman Domas Cesevičius was also puzzled as to the form of government the Catholics favored. See *Lietuvos Aidas*, January 11, 1940, p. 6.

3. See Stasys Šalkauskis, "Katalikiškosios pasaulėžiūros reikšmė Lietuvos ateičiai" (The Significance of the Catholic World View for Lithuania's Future), in *Krikščionybė Lietuvoje: praeitis, dabartis, ateitis* (Christianity in Lithuania: The Past, the Present, the Future), ed. Mantvydas, Kaunas: Šv. Kazimiero Draugija, 1938, pp. 85-86.

4. See *XX Amžius*, January 11, 1940, p. 12.

5. Ibid., November 14, 1939, p. 10.

6. Ibid., May 4, 1940, p. 6.

7. Juozas Brazaitis, personal letter to author, October 31, 1961.

8. See J[uozas] Girnius ed., *Lietuvių enciklopedija* (Lithuanian Encyclopedia; South Boston, Massachusetts: Lietuvių enciklopedijos leidykla, 1960), XXII, 198; *Ateitis* (The Future), no. 9 (April, 1939), p. 516; *Draugija*, March 30, 1939, pp. 406-407; *Mūsų Laikraštis* (Our Newspaper), December 14, 1939, p. 16; *Naujoji Vaidilutė* (The New Priestess), no. 7 (July, 1939), p. 342.

9. See pp. 66-74.

10. Juozas Audėnas, unpublished memoirs, pp. 72-83.

11. See *Žygis* (Action), December 17, 1938, pp. 7, 10-11.

12. Professor Augustinas Voldemaras was an influential figure in Lithuanian politics of the first interwar decade. Head of the ephemeral first cabinet formed on November 11, 1918, Voldemaras also led his country's delegation to the Paris peace conference and served as Minister of Foreign Affairs in the first five cabinets. After the coup in 1926, he once more became the Prime Minister and held that post until his forced resignation on September 19, 1929. The rightist Voldemaras deprived the national minorities of some of their rights, vigorously pursued an anti-Polish policy, and endeavored to build a personal following among the younger nationalist officers who were favorably impressed by emergent Fascism.

13. See *Bendras Žygis* (Joint Action), January 8, 1939, pp. 1-2, 7, and 16.

14. See *XX Amžius*, March 30, 1939, p. 2.

15. Interview with Kipras Bielinis, August 31, 1961; Kipras Bielinis, "Socialdemokratija Lietuvoje" (Social Democracy in Lithuania), paper prepared for publication in *Lithuanian Encyclopedia*, South Boston, Massachusetts.

16. See Stasys Raštikis, *Kovose dėl Lietuvos: kario atsiminimai* (In the Struggles for Lithuania: Memoirs of a Soldier; Los Angeles: Lietuvių Dienos, 1956), I, 529.

17. See *Lietuvos Aidas*, April 17, 1940, p. 5.

18. See Benedict V. Mačiuika ed., *Lithuania in the Last 30 Years*, Human Relations Area Files, Inc., (New Haven, Connecticut, 1955), p. 58.

V. THE COMMUNIST UNDERGROUND

1. The term "nationalists" here refers to those who wished to constitute the Lithuanian people into a single independent state. It is not synonymous with Smetona's Nationalist party.

2. See S. Lopajevas, *Lietuvos komunistų partijos idėjinis ir organizacinis stiprėjimas* (The Increase in Ideological and Organizational Strength of the Communist Party of Lithuania; Vilnius: Valstybinė politinės ir mokslinės literatūros leidykla, 1964), p. 95.

3. See G. Feigelsonas and others (eds.), *Lietuvos komunistų partijos atsišaukimai* (Appeals of the Communist Party of Lithuania; Vilnius: Valstybinė politinės ir mokslinės literatūros leidykla, 1962), I, 222-229; Lopajevas, pp. 52-53; A. Gaigalaitė and others (eds.), *Lietuvos*

TSR istorija (History of the Lithuanian SSR; Vilnius: Mintis, 1965), III, 153.

4. See Gaigalaitė and others (eds.), III, 158-159.

5. Ibid., p. 163.

6. Ibid., p. 164. Leaders of the Communist Party occasionally deviated from the established tactics by suggesting to the leaders of the Social Democratic Party the advisability of cooperation between the two parties. They made overtures to that effect in August 1925, March 1933, September 1934, and at other times. Ibid., 169 and 287; J[uozas] Žiugžda ed., *Lietuvos TSR istorijos šaltiniai* (Sources for the History of the Lithuanian SSR; Vilnius: Lietuvos TSR mokslų akademija, 1961), IV, 548.

7. The argument that there was no crisis is contained in E. Bilevičius, "Vienu Lietuvos KP istorijos klausimu" (Concerning One Question in the History of the Communist Party of Lithuania), *Komunistas* (The Communist), no. 11 (November, 1965), pp. 51-54.

8. See K[onstantinas] Jablonskis and others (eds.), *Lietuvos TSR istorija* (History of the Lithuanian SSR; Vilnius: Lietuvos TSR mokslų akademija, 1958), p. 364; Žiugžda ed., IV, 354; Gaigalaitė and others (eds.), III, 264-265; R. Šarmaitis ed., *Revoliucinis judėjimas Lietuvoje* (Revolutionary Movement in Lithuania; Vilnius: Partijos istorijos institutas prie LKP CK, 1957), pp. 388-389.

9. At the time these decisions were made Lithuania had some 52,202 workers in industry, commerce, and transport, and approximately 153,764 hired agricultural laborers who permanently worked on the farms. See *Statistikos Biuletenis* (Bulletin of Statistics), no. 3 (March, 1939), p. 99; A. Musteikis ed., *Lietuvos žemės ūkis ir statistika* (Lithuanian Agriculture and Statistics); Dillingen: Žemės ūkio darbuotojų sąjunga, 1948), pp. 94-95; Jurgis Krikščiūnas, *Agriculture in Lithuania*, trans. Vikt. Kamantauskas (Kaunas: The Lithuanian Chamber of Agriculture, 1938), p. 43.

10. See *Balsas* (Voice), August 25, 1928, p. 428; *Šaltinis* (The Fountainhead), January 27, 1940, p. 75.

11. See *Liet. Komunistų Partijos V konferencijos rezoliucijos* (Resolutions of the Fifth Conference of the Communist Party of Lithuania; n.p.: LKP CK, 1934), pp. 9, 11, and 14; Žiugžda (ed.), IV, 476-480.

12. As attested to by a top Lithuanian Communist, some four months before the Comintern congress the Central Committee of the Communist Party of Lithuania had drawn up a letter which was intended to

258

pave the way for the popular front. However, for undisclosed reasons, the letter remained unpublished and nothing was done until the congress. The Central Committee termed this failure to implement its earlier decision a "political error." See Z[igmas] Angarietis, "Lietuvos komunistų partijos darbas VII kongreso tarimų šviesoj" ('l'he Work of the Communist Party of Lithuania in the Light of the Decisions of the Seventh Congress), *Priekalas* (Anvil), no. 10 (October, 1935), p. 594. Other sources indicate that the Communist Party of Lithuania began to spread the idea of a popular front as early as the spring of 1935. See V. Brazaitytė and others (eds.), *Lietuvos komunistų partijos atsišaukimai* (Appeals of the Communist Party of Lithuania; Vilnius: Valstybinė politinės ir mokslinės literatūros leidykla, 1963), IV, 49-57; Gaigalaitė and others (eds.), III, 294 and 306; S. Atamukas, *LKP kova prieš fašizmą, už tarybų valdžią Lietuvoje 1935-1940 metais* (The Struggle of the Communist Party of Lithuania Against Fascism, for the Soviet Government in Lithuania, 1935-1940; Vilnius: Valstybinė politinės ir mokslinės literatūros leidykla, 1958), pp. 55-56.

13. See Žiugžda ed., IV, 573-575.

14. For an account of Communist activities in 1918-1919, see Alfred Erich Senn, *The Emergence of Modern Lithuania* (New York: Columbia University Press, 1959), pp. 34-107.

15. See B[oleslovas] Baranauskas, *Devyniolika metų pogrindyje* (Nineteen Years in the Underground; Vilnius: Vaga, 1965), p. 162.

16. See Lopajevas, p. 31; V. Kapsukas, "Karolis Požela" in *Karolis Požela: Raštai* (Karolis Pozela: Writings), ed. R. Šarmaitis, (Vilnius: Mintis, 1966), pp. 28 and 30-31.

17. See Lopajevas, pp. 56 and 81.

18. Ibid., p. 62.

19. See *Balsas*, August 25, 1928, p. 428; ibid., September 25, 1929, p. 845; Žiugžda ed., IV, 413.

20. See report by Antanas Sniečkus quoted in A. Butkutė-Ramelienė, *Lietuvos komunistų partijos kova už tarybų valdžios įtvirtinimą respublikoje 1940-1941 m.* (The Struggle of the Communist Party of Lithuania for the Consolidation of Soviet Power in the Republic, 1940-1941; Vilnius: Valstybinė politinės ir mokslinės literatūros leidykla, 1958), pp. 166-167. However, correspondence with a prominent Communist suggests that according to new data at their disposal total membership was close to 2,000.

21. Ibid., pp. 98-99 and 168. Communist failure to attract industrial

workers is amply documented. See Andrius Valuckas, *Kolektyvinė tironija* (The Collective Tyranny; Kaunas: Valstybinė leidykla, 1943), p. 19; Žiugžda ed., IV, 634; *Šaltinis*, January 13, 1940, p. 43; interview with Jonas Vilkaitis, September 25, 1961.

22. Žiugžda ed., IV, 634 and 726.

23. See Baranauskas, p. 172.

24. Atamukas, p. 63.

25. B. Sudavičius, *LKP kova už darbininkų klasės vienybę, 1934-1937* (The Struggle of the Communist Party of Lithuania for the Unity of the Working Class, 1934-1937; Vilnius: Valstybinė politinės ir mokslinės literatūros leidykla, 1961), pp. 12-13.

26. See An. Ramutis, "Lietuvos darbininkų padėtis ir jų kova 1935 m." (The State of Lithuanian Workers and Their Struggle in 1935), *Priekalas*, no. 5 (May, 1936), pp. 284-291; *Priekalas*, no. 4 (April, 1936), pp. 253-254; Atamukas, p. 80.

27. See Communist sources quoted in Juozas Daulius [Stasys, Yla], *Komunizmas Lietuvoje* (Communism in Lithuania; Kaunas: Šviesa, 1937), pp. 89-90.

28. See "LKP atstovo drg. Adomo kalba KJS VI kongrese" (Speech by the Representative of the Communist Party of Lithuania Comrade Adomas Before the VI Congress of the Communist League of Youth), *Priekalas*, no. 1 (January, 1936), pp. 14-17.

29. See Lopajevas, p. 83; E. Dirvelė and others (eds.), *Lietuvos komjaunimas* (The Communist Youth of Lithuania; Vilnius: Vastybinė politinės ir mokslinės literatūros leidykla, 1962), p. 63.

30. The Lithuanian Red Aid was commonly referred to by its Russian abbreviation as MOPR—Mezhdunarodnaia organizatsiia pomoshchi revoliutsioneram (International Organization of Aid to Revolutionaries).

31. See Butkutė-Ramelienė, p. 174; *Balsas*, June 10, 1931, p. 342; *Priekalas*, no. 10 (October, 1936), p. 656.

32. Anna Louise Strong, *Lithuania's New Way* (London: Lawrence and Wishart Ltd., 1941), p. 26.

33. See *Priekalas*, no. 10 (October, 1936), p. 657.

34. The table does not include contributions from abroad intended for the Party. In 1927 the Party received about $10,000 from its supporters in the United States, and it is also known that it obtained some assistance in the years that followed. Figures, however, are not available. A. Beržinskaitė, *LKP veikla auklėjant Lietuvos darbo žmones proletarinio internacionalizmo dvasia, 1927-1940* (The Activities of the Communist

Party of Lithuania in Educating the Working People of Lithuania in the Spirit of Proletarian Internationalism, 1927-1940; Vilnius: Valstybinė politinės ir mokslinės litcratūros leidykla, 1962), p. 93; Gaigalaitė and others (eds.), III, 257.

35. See Atamukas, p. 178.

36. Part IV discusses the surrender of Klaipėda, and Part V deals with the return of Vilnius and the arrival of the Red Army.

37. These Lithuanians of Russian descent, goaded by the Communists, caused labor problems that delayed the work. They served as a pretext for Soviet charges that Lithuanians were guilty of sabotage. See Jonas Audrūnas [Bronius Dirmeikis] and Petras Svyrius [Vincas Rastenis], *Lietuva tironų pančiuose* (Lithuania in Chains of Tyrants; Cleveland: Lietuvai vaduoti sąjunga, 1946), I, 39; Stasys Raštikis, *Kovose dėl Lietuvos: Kario atsiminimai* (In the Struggles for Lithuania: Memoirs of a Soldier; Los Angeles: Lietuvių Dienos, 1956), I, 629 and 692; U.S. Congress, Select Committee to Investigate the Incorporation of the Baltic States into the U.S.S.R., *Hearings, Baltic States Investigation*, Part 1, 83rd Cong., 1st Sess., 1954, p. 44; Valuckas, p. 19; Audėnas, unpublished memoirs, pp. 106-107.

38. See Žiugžda ed., IV, 740-741.

39. Ibid.

40. See Baranauskas, pp. 182, 196, 218, and 220.

VI. Problems on the Land

1. See Appendix C.

2. See P. Cimbolenka, ed., *20 metų Tarybų Lietuvos liaudies ūkiui* (Twenty Years of People's Economy in Soviet Lithuania; Vilnius: Lietuvos TSR mokslų akademija, 1960), pp. 14-15; K. Meškauskas, *Tarybų Lietuvos industrializavimas* (The Industrialization of Soviet Lithuania; Vilnius: Lietuvos TSR mokslų akademija, 1960), p. 58; see Nationalist resolutions published in *Lietuvos Aidas*, January 7, 1940, p.4.

3. See Maciuika ed., *Lithuania in the Last Thirty Years*, Human Relations Area Files, Inc. (New Haven, Connecticut, 1955), p. 166.

4. See V[alerionas] Balčiūnas, *Lietuvos kaimų žemės tvarkymas istorijos, ūkio ir statistikos šviesoje* (The Organization of Lithuanian Rural Land in the Light of History, Economy, and Statistics; Kaunas: Žemės reformos valdyba, 1938), p. 101; St. Elsbergas, "Žemės reforma

Lietuvoje" (Land Reform in Lithuania), *Židinys* (Hearth), no. 2 (February, 1940), p. 194.

5. See J. Krikščiūnas, *Agriculture in Lithuania*, trans. by V. Kamantauskas (Kaunas: Lithuanian Chamber of Agriculture, 1938), p. 33; *Tautos Ūkis* (National Economy), June 1, 1940, pp. 430-431.

6. See L. Truska, "Visuomenės klasinės sudėties pakitimas Lietuvoje socializmo statybos metais" (Change in the Class Structure of Lithuanian Society During the Years of Socialist Construction), in *Lietuvos TSR Mokslų Akademijos Darbai* (Works of the Academy of Sciences of the Lithuanian SSR), series A, no. 1 (1965), p. 118.

7. See J. P., "Lietuvos ūkių skaičius ir jų dydis" (The Number of Lithuanian Farms and Their Size), *Žemės Ūkis* (Agriculture), no. 7 (July, 1931), p. 430.

8. See Elsbergas, p. 205; K. Tiškevičius, "Fašistinės santvarkos krizė Lietuvoje tarybų valdžios atkūrimo išvakarėse, 1938-1940 m." (The Crisis of the Fascist Regime in Lithuania on the Eve of the Restoration of Soviet Government, 1938-1940), in J[uozas] Jurginis, R[omas] Šarmaitis, and J[uozas] Žiugžda, eds., *Už socialistinę Lietuvą* (For a Socialist Lithuania; Vilnius: Valstybinė politinės ir mokslinės literatūros leidykla, 1960), p. 264; J. Krikščiūnas, "Kokio didumo ūkiai—stambūs, vidutiniai ar smulkūs—našiausi" (What Size Farms—Large, Medium, or Small—Are Most Productive), *Tautos Ūkis*, January 27, 1940, p. 61; A. Lukošaitis, "Kokio dydžio žemės ūkiai mums naudingiausi" (What Size Farms Are Most Beneficial to Us), *Tautos Ūkis*, January 20, 1940, p. 39; *Lietuvos Ūkininkas* (The Lithuanian Farmer), May 4, 1939, p. 3; *Panevėžio Garsas* (The Sound of Panevėžys), November 18, 1939, p. 1.

9. See Elsbergas, p. 200; *Žemės Ūkio Ministerijos metraštis, 1918-1938* (Yearbook of the Ministry of Agriculture, 1918-1938; np.: n.d.), p. 329.

10. Ibid., pp. 378-379; *Statistikos Biuletenis*, no. 1 (January, 1937), p. 33; ibid., no. 1 (January, 1938), p. 35; ibid., no. 1 (January, 1939), p. 33; ibid., nos. 5 and 6 (May-June, 1940), p. 49; Gaigalaitė and others (eds.), *Lietuvos TSR istorija* (History of the Lithuanian SSR; Vilnius: Mintis, 1965), III, 221.

11. See Balčiūnas, p. 186.

12. On January 6, 1940, the Nationalists themselves went on record as favoring the abolition of the experimental farm. See *Lietuvos Aidas*, January 7, 1940, p. 4.

13. See Elsbergas, p. 202; Butkutė-Rameliené, *Lietuvos Komunistų partijos kova už valdžios įtvirtinimą respublikoje, 1940-1941 m.* (The Struggle of the Communist Party of Lithuania for Consolidation of Soviet Power in the Republic, 1940-1941; Vilnius: Valstybinė politinės ir mokslinės literatūros leidykla, 1958), p. 113; *Lietuvos Ūkininkas,* July 6, 1939, p. 1.

14. See Balčiūnas, pp. 189-192; Elsbergas, p. 198; S. Jakubauskas, "Dėl žemės reformos gilinimo"(Concerning the Intensification of Land Reform), *Vairas,* May 4, 1939, pp. 323-324; *Lietuvos Ūkininkas,* May 9, 1940, p. 4.

15. See Krikščiūnas, *Agriculture in Lithuania,* p. 43.

16. See M[arijonas] Gregorauskas, *Tarybų Lietuvos žemės ūkis, 1940-1960* (Agriculture of Soviet Lithuania, 1940-1960; Vilnius: Valstybinė politinės ir mokslinės literatūros leidykla, 1960), p. 68; Truska, p. 123.

17. One thousand workers entered Germany illegally in the summer of 1939; figures for similar seasonal migrations into Latvia are lacking. The agreement of March 8, 1940, had authorized the Estonian government to recruit its labor force from the ranks of war refugees residing in Lithuania, but the possibility of hiring Lithuanian citizens too was not excluded. By mid-April 1940, as many as 5,000 rural workers set out for Estonia. See *Lietuvos Aidas,* June 2, 1940, p. 2; *Vilniaus Balsas* (Voice of Vilnius), April 17, 1940, p. 6; *Šaltinis,* July 8, 1939, p. 562; *Lietuvos Ūkininkas,* March 14, 1940, p. 1.

18. See A. Kondrotas, "Žemės ūkis ir bedarbiai" (Agriculture and the Unemployed), *Lietuvos Aidas,* February 22, 1940, p. 3.

19. Ibid.; *Lietuvos Ūkininkas,* March 7, 1940, p. 5.

20. *Panevėžio Garsas,* December 23, 1939, p. 4.

21. See *Vilniaus Balsas,* May 26, 1940, p. 1.

22. *Mūsų Laikraštis* (Our Newspaper, Kaunas), December 21, 1939, p. 21.

23. See *Lietuvos Aidas,* February 5, 1940, quoted in *Lietuvos Ūkininkas,* February 8, 1940, p. 3.

24. See Z. Ruseckas, "Žemės ūkio darbininkų klausimu" (Concerning the Question of Agricultural Labor), *Vairas,* April 20, 1939, p. 300.

25. See J[onas] Pikčilingis, "Idėjiniai pagrindai Lietuvos socialinei politikai" (Theoretical Bases for Lithuania's Social Policies), *Vairas,* June 8, 1939, p. 415.

26. Imports of agricultural machinery in 1939 totalled 4,699,900 lits, an increase of 26 per cent over 1938. Moreover, it was reported in

April 1940 that the Chamber of Agriculture would increase its subsidies to purchasers of agricultural machinery from 50 to 75 per cent of the total sales value. See *Tautos Ūkis*, April 6, 1940, p. 252.

27. *Lietuvos Ūkininkas*, May 9, 1940, p. 4.

28. See *Šaltinis*, January 27, 1940, p. 71.

29. See *Lietuvos Ūkininkas*, February 15, 1940, p. 9.

30. Ibid., December 7, 1939, p. 2.

31. See Vl. Balsys, "Dėl priemonių, kovojant su darbininkų bėgimu iš kaimo" (Concerning the Means in Combating Labor Flight from the Village), *Tautos Ūkis*, June 3, 1939, pp. 487-488.

32. See *Mūsų Laikraštis*, February 22, 1940, p. 13; *Lietuvos Ūkininkas*, February 8, 1940, p. 3. The government move to drive the profit-making middleman out of business also typifies the prevailing frame of mind of a large segment of rural society.

33. See *Vyriausybės Žinios* (Government News), May 6, 1940, p. 331.

34. See *Lietuvos Aidas*, March 21, 1940, p. 4; ibid., June 2, 1940, p. 2; *Lietuvos Ūkininkas*, March 7, 1940, p. 8.

VII. URBAN CONDITIONS

1. References in this essay to a study conducted by the Central Bureau of Statistics and published in Kaunas in 1937 under the title of *Résultats de l'enquête organisée en Lithuanie durant les années 1936-1937, sur les budgets de 297 familles ouvrières, d'employés et de fonctionnaires* will be minimal, for its scope is limited and insufficiently representative.

2. See *Lietuvos Aidas*, March 22, 1940, p. 1; *Lietuvos Žinios*, April 12, 1940, p. 9.

3. See *XX Amžius*, December 21, 1939, p. 7.

4. Compared with 1939, production in mid-January 1940 had decreased as follows: rubber, 50 to 70 per cent; knitwear, 50 per cent; furniture, 25 per cent; textiles, metals and machinery, candy and chocolate, 20 per cent. Four months later the outlook changed. Grain mills were reported to have increased their operations 20 per cent; textile, leather, and footwear industries were producing at their 1939 capacity; but other industries still registered a decline in production: knitwear, 25 per cent; rubber, 15 per cent; furniture, 10 to 15 per cent; candy and chocolate, 10 to 15 per cent; metals and machinery, 10 per

cent. See *Lietuvos Banko Biuletenis* (Bulletin of the Bank of Lithuania), February 20, 1940, p. 2; ibid., May 24, 1940, p. 2.

5. See *Tautos Ūkis*, June 29, 1940, p. 467.

6. See *Lietuvos Žinios*, October 10, 1939, p. 7.

7. See *Tautos Ūkis*, June 29, 1940, pp. 467-468.

8. R. Šarmaitis ed., *Revoliucinis judėjimas Lietuvoje* (Revolutionary Movement in Lithuania; Vilnius: Partijos istorijos institutas prie LKP CK, 1957), p. 578; A. Butkutė-Ramelienė, *Lietuvos Komunistų partijos kova už tarybų valdžios įtvirtinimą respublikoje, 1940-1941 m.* (The Struggle of the Communist Party of Lithuania for the Consolidation of Soviet Power in the Republic, 1940-1941, Vilnius: Valstybinė politinės ir mokslinės literatūros leidykla, 1958), p. 105.

9. See *Lietuvos Aidas*, June 2, 1940, p. 2.

10. See Butkutė-Ramelienė, p. 105; Šarmaitis ed., p. 578; *Priekalas*, no. 1 (January, 1936), p. 53.

11. See *Statistikos Biuletenis*, no. 8 (August, 1940), p. 94.

12. See *Lietuvos Aidas*, March 10, 1940, p. 4.

13. Ibid.; *XX Amžius*, March 9, 1940, p. 12.

14. See *Mūsų Laikraštis*, December 21, 1939, p. 19; ibid., February 29, 1940, p. 2; *Panevėžio Garsas*, December 2, 1939, p. 3.

15. *Šaltinis*, December 16, 1939, p. 920.

VIII. THE COOPERATIVE MOVEMENT

1. *Talka* (Collective Action), June 15, 1939, p. 247.

2. M. Ragevičius, "Kooperatyvų revizavimas-instruktavimas" (The Auditing-Instructing of Cooperatives), *Talka*, June 15, 1939, p. 261.

3. *Talka*, June 15, 1940, p. 1.

4. Ibid., August 1, 1939, p. 303.

5. See J[onas] Glemža, "Kooperatyvų uždaviniai gyvenamuoju momentu" (The Tasks of the Cooperatives at the Present Time), *Talka*, November 15, 1939, p. 473.

6. See *Tautos Ūkis*, April 27, 1940, p. 305.

7. See Jonas Biržys, "Kooperatinio dinamizmo siekiant" (In Quest of Cooperate Dynamism), *Talka*, June 1, 1939, p. 222.

8. See P. Vasinauskas, "Gabūs žmonės kooperacijoje" (Able People in Cooperation), *Talka*, April 1, 1939, pp. 125-126; K. Bartkus, "Tiesos beieškant" (In Quest of Truth), *Talka*, June 15, 1939, pp. 244-245.

9. See *Lietuvos Aidas*, April 9, 1940, p. 10.

10. *Talka*, April 30, 1940, p. 235; see also V. Pauliukonis, "Koopera-cijos įaugimas į valstybinio-monopolistinio kapitalizmo sistemą buržua-zinėje Lietuvoje" (The Incorporation of the Cooperatives into the System of State-Monopolistic Capitalism in Bourgeois Lithuania), *Lietuvos TSR Aukštųjų Mokyklų Mokslo Darbai: Ekonomika* (Works of the Higher Schools of the Lithuanian SSR: Economics), II (1962), 94; A. Venckus, "Prekybinės kooperacijos socialinis bei ekonominis vaid-muo buržuazinėje Lietuvoje" (The Social and Economic Role of the Trade Cooperatives in Bourgeois Lithuania), *Lietuvos TSR Aukštųjų Mokyklų Mokslo Darbai: Ekonomika* (Works of the Higher Schools of the Lithuanian SSR: Economics), III, Part 2 (1963), 72.

11. *Talka*, April 30, 1940, p. 235.

12. See *Talka*, June 1, 1939, pp. 223-224; P. G., "Tarnautojų darbo sąlygos" (The Employees' Conditions of Work), *Talka*, April 15, 1939, pp. 152-153.

13. See *Talka*, April 15, 1939, p. 162; *Lietuvos Ūkininkas*, December 21, 1939, p. 16.

14. Ibid.

15. *Talka*, May 30, 1940, p. 1.

16. A. G-nas, "Suvažiavimą prisiminus" (Recollections of the Con-vention), *Talka*, April 1, 1939, p. 128.

IX. THE GREAT DEBATE

1. See A[lbertas] Tarulis, "Viešieji darbai ir pramoninės investicijos" (Public Works and Investments in Industry), *Tautos Ūkis*, April 13, 1940, p. 260.

2. V. Mačys, "Reikalinga prekybos įmonių steigimo priežiūra" (The Need for Supervision of the Establishment of Trading Firms), *Tautos Ūkis*, May 20, 1939, p. 438.

3. For a detailed criticism of the development of industry and trade, see K. Stapulionis, "Pramonės racionalizavimas" (The Rationalization of Industry), *Tautos Ūkis*, May 13, 1939, pp. 411-413; J. Miknevičius, "Steigtinas ūkio racionalizacijos institutas" (The Case for an Institute to Rationalize the Economy), *Tautos Ūkis*, January 13, 1940, pp. 22-23; Mačys, pp. 438-439; Cimbolenka, ed., *20 metų Tarybų Lietuvos liaudies ūkiui* (Twenty Years of People's Economy in Soviet Lithuania;

Vilnius: Lietuvos TSR mokslų akademija, 1960), p. 21; A. Nasvytis, "Mūsų pramonės racionalizavimas" (Rationalization of Our Industry), *Tautos Ūkis*, March 16, 1940, pp. 202-203.

4. See *Talka*, November 15, 1939, p. 471.

5. See J[onas] Pikčilingis, "Viešosios labdaros etika socialinės pagalbos įstatymo projekte" (Ethics of Public Charity in the Social Assistance Bill), *Vairas*, December 7, 1939, p. 910; V[incas] Vileišis, "Ūkiniams uždaviniams ryškėjant" (While the Economic Tasks Become Clear), *Vairas*, October 19, 1939, pp. 803-805.

6. A. Andrašiūnas, "Planingas tautos ūkis" (Planned National Economy), *Naujoji Romuva*, May 28, 1939, pp. 469-470.

7. See *Talka*, June 1, 1939, pp. 221 and 228.

8. Ibid., p. 222.

9. See *Lietuvos Aidas*, May 1, 1940, p. 3.

10. See *Talka*, May 10, 1940, p. 279.

11. Ibid., November 15, 1939, pp. 471-472.

12. See *Lietuvos Žinios*, March 6, 1940, p. 1.

13. For resolutions adopted by the Nationalists on January 6, 1940, see *Lietuvos Aidas*, January 7, 1940, p. 4.

14. See *XX Amžius*, December 14, 1939, p. 3.

15. See *Lietuvos Aidas*, April 9, 1940, p. 10.

16. J.P., "Žmoniškumo variantai" (The Variants of Humaneness), *Vairas*, November 9, 1939, p. 851.

17. Ibid., pp. 851-852.

18. See interview with Finance Minister Jonas Sutkus published in *Tautos Ūkis*, July 22, 1939, p. 579; also the Finance Minister's speech in *Tautos Ūkis*, April 22, 1939, p. 339; J. Raistys, "Lietuvos ūkio keliai" (The Ways of Lithuanian Economy), *Vairas*, April 20, 1939, p. 295.

19. See *Lietuvos Ūkininkas*, July 20, 1939, p. 3; *Tautos Ūkis*, January 27, 1940, p. 76.

20. *Lietuvos Aidas*, April 8, 1940, p. 6.

21. See *Vyriausybės Žinios*, May 11, 1940, pp. 335-337.

22. See *Lietuvos Aidas*, April 8, 1940, p. 6.

23. See *Lietuvos Žinios*, April 12, 1940, p. 1; *Talka*, April 30, 1940, p. 236.

X. Authoritarianism in Retreat

1. See memorandum by Foreign Minister Stasys Lozoraitis prepared for the President in 1935 and published in A. Merkelis, *Antanas Smetona: jo visuomeninė kultūrinė ir politinė veikla* (Antanas Smetona: His Civic, Cultural and Political Activities; New York: Amerikos lietuvių tautinė sąjunga, 1964), pp. 485-489.
2. Petras Mačiulis, *Trys ultimatumai* (Three Ultimatums; New York: Darbininkas, 1962), p. 54.
3. See *Vyriausybės Žinios*, March 22, 1939, p. 74. The state of emergency in the city and district of Kaunas had been in effect since December, 1938.
4. *XX Amžius*, March 22, 1939, p. 1.
5. For an account of Catholic-Populist collaboration against the ruling Nationalists, see pp. 43-44.
6. *Lietuvos Žinios*, March 24, 1939, quoted in *Pasaulio Lietuvis* (The World Lithuanian), April 15, 1939, p. 126.
7. A reference to those who in 1918 volunteered to fight for independent Lithuania.
8. *Žemaičių Prietelius* (The Friend of *Žemaičiai*), March 23, 1939, p. 8.
9. *Lietuvos Aidas*, March 22, 1939, p. 1.
10. *Karys*, March 23, 1939, p. 378; *Lietuvos Aidas*, March 24, 1939, p. 4.
11. General Raštikis asserted that President Smetona had asked him to deliver this radio address in order to pacify the population. See S. Raštikis, *Kovose dėl Lietuvos: kario atsiminimai*; (In the Struggles for Lithuania: Memoirs of a Soldier; 2 vols; Los Angeles: Lietuvių Dienos, 1956-1957), I, 545. However, it is unlikely that the President had seen the message before it became public.
12. *Karys*, March 23, 1939, p. 380.
13. *Lietuvos Aidas*, March 28, 1939, p. 5.
14. See *Lietuvos Ūkininkas*, April 27, 1939, p. 3.
15. See speech by the director of the Bank of Lithuania published in *Tautos Ūkis*, March 9, 1940, pp. 179-183.
16. See Albertas Tarulis, "Klaipėdos krašto pramonės netekus" (Having Lost the Klaipėda Industries), *Tautos Ūkis*, April 1, 1939, p. 293.
17. See Jurgis Krikščiūnas, "Kiek nukentėjo mūsų žemės ūkis,

atskyrus Klaipėdos kraštą" (What Losses Has Our Agriculture Sustained After the Detachment of the Klaipėda Area), *Tautos Ūkis*, April 1, 1939, p. 293.

18. See Juozas Audėnas, unpublished memoirs, p. 99.

19. After the loss of Klaipėda the Communist Party of Lithuania was known to have favored the creation of a patriotic front and to have urged the populace to take up arms against the danger of German occupation. See K. Jablonskis and others (eds.), *Lietuvos TSR istorija* (History of the Lithuanian SSR; Vilnius: Lietuvos TSR mokslų akademija, 1958), p. 378.

20. See Raštikis, I, 55?

21. Ibid., pp. 552-554.

22. *Lietuvos Aidas*, March 28, 1939, p. 3; Jonas Statkus, "Pervertinimų šviesoje" (In the Light of Reappraisal), *Vairas*, June 15, 1939, p. 450.

23. *Šaltinis*, April 9, 1939, p. 243.

24. *Lietuvos Aidas*, March 30, 1939, p. 3.

25. *Vairas*, March 30, 1939, p. 256.

26. See *Šaltinis*, May 6, 1939, p. 299. It is known that the Communist Party, too, had favored the idea of a Patriotic Front. This could have been one reason the government frowned on the effort. See Jablonskis and others (eds.), p. 378; V. Brazaitytė, G. Feigelsonas and others (eds.), *Lietuvos komunistų partijos atsišaukimai* (Appeals of the Communist Party of Lithuania; Vilnius: Valstybinė politinės ir mokslinės literatūros leidykla, 1963), IV, 392.

27. See *Lietuvos Aidas*, April 4, 1939, p. 1.

XI. THE NEW DEAL

1. See *Lietuvos Ūkininkas*, April 6, 1939, p. 3.
2. Ibid.
3. *XX Amžius*, April 6, 1939, p. 13.
4. Ibid.
5. See Tiškevičius, K., "Fašistinės santvarkos krizė Lietuvoje tarybų valdžios atkūrimo išvakarėse, 1938-1940 m." (The Crisis of the Fascist Regime in Lithuania on the Eve of the Restoration of Soviet Government, 1938-1940), in J. Jurginis, R. Šarmaitis and J. Žiugžda (eds.), *Už Socialistinę Lietuvą* (For a Socialist Lithuania; Vilnius: Valstybinė politinės ir mokslinės literatūros leidykla, 1960), p. 270; K. Jablonskis

and others (eds.), *Lietuvos TSR istorija* (History of the Lithuanian SSR; Vilnius: Lietuvos TSR mokslų akademija, 1958), p. 378.

6. See *Lietuvos Ūkininkas*, April 6, 1939, p. 1.

7. Deputy Prime Minister Kazys Bizauskas arrived in Ukmergė on April 21; Agriculture Minister Jurgis Krikščiūnas visited Alytus on April 23; Ministers Kazys Musteikis and Leonas Bistras shared the rostrum in Vilkaviškis on April 23; Justice Minister Antanas Tamošaitis travelled that same day to Kėdainiai; on April 29 Finance Minister Jonas Sutkus addressed a meeting at Šiauliai; the following day Bistras spoke at Panevėžys, Tamošaitis at Raseiniai, and Interior Minister Kazys Skučas at Šakiai; on May 7 Bizauskas was greeted at Tauragė; and a week later both Bistras and Krikščiūnas made a trip to Šiauliai.

8. Mykolas Krupavičius, personal letter, November 3, 1961.

9. For an account of the Council, see p. 107.

10. *Lietuvos Ūkininkas*, April 13, 1939, p. 3.

11. Ibid.; *Lietuvos Ūkininkas*, April 27, 1939, pp. 3 and 5.

12. On April 30 Interior Minister Skučas upbraided the public for making irrational demands and on May 1 Prime Minister Černius aired his misgivings about alleged excesses some speakers had committed. See D[omas] Cesevičius, "Kalbos ir nuotaikos" (Speeches and Tempers), *Vairas*, May 4, 1939, p. 321.

13. Musteikis, personal letter to author, November 19, 1961.

14. Cesevičius, p. 321.

15. See *Vairas*, May 4, 1939, p. 335.

16. See *Lietuvos Ūkininkas*, May 11, 1939, p. 1.

17. *Naujoji Romuva*, April 1, 1939, p. 289.

18. The Social Democrats, who applauded the new administration, named freedom of the press as the one aspiration which they hoped the coalition government would realize. See *Mintis* (Thought), March 1939, pp. 42-43.

19. A protracted tug of war between the Nationalist censors and the Catholic editors was largely responsible for the appearance in 1936 of *XX Amžius*. Its immediate predecessor, the rebellious *Rytas*, did not get along very well with the authorities, shunned their texts, and eventually disappeared altogether.

20. See *Vyriausybės Žinios*, November 16, 1935, pp. 1-4; J. Žiugžda ed., *Lietuvos TSR istorijos šaltiniai* (Sources for the History of the Lithuanian SSR, Vol. IV; Vilnius: Lietuvos TSR mokslų akademija, 1961), p. 611; Audėnas, unpublished memoirs, p. 74.

21. Žiugžda ed., IV, 609, 616, and 617.

An illustrious case, pointing out both government sensitivity to press handling of matters affecting foreign powers and the reasons which in part were responsible for it, occurred on May 4, 1940, when the refractory *XX Amžius* carried a front page political cartoon, plainly identifying the Soviet whip as a source of inspiration to some leftist writers in Lithuania. The newspaper paid a fine for potentially endangering relations with Lithuania's eastern neighbor, and it was thought the incident was over. However, Vyacheslav Molotov, Chairman of the Council of People's Commissars, referred to it when the Lithuanian Prime Minister visited Moscow in June. For half an hour the Soviet leader reproached his guest for permitting the press to foment a public opinion unfriendly to the USSR. See *Lietuvos Žinios*, May 31, 1940, p. 8; Antanas Smetona, unpublished pro memoria, p. 7.

22. For an account of the problem, see pp. 146-147.

23. Interview with Vincas Rastenis, October 5, 1961.

24. *Vairas*, November 9, 1939, p. 860.

25. See Raštikis, *Kovose dėl Lietuvos: karių atsiminimai* (In the Struggles for Lithuania: Memoirs of a Soldier, 2 vols.; Los Angeles: Lietuvių Dienos, 1956-1957), I, 675; Stasys Raštikis, personal letter, October 24, 1961.

26. Interview with Vincas Rastenis; Razma, "Nepateisinti lūkesčiai ir propaganda," pp. 307-309.

27. See *Lietuvos Ūkininkas*, April 20, 1939, p. 1.

28. See *Vairas*, May 11, 1939, p. 331. Effective May 1, a second Secretary-General within the Ministry of the Interior was entrusted with the supervision of press and public organizations. See *Vyriausybės Žinios*, May 10, 1939, p. 302.

29. One such little weekly, published in a provincial town, was uncommonly predisposed to violate propriety. Apparently evading the censor, it publicly sympathized with the Czechs in their conflict with Germany, and had no difficulty whatever in finding a suitable occasion to write about the "ugly and abominable" face of Communism. See *Šaltinis*, March 25, 1939; ibid., July 1, 1939, p. 443.

30. See *Vairas*, December 21, 1939, p. 950.

31. Justice Minister Tamošaitis estimated that by the beginning of 1939 some 4,268 people were behind bars. The total includes 500 political prisoners, 80 of whom were charged with espionage and high treason. See *Lietuvos Aidas*, April 27, 1939, p. 3; *Lietuvos Ūkininkas*, April 27, 1939, p. 2.

32. See *Lietuvos Ūkininkas*, June 15, 1939, p. 11; ibid., July 27, 1939, p. 1.
33. Musteikis, personal letter to author, November 19, 1961.
34. See *Lietuvos Ūkininkas*, May 4, 1939, p. 9.
35. See *Vyriausybės Žinios*, May 10, 1939, pp. 303-304.
36. See *Lietuvos Ūkininkas*, June 29, 1939, p. 2.

XII. THE NATION PREPARES FOR THE WORST

1. See *Karys*, April 6, 1939, p. 445.
2. Ibid., March 30, 1939, p. 405.
3. Ibid., April 20, 1939, p. 491; ibid., May 11, 1939, p. 573.
4. See *Lietuvos Ūkininkas*, April 20, 1939, p. 12.
5. *Karys*, April 13, 1939, p. 479.
6. Contributions in kind, expected receipts from Lithuanians living abroad, and incomplete statistics make it difficult to estimate the total contribution to the Fund. Its partial income for the first six weeks was as follows:

Donors	Totals in lits
Workers	130,000
Farmers	260,000
Primary schools	30,000
Secondary schools	42,000
Government and military	355,000
Kaunas manufacturers and retailers	117,000

The total for 1939 is estimated at 2,027,419 lits. See *Karys*, May 11, 1939, p. 573; *Lietuvos Aidas*, June 13, 1940, p. 4.

7. See *Lietuvos Ūkininkas*, March 7, 1940, p. 4.
8. *Karys*, June 15, 1939, p. 717.
9. Ibid., May 22, 1939, p. 599.
10. Ibid., June 15, 1939, p. 724.
11. A brief survey of *Karys* indicates that by the middle of the 1939-1940 academic year national guard companies in secondary schools, both gymnasia and professional schools, appeared in the following towns: Belvederis, Biržai, Dotnuva, Joniškis, Kaunas, Kėdai-

272

niai, Kelmė, Kretinga, Kybartai, Pasvalys, Prienai, Šiauliai, Tauragė, Ukmergė, Utena, Vilkaviškis, Vilnius, and Zarasai.

12. See *Lietuvos Ūkininkas*, March 7, 1940, p. 8. For an account of other reasons responsible for the increase in membership, see p. 36.

13. R[omualdas] Medelis, "Kariškas parengimas pradžios mokykloje" (Military Training in Primary Schools), *Tautos Mokykla*, May 1, 1939, p. 191.

14. Ibid.

15. Alfa Sušinskas, "Trys milijonai lietuviškų tankų" (Three Million Lithuanian Tanks), *Ateities Spinduliai* (Rays of the Future), November 1939, p. 99.

16. *Karys*, February 8, 1940, p. 180.

17. Ibid., March 30, 1939, p. 420.

18. Ibid., April 20, 1939, p. 504.

19. *Tautos Mokykla*, May 1, 1939, p. 210.

20. See *Skautų Aidas* (Echo of the Scouts) June 1939, p. 272.

21. See *Karys*, May 9, 1940, p. 520.

XIII. THE NATIONALIST COUNTERDRIVE

1. See D[omas] Cesevičius, "Tautiškumo perspektyvos" (The Perspectives of National-Mindedness), *Vairas*, November 30, 1939, p. 895; Cesevičius, "Mūsų politinės sąmonės evoliucija" (The Evolution of Our Political Thought), *Vairas*, June 8, 1939, p. 409; Smetona, unpublished pro memoria, p. 2; *Vairas*, November 30, 1939, p. 893; E. Jacovskis and others (eds.), *Tarybų valdžios atkūrimas Lietuvoje 1940-1941 metais: dokumentų rinkinys* (The Restoration of Soviet Power in Lithuania, 1940-1941: collection of documents; Vilnius: Mintis, 1965), p. 34.

2. Interview with Vincas Rastenis, October 5, 1961.

3. See A. Smetona, *Pasakyta parašyta, 1927-1934* (Spoken Written, 1927-1934; Kaunas: Pažanga, 1935), pp. 101 and 325; Alantas, "Politinė tautos vienybė" (The Nation's Political Unity), *Vairas*, December 14, 1939, p. 930.

4. Jonas Statkus, "Momento reikalavimai" (The Demands of the Moment), *Vairas*, August 31, 1939, p. 674.

5. Jonas Statkus, "Gyvybinė sąlyga" (The Vital Condition), *Vairas*, October 19, 1939, p. 798; Cesevičius, "Tautiškumo perspektyvos"

p. 895; Alantas, "Politinė tautos vienybė," p. 930; *Lietuvos Aidas*, March 11, 1940, p. 3.

6. *Vairas*, September 21, 1939, p. 723.

7. Former party secretary Rastenis was quite right when he conceded that *Vairas* had not published a single article suggesting the need to review the basic tenets of authoritarianism. See Vincas Rastenis, "Reikia, bet ir užtenka" (Necessary and Sufficient), *Vairas*, June 8, 1939, p. 437; K. Galinis, "Reikia apsispręsti" (It is Necessary to Make up Our Minds), *Vairas*, July 20, 1939, p. 672.

8. See pp. 146-147.

9. Vyt[autas] Alantas, "Nacionalizmo baimė" (Fear of Nationalism), *Vairas*, September 21, 1939, p. 719.

10. Alantas, "Žygiuojanti tauta" (A Nation on the March), *Vairas*, June 8, 1939, p. 437.

11. *Vairas*, December 14, 1939, p. 926.

12. See *Lietuvos Aidas*, January 7, 1940, p. 4.

13. Cesevičius, "Tautiškumo perspektyvos," p. 896.

14. Ibid.

15. See pp. 167-168.

16. *Tautos Mokykla*, January 15, 1940, pp. 36-37.

XIV. THE DECISION TO REMAIN NEUTRAL

1. S. Raštikis, *Kovose dėl Lietuvos: kario atsiminimai* (In the Struggles for Lithuania: Memoirs of a Soldier, 2 vols.; Los Angeles: Lietuvių Dienos, 1956-1957), I, 596-597 and 612.

2. See *Vairas*, August 24, 1939, p. 667.

3. See J[onas] S[tatkus], "Lietuvos neutralumas" (Lithuania's Neutrality), *Vairas*, August 24, 1939, pp. 657-658.

4. J. Statkus, "Momento reikalavimai" (The Demands of the Moment), *Vairas*, August 31, 1939, p. 673.

5. See p. 127.

6. See his series of articles entitled "Vilnius—nepriklausomybės raktas" (Vilnius—Key to Independence) published in *Sėja* in 1956 and 1957.

7. See Raštikis, I, 591-592; Raštikis, personal letter to author, October 24, 1961; interview with Kazys Škirpa, October 14, 1961; U.S. Department of State, *Documents on German Foreign Policy 1918-1945*, series D, vol. VIII, Washington, 1953-1954, pp. 55, 63, and 75;

Kazys Musteikis, *Prisiminimų fragmentai* (Fragments of Reminiscences; London: Nida, 1970), pp. 43-44.

8. See Raštikis, I, 592; Pranas Ancevičius, "Istorija be pagražinimų" (History Without Trimmings), *Naujienos* (News), September 14, 1960, p. 3.

9. Raštikis, I, 591-592.

10. See *Sėja*, no. 1 (1957), pp. 11-12; interview with Kazys Škirpa. Even after the government decision to hold back from any military measures, the Prime Minister toyed with the idea of provoking guerilla activities in the area and using them as a pretext for Lithuanian intervention. Interview with Kazys Škirpa; *Documents on German* . . . VIII, 63.

11. Interview with Vincas Mašalaitis, October 19, 1961.

12. Interview with Kazys Škirpa, October 10, 1961.

13. See U.S. Department of State, House of Representatives, Select Committee to Investigate the Incorporation of the Baltic States into the USSR, *Hearings, Baltic States Investigation*, Part 1, 83rd. Congress, 1st. Session, Washington, 1954, p. 287.

14. See *Sėja*, no. 5 (1957), p. 10.

15. Ibid., no. 6 (1957), p. 14; interview with Kazys Škirpa.

16. See U.S., Congress, House, *Third Interim Report of the Select Committee on Communist Aggression*, 83rd Congress, 2d Session, Washington, 1954, H.R. 346 and H.R. 438, p. 444.

XV. Arrival of Russian Troops and the Return of Vilnius

1. See *Lietuvos Aidas*, October 3, 1939, p. 1.

2. A reference to Poland. The implication was that Moscow would be well-advised to transfer Vilnius to Lithuania.

3. *XX Amžius*, October 7, 1939, p. 12.

4. See *Lietuvos Ūkininkas*, October 5, 1939, p. 3.

5. See S. Raštikis, *Kovose dėl Lietuvos: Kario atsiminimai* (In the Struggles for Lithuania: Memoirs of a Soldier, 2 vols.; Los Angeles: Lietuvių Dienos, 1956-1957), I, 605-618; Vincas Mašalaitis, Former Secretary-General of the Lithuanian Council of Ministers, an unpublished statement, Bryn Mawr, Pennsylvania, October 25, 1953.

6. Raštikis, I, 613.

7. *Lietuvos Aidas*, October 16, 1939, p. 1.

8. *Lietuvos Žinios*, October 10, 1939, p. 1.

9. *Vairas*, October 12, 1939, p. 758.

275

10. See J[uozas] Gobis, "Vilnius, Lietuva ir SSSR" (Vilnius, Lithuania and the USSR), *Draugija*, December 21, 1939, p. 1225; *Panevėžio Garsas*, November 11, 1939, p. 1.

11. J[uozas] Gobis, "Mažosios tautos dabartinio karo akivaizdoje" (The Small Nations in the Presence of the Current War), *Draugija*, May 5, 1940, p. 438.

12. See *XX Amžius*, October 11, 1939, p. 12; *Lietuvos Ūkininkas*, October 12, 1939, p. 3.

13. See *XX Amžius*, October 16, 1939, p. 2; K. Jablonskis and others (eds.), *Lietuvos TSR istorija* (History of the Lithuanian SSR; Vilnius: Lietuvos TSR mokslų akademija, 1958), p. 379. According to the State Security Department, quoted in Communist sources, the number of those arrested in Kaunas on October 11-13 climbed to 161. Of this total some 57 Communists were sent to concentration camps. See Tiškevičius, "Fašistinės santvarkos krizė Lietuvoje tarybų valdžios atkūrimo išvakarėse, 1938-1940 m." (The Crisis of the Fascist Regime in Lithuania on the Eve of the Restoration of Soviet Government, 1938-1940, in J. Jurginis, R. Šarmaitis, and J. Žiugžda (eds.), *Už socialistinę Lietuvą* (For a Socialist Lithuania; Vilnius: Valstybinė politinės ir mokslinės literatūros leidykla, 1960, p. 276.

14. See *Draugija*, October 20, 1939, p. 1081; ibid., November 1, 1939, p. 1126; *Šaltinis*, October 28, 1939, p. 822.

15. See *Lietuvos Ūkininkas*, October 19, 1939, p. 1.

16. U.S. Department of State, *Documents on German Foreign Policy 1918-1945*, Series D, vol. VIII, Washington, 1953-1954, p. 285.

17. See *Lietuvos Ūkininkas*, November 2, 1939, p. 3.

18. *Foreign Relations of the United States: Diplomatic Papers. The Soviet Union, 1933-1939*, Department of State Publication 4539 (Washington: Government Printing Office, 1952), p. 967.

19. Kazys Musteikis, personal letter, November 1, 1961.

20. *Mūsų Žinynas* (Our Record), no. 10 (October, 1939), pp. 345-346.

21. Ibid., pp. 347-350.

22. See *Panevėžio Garsas*, November 11, 1939, p. 1.

23. Vincas Mašalaitis, an unpublished statement; Raštikis, I, 628; Raštikis, personal letter.

24. See Raštikis, I, 628. General Raštikis recalls that Moscow was not entirely pleased with the outcome of the military talks and that, consequently, it dismissed the delegation chairman, Kovalev, from his post as commander of the Minsk military district. According to Lithu-

anian sources, the delegation's arrogant vice-chairman, division com-
mander Pavlov, on June 15, 1940, occupied the country with two
Russian armies. See Raštikis, I, 630; Raštikis, personal letter to author,
October 24, 1961.

25. Vincas Mašalaitis, an unpublished statement.

26. *Foreign Relations of the United States*, p. 981; Raštikis, I, 629.

27. See Tiškevičius, p. 284; Jacovskis and others (eds.), *Tarybų
valdžios atkūrimas Lietuvoje 1940-1941 metais: dokumentų rinkinys*
(Restoration of Soviet Power in Lithuania, 1940-1941: Collection of
Documents; Vilnius: Mintis, 1965), pp. 47-49.

28. See *Lietuvos Ūkininkas*, November 23, 1939, p. 12.

29. Musteikis, personal letter to author, November 19, 1961.

30. See *Vilniaus Balsas*, January 9, 1940, p. 3.

31. Ibid., April 18, 1940, p. 3.

32. *Lietuvos Aidas*, June 10, 1940, p. 1.

33. Ernestas Galvanauskas, personal letter, December 30, 1961.

34. One historian recalls that "Vilnius was transferred to Lithuania
only on October 28, 1939, eighteen days after the signing of the treaty.
Those days seemed very long for the nation, but even longer for the
denizens of Vilnius beset with the Bolshevik terror and pillage. No
merchandise was left in the city, not even bread. The inhabitants were
suffering from hunger and lived in perennial fear lest any night they
should be spirited away like so many of their neighbours and acquain-
tances. Not content with the imposition of their usual Bolshevik regime,
the Russians plundered everything and sent the spoils to Russia; they
carried off even the archives, libraries, other cultural treasures, and
door knobs, window and plumbing fixtures of public buildings."
Adolfas Šapoka, *Vilnius in the Life of Lithuania*, trans. E. J. Harrison
(Toronto: Lithuanian Association of the Vilnius Region, 1962), p. 158.

35. According to Polish sources, the ethnic differentiation in the
returned portion of the Vilnius area was as follows (in thousands,
October 1939):

Lithuanians	31.3
Jews	107.6
Germans	1.1
Poles	321.7
White Russians	75.2
Great Russians	9.9
Others	2.2
Total	549.0

A. W. De Porte writes that "since the area was so important a source of contention between Poland and Lithuania, and the nationality of its population so much disputed, these figures—which are based on the census of an interested party—are not to be taken at face value. The extremely high Polish population and the very small proportion of Lithuanians are particularly suspect, for it was commonly understood by impartial observers that there were more Lithuanians than Poles in the countryside, but more White Russians than either, and that in the city itself, which accounted for considerably less than half of the population of this area, there were more Poles than Lithuanians, but more Jews than either. However, there seems no method to go behind these figures, or to assign any given number of persons listed as 'Poles' to other categories, but it should be remembered in later breakdowns of the Lithuanian population that there are considerably fewer Poles and more Lithuanians, and perhaps White Russians, than are stated." A. W. De Porte, "Population," *Lithuania in the Last 30 Years*, ed. Benedict V. Mačiuika (New Haven, Connecticut: Human Relations Area Files, Inc., 1955), p. 18; see also K. M. Smogorzewski, "The Russification of the Baltic States," *World Affairs*, IV, October 1950, 468-481. The census of 1942 taken by the German occupation authorities is quoted in Šapoka, pp. 136-137; also in Kazys Pakštas, "National and State Boundaries," *Lituanus*, no. 3, September 1959, p. 71.

36. The action against the area's large proprietors appears to have received popular support among the Lithuanians. At a discussion held in Vilnius on April 17, a Christian Democratic leader suggested that the large landowners be dispossessed of all their holdings. The audience responded with unanimous approval. See *Vilniaus Balsas*, April 19, 1940, p. 6. Cf. p. 222-223.

37. See V. Vazalinskas, "Žemės reformos klausimu" (Concerning the Question of Land Reform), *Naujoji Romuva*, November 26, 1939, pp. 845-849.

38. See *Tautos Ūkis*, March 16, 1940, p. 212.

39. See *Lietuvos Ūkininkas*, December 14, 1939, p. 2; ibid., November 23, 1939, p. 2; *Lietuvos Banko Biuletenis*, May 24, 1940, p. 10.

40. *Lietuvos Aidas*, April 16, 1940, p. 1. See also Justas Paleckis, *Gyvenimas prasideda* (Life Begins; Vilnius: Vaga, 1967), pp. 204, 210, and 224-225. A prominent Lithuanian recalls, however, that he found much sympathy toward Lithuania among the residents of the area.

See Rapolas Skipitis, *Nepriklausoma Lietuva: atsiminimai* (Independent Lithuania: Memoirs; Chicago, 1967), pp. 161 and 164-165.

41. Maceina, "Tauta ir valstybė" (The Nation and the State), *Naujoji Romuva*, March 19, 1939, p. 229.

42. A[ntanas] Maceina, "Tautinis auklėjimas nutautintoje Vilniaus aplinkoje" (National Education in Denationalized Vilnius Surroundings), *Lietuvos Mokykla* (The Lithuanian School), no. 1 (January, 1940), pp. 8-9.

43. A[lbertas] Tarulis, "Lietuvių kultūrai saugoti įstatymas" (The Law to Protect Lithuanian Culture), *Naujoji Romuva*, December 10, 1939, p. 908.

44. See *XX Amžius*, March 13, 1940, p. 10.

45. See *Vilniaus Balsas*, April 11, 1940, p. 6; ibid., April 19, 1940, p. 6.

46. See *Lietuvos Žinios*, May 3, 1940, p. 2.

XVI. END OF JOINT ACTION

1. S. Raštikis, *Kovose dėl Lietuvos: kario atsiminimai:* (In the Struggles for Lithuania: Memoirs of a Soldier, 2 vols.; Los Angeles: Lietuviu Dienos, 1956-1957) I, 557-558 and 631-632; Raštikis, personal letter to author, October 24, 1961.

2. See *XX Amžius*, June 14, 1939, p. 4.

3. For a detailed analysis of what size farms were most suitable for Lithuanian agriculture, see J. Krikščiūnas, "Kokio didumo ūkiai - stambūs, vidutiniai ar smulkūs—našiausi" (What Size Farms are Most Productive—Large, Medium or Small), *Tautos Ūkis*, January 27, 1940, pp. 59-61; A. Luksošaitis, "Kokio dydžio žemės ūkiai mums naudingiausi?" (What Size Farms are Most Beneficial to Us?), *Tautos Ūkis*, January 20, 1940, pp. 39-40.

4. See *Lietuvos Ūkininkas*, October 19, 1939, p. 8.

5. See *XX Amžius*, October 21, 1939, p. 12.

6. A. Valuckas, *Kolektyvinė tironija* (Collective Tyranny; Kaunas: Valstybinė leidykla, 1943), pp. 18-19.

7. See *Karys*, December 7, 1939, pp. 1419-1422.

8. J. Audėnas, unpublished memoirs, p. 125.

9. See *Lietuvos Aidas*, January 11, 1940, p. 7.

10. Interview with Vincas Rastenis, October 5, 1961.

11. See U.S. House of Representatives, *Hearings, Baltic States*

Investigation, Part 1, 83rd Congress, 1st. Session, 1954, p. 283; interview with Vincas Mašalaitis, October 19, 1961.

12. For an account of the formation of the Merkys cabinet, see Raštikis, I, 632-636. A different version of the formation of the new cabinet appears in Merkelis, *Antanas Smetona: jo visuomeninė, kultūrinė ir politinė veikla* (Antanas Smetona: His Civic, Cultural and Political Activities; New York: Amerikos lietuvių tautinė sąjunga, 1964), pp. 560-562 and 564.

13. See *Lietuvos Aidas*, November 22, 1939, p. 1.

14. See *XX Amžius*, November 22, 1939, p. 10.

15. Ibid., December 7, 1939, p. 12.

16. See p. 127.

17. See Raštikis, I, 673-677; ibid., II, 20; *Lietuvos Ūkininkas*, January 25, 1940, p. 12.

18. See Raštikis, I, 693-694.

19. See *Lietuvos Aidas*, January 7, 1940, p. 4; ibid., January 11, 1940, p. 6.

20. *Šaltinis*, June 10, 1939, p. 389; ibid., June 17, 1939, p. 406.

21. See *XX Amžius*, February 13, 1940, p. 4.

22. See *Draugija*, April 20, 1940, pp. 45-49.

23. See *Tiesos Kelias* (The Road of Truth), no. 6, June 1940, pp. 22-27.

24. See Audėnas, unpublished memoirs, pp. 113-114.

25. See *Lietuvos Ūkininkas*, May 9, 1940, p. 3.

26. See Audėnas, unpublished memoirs, pp. 112-113; *Lietuvos Žinios*, April 18, 1940, pp. 1 and 5; *XX Amžius*, April 23, 1940, p. 12.

XVII. THE PRECIPITATE END

1. See *Lietuvos Aidas*, April 2, 1940, p. 2.

2. See Audrūnas and Svyrius, *Lietuva tironų pančiuose* (Lithuania in Chains of Tyrants, vol. I; Cleveland: Lietuvai vaduoti sąjunga, 1946), p. 37.

3. See J. Audėnas, unpublished memoirs, p. 175.

4. *Lietuvos Ūkininkas*, June 6, 1940, p. 12.

5. Ibid.

6. Ibid.; Vincas Mašalaitis, unpublished statement relative to Lithuania's occupation; Bryn Mawr, Pennsylvania, October 25, 1953;

Juozas Audėnas, former Minister of Agriculture, unpublished statement, New York, October 21, 1953.

7. See *Lietuvos Aidas*, May 30, 1940, p. 1; *Lietuvos Žinios*, May 30, 1940, quoted in *XX Amžius*, May 31, 1940, p. 6; *Vilniaus Balsas*, May 31, 1940, p. 1; *XX Amžius*, May 30, 1940, p. 12.

8. U.S. Department of State, *Documents on German Foreign Policy 1918-1945*, IX, 475.

9. Smetona, pro memoria, p. 6.

10. The question of a military alliance with Latvia and Estonia was repeatedly brought up by the Russians. "An official Russian statement describes the ultimatum [the Russian ultimatum to Lithuania on June 14] as having charged Lithuania with violation of the spirit of the mutual assistance pact concluded with the Soviets last year by signing a secret military treaty with Estonia and Latvia." *The New York Times*, June 16, 1940, p. 1; ibid., June 17, 1940, p. 6.

The Treaty of Good Understanding and Cooperation between the three Baltic states, which was applauded by Soviet commentators at the time of its conclusion in 1934, did not terminate in a military alliance. Former Minister of Defense Musteikis recalls that by the end of 1939 the Baltic governments had agreed to standardize military equipment and ammunition. However, it was apparently too late to give effect to this decision. Musteikis, personal letter, November 19, 1961.

11. Smetona, pro memoria, p. 7.

12. *Foreign Relations of the United States: Diplomatic Papers, 1940*, Department of State Publication 6818 (Washington: Government Printing Office, 1959), I, 366.

13. See Audėnas, unpublished memoirs, p. 183; *Nepriklausoma Lietuva* (Independent Lithuania), June 15, 1955, p. 2; interview with Bronius Dirmeikis, March 10, 1961; Kazys Musteikis, *Prisiminimų fragmentai* (Fragments of Reminiscences; London: Nida, 1970), p. 95.

14. See *Lietuvos Aidas*, June 9, 1940, p. 1; ibid., June 10, 1940, p. 1.

15. See *Lietuvos Ūkininkas*, June 20, 1940, p. 2.

16. James W. Gantenbein ed., *Documentary Background of World War II, 1931 to 1941* (New York: Columbia University Press, 1948), p. 752.

17. For a concise account of government deliberations on the eve of Russian occupation, see statement by Vincas Mašalaitis; see also Smetona, pro memoria, pp. 10-20; statement by Juozas Audėnas;

Audėnas, unpublished memoirs, pp. 193-205; Raštikis, *Kovose dėl Lietuvos: kario atsiminimai* (In the Struggles for Lithuania: Memoirs of a Soldier, 2 vols.; Los Angeles: Lietuvių Dienos, 1956-1957), II, 21-25; Musteikis, *Prisiminimų fragmentai*, pp. 101-108.

18. President Smetona, who had stayed briefly in Germany, was permitted to come to the United States. He died in Cleveland on January 9, 1944.

19. See Smetona, pro memoria, p. 1.

20. Ernestas Galvanauskas, personal letter to author, December 30, 1961.

21. Ibid.; Smetona, pro memoria, pp. 1-2; U.S. House of Representatives, *Hearings, Baltic States Investigation*, Part 1, 83rd. Congress, 2nd. Session, Washington 1954, p. 43; see also Musteikis, *Prisiminimų fragmentai*, pp. 86-87 and 103.

22. See *Nepriklausoma Lietuva*, June 15, 1955, p. 2.

23. Ibid.

24. Ernestas Galvanauskas, personal letter to author, December 30, 1961.

25. See Raštikis, II, 27

XVIII. COLLABORATION BY COMPULSION:
THE ALLIANCE OF THE LEFT

1. See *Lietuvos Žinios*, June 17, 1940, p. 10.

2. *Lietuvos Ūkininkas*, June 20, 1940, p. 1.

3. *XX Amžius*, quoted in *Lietuvos Žinios*, June 17, 1940, p. 6.

4. *Vilniaus Balsas*, June 18, 1940, p. 1.

5. See *Lietuvos Aidas*, June 16, 1940, p. 1; ibid., June 17, 1940, p. 1.

6. The Soviet envoy arrived in Kaunas on June 15. His counterpart in Estonia was A. A. Zhdanov and in Latvia, A. Y. Vyshinski. Dekanozov was liquidated by the Russians after the fall of Lavrenti Beria in 1953.

7. Vincas Mašalaitis, unpublished statement relative to Lithuania's occupation, Bryn Mawr, Pennsylvania, October 25, 1953; Juozas Audėnas, unpublished statement relative to Lithuanian-Soviet tension in 1939-1940, New York, October 21, 1953; Ernestas Galvanauskas personal letter to author, December 30, 1961.

8. See Appendix B.

9. Ernestas Galvanauskas, personal letter to author, December 30, 1961.

10. See V[incas] Krėvė-Mickevičius, "Bolševikų invazija ir Liaudies vyriausybė" (The Bolshevik Invasion and the People's Government), *Lietuvių archyvas: bolševizmo metai*, ed. J. Balčiūnas (Lithuanian Archives: The Bolshevik Years; 2d. ed.; Kaunas: Studijų biuras, 1942), III, 7-9.

11. Reminiscing in the Soviet Union twenty years after the events under consideration, former Defense Minister Vincas Vitkauskas divulged that even before the Bolshevik onset in 1940 he was already secretly engaged in the Communist cause. See Vincas Vitkauskas, "Tą neužmirštamą vasarą" (That Unforgettable Summer), *Švyturys* (The Beacon), June 30, 1960, p. 11. However, the disclosure is widely discounted as an inconsequential misrepresentation of history inspired by the peculiar needs of the society to which he belonged.

12. See Krėvė, "Bolševikų invazija," p. 8.

13. See Krėvė, "Pasikalbėjimas Maskvoje su V. Molotovu" (The Conversation with V. Molotov in Moscow), *Aidai* (Echoes), no. 3, March 1953, p. 122.

14. See *Lietuvos Ūkininkas*, June 20, 1940, p. 3.

15. Ibid., July 4, 1940, p. 1; ibid., June 20, 1940, p. 12; ibid., June 27, 1940, p. 1.

16. Ibid., July 4, 1940, pp. 1 and 5.

17. See *Lietuvos Ūkininkas*, July 4, 1940, p. 5; ibid., July 25, 1940, p. 12.

18. See *Darbo Lietuva* (Labor Lithuania), July 18, 1940, p. 4.

19. See *Vilniaus Balsas*, June 19, 1940, p. 1.

20. Ibid., June 28, 1940, p. 1.

21. *XX Amžius*, June 26, 1940, p. 10.

22. See *Darbo Lietuva*, July 16, 1940, p. 1; *Lietuvos Žinios*, August 1, 1940, p. 1; *XX Amžius*, August 1, 1940, p. 10.

23. *Lietuvos Ūkininkas*, June 27, 1940, p. 1.

24. Ibid.

25. See *Vilniaus Balsas*, July 2, 1940, p. 1.

26. Ibid., July 3, 1940, p. 6; *Lietuvos Žinios*, July 3, 1940, p. 10.

27. *Ūkininko Patarėjas* quoted in *Vilniaus Balsas*, July 6, 1940, p. 6; *Tiesa* quoted in *Lietuvos Ūkininkas*, July 4, 1940, p. 2.

28. See *Darbininkų Žodis* (The Workers' Word), June 30, 1940, p. 5.

29. The Communist Party had tried to repress lawlessness by threatening with expulsion all members guilty of arbitrary acts. However, the

admonition appears to have carried little weight. See *Darbininkų Žodis*, July 6, 1940, p. 10.

30. See Krėvė, "Pasikalbėjimas Maskvoje," pp. 122-123.

31. Ibid., p. 127; Krėvė, "Bolševikų invazija," p. 11. Krėvė's account of his talks with Molotov appears in U.S. Congress, House, *Third Interim Report of the Select Committee on Communist Aggression*, 83rd. Congress, 2nd. Session, 1954, H.R. 346 and H.R. 438, pp. 454-460.

32. *Vilniaus Balsas*, July 6, 1940, p. 1.

33. Ibid.

34. See Krėvė, "Bolševikų invazija," p. 14.

35. Ibid., p. 15. Writing in Soviet-occupied Lithuania some twenty-five years after the events under consideration, Paleckis recalls that those were "complex, difficult, and moving" days, and that his responsibilities were a "heavy burden." He further states that each day brought "an unusual nervous tension." See J. Paleckis, *Gyvenimas prasideda* (Life Begins; Vilnius: Vaga, 1967), p. 233.

36. See Krėvė, "Bolševiku invazija . . .," pp. 14-15.

37. Ibid., p. 16.

38. See *Lietuvos Ūkininkas*, July 11, 1940, p. 1.

39. Ibid., p. 2; for a short analysis of the electoral law, see X. Y. [Mykolas Römeris], *Lietuvos sovietizacija 1940-1941 m.* (The Sovietization of Lithuania in 1940-1941; Augsburg: Lietuvos Teisininkų Tremtinių Draugija, 1949), pp. 19-21.

40. See *Lietuvos Ūkininkas*, July 11, 1940, p. 3.

41. See Liudas Dovydėnas, "Mano kelias į Liaudies Seimą" (My Road to the People's Diet), *Lietuvių archyvas: bolševizmo metai*, III, 51; A[ntanas] Garmus, "Lietuvos įjungimas į SSSR—Maskvos diktatas" (Lithuania's Incorporation into the USSR—Moscow's Dictate), *Lietuvių archyvas: bolševizmo metai*, ed. J. Prunskis (Lithuanian Archives: The Bolshevik Years; Brooklyn, N. Y.: Tėvų Pranciškonų spaustuvė, 1952), p. 11. The book compiled by Prunskis is an abridged edition of the report on Bolshevik occupation published in 1942.

42. See A. Butkutė-Ramelienė, *Lietuvos komunistų partijos kova už tarybų valdžios įtvirtinimą respublikoje, 1940-1941 m.* (The Struggle of the Communist Party of Lithuania for the Consolidation of Soviet Power in the Republic, Vilnius: 1958), pp. 37-38.

43. See Dovydėnas, p. 51; Garmus, p. 9.

44. A former legislator refers to an unsuccessful effort, on the part of the Populists, to put forward their own contestants for People's

deputies. See Garmus, p. 11. However, the assertion cannot be verified, as the émigré Populists who were asked for comment denied either the existence of such an attempt or any knowledge of it. Liudas Šmulk-štys, personal letter, October 1, 1961; Jonas Kardelis, personal letter, January 5, 1962; interview with Juozas Audėnas, October 24, 1961.

45. See S. Raštikis, *Kovose dėl Lietuvos: kario atsiminimai* (In the Struggles for Lithuania: Memoirs of a Soldier, 2 vols. Los Angeles: Lietuvių Dienos, 1956-1957), II, 87.

46. *Darbininkų Žodis,* July 6, 1940, p. 2.

47. See *Lietuvos Aidas,* July 11, 1940, p. 1; *Lietuvos Žinios,* July 12, 1940, p. 5.

48. See U.S. House of Representatives, Committee to Investigate Communist Aggression in the Baltic States *Third Interim Report,* Washington, 1954, pp. 468-470; Mykolas Krupavičius and Vaclovas Sidzikauskas, *Appeal by Representatives of the Baltic Nations to the General Assembly of the United Nations,* presented November 24, 1947 (n.p.: n.d.), p. 8; unpublished testimony by MM, Lithuanian National Martyrological Archives, Chicago, Illinois.

49. See Audrūnas and Svyrius, *Lietuva tironų pančiuose* (Lithuania in Chains of Tyrants, vol. I, Cleveland, 1946), pp. 105-107; Pranas Mickus, "Liaudies Seimo rinkimų duomenų klastojimas," (The Falsi-fication of Returns of Elections to the People's Diet), *Lietuvių archyvas: bolševizmo metai,* III, 21.

50. *Lietuvos Ūkininkas,* July 11, 1940, p. 1.

51. Ibid., July 18, 1940, p. 1.

52. See *XX Amžius,* July 20, 1940, p. 8.

53. See Liudas Dovydėnas, *Užrašai* (Diary; 2nd. ed.; Kaunas: Br. Daunoro leidykla, 1944), pp. 185-186.

54. In a statement of August 30, 1942, a group of former members of the People's Government and the People's Diet placed the total count at approximately 18 per cent. It is this figure that is usually quoted in non-Communist sources. However, it appears that this is a conservative estimate, based on the lowest number of votes registered in some electoral districts; it does not take into account the higher percentages believed to have been cast in urban communities.

55. See Audrūnas and Svyrius, p. 201.

56. See *Darbo Lietuva,* July 17, 1940, p. 2; ibid., July 19, 1940, p. 4.

57. See *XX Amžius,* July 20, 1940, p. 8.

58. See Dovydėnas, *Užrašai,* p. 197; X. Y., p. 26.

285

59. For some eloquent passages on the attitudes of the legislators before the opening session, see Dovydėnas, *Užrašai*, pp. 179-197; see also Garmus, p. 14.

60. See Dovydėnas, *Užrašai*, p. 198; Garmus, pp. 19-20.

61. See Dovydėnas, "Mano kelias į Liaudies Seimą" (My Road to the People's Diet), in J. Balčiūnas ed., *Lietuvių archyvas: bolševizmo metai*, vol. III; Kaunas: Studijų biuras, 1942), pp. 53-54.

62. Dovydėnas, *Užrašai*, p. 195.

63. Large-scale digressions from the ethics appropriate to free elections are amply documented. For evidences of intimidation of voters, the application of physical force, the presence of foreign soldiers at polling places, and the generous addition of ballots by members of the electoral commissions in order to augment the total count, see World Lithuanian Archives, Chicago, Ill., 4451, 4621, 4956; unpublished testimony by LL and MM, Lithuanian National Martyrological Archives, Chicago, Ill.; P. Mickus, "Liaudies Seimo rinkimų duomenų klastojimas" (The Falsification of Returns of Elections to the People's Diet), in J. Balčiūnas ed., p. 34.

XIX. CONCLUSION

1. *Lietuvos Ūkininkas*, July 25, 1940, p. 12.

293